THE ROOTS OF DISUNITY

REVISED EDITION

THE ROOTS OF DISUNITY

A Study of Canadian Political Culture

DAVID V.J. BELL

Toronto
OXFORD UNIVERSITY PRESS
1992

Oxford University Press, 70 Wynford Drive, Don Mills, Ontario M3C 1J9

Toronto   Oxford   New York
Delhi Bombay Calcutta Madras Karachi Kuala Lumpur
Singapore Hong Kong Tokyo Nairobi Dar es Salaam
Cape Town Melbourne Auckland

and associated companies in
Berlin   Ibadan

This book is printed on permanent (acid free) paper.

Canadian Cataloguing in Publication Data

Bell, David V.J., 1944-
    The roots of disunity
rev. 2nd ed.
Includes bibliographical references and index.
ISBN 0-19-540858-6

1. Federal government - Canada. 2. Regionalism - Canada. 3. Canada -
Politics and government. 4. Biculturalism - Canada. 5. Multiculturalism -
Canada.* I. Title.

JL65.1992.B4 1992   320.971   C91-095797-5

Contents

To my students, from whom I have learned a great deal

Docendo discimus

Tables

Preface

The current crisis of Canadian disunity holds both danger and opportunity. The greatest danger lies in ignorance and amnesia—Canadians know little about each other or about their collective past. Much attention is being focused on the failure of our economic system to adjust to global pressures and fundamental restructuring, and on our political system's failure to respond to internal strains and pressures. This book has little to say about the former, quite a lot to say about the latter. However, it highlights a deeper if less visible failure in our political socialization systems. For this book is concerned with Canadian political culture—what Canadians think and feel about politics—and the language of political action. Changes in our political structures must be accompanied by a transformation in our political culture if we are to survive as a sovereign country over the next decade. Yet culture changes slowly and sometimes painfully. We have ignored culture at our peril and now the consequences await us.

Would an appropriate cultural mutation save Canada from disintegration? Perhaps not. But there still remains an opportunity for new thinking, a reassessment of our fundamental values, a rediscovery of positive elements of our tradition, and the maturing of a new language of co-operation, understanding and tolerance. In this spirit, this book is offered as a contribution to the ongoing debate about Canada's future.

Large multi-ethnic federal systems have not fared very well in the past few years. Many are disintegrating, some of them bloodily. Canada is no less under strain, but we do have a tradition of compromise and negotiation from which we may be able to salvage at least an amicable method of resolving these tensions, and hopefully find a future that is better than our recent past.

Acknowledgements

I would like to thank Richard Teleky and Lorne Tepperman for encouraging me to undertake this revision; Olive Koyama, for intelligent editorial advice and guidance; Michaela Otto, for her critical reading of the chapters that were published in the first edition; Andrew Spurgeon, for assistance in updating the quantitative data; my colleagues in the Department of Political Science at York, for their constant intellectual stimulation and support; and finally my family, Kaaren, Kristin, and Jason, whose affection sustains the whole enterprise.

Introduction

An American who overheard two Canadians talking about the 'death of Meech Lake' could be forgiven for assuming the conversation was about ecology rather than politics. To make sense of political talk requires knowledge of the underlying political culture that gives it meaning. Yet we are so thoroughly immersed in our own political culture that often we fail to see it at all. Like a fish in water, we are oblivious to the medium that sustains our political life.

This book is about Canadian political culture and how it can help us understand the problem of Canadian disunity. Axiomatic to this approach is the assumption that what's in people's heads matters a great deal. Political actions uninformed by thought inspire either laughter or contempt. What we do depends on what we think and feel and believe. Actions, unless they are thoughtless reactions, reflect and involve these elements of culture. In all of this, language is absolutely crucial. We formulate and express both thoughts and beliefs in language. To be sure, anger sometimes leaves us speechless and love can overwhelm our reason, but feelings also evoke elaborate vocabularies of description and evaluation inscribed in poetry and song.

Without language, political culture would not exist. Neither would politics itself! Some readers might instantly disagree, insisting that politics is about actions not thoughts, about deeds not words, about conflict not conversation. A moment's reflection corrects this understandable impulse, however. The distinction between words and deeds is largely misleading. Most political actions involve speech or writing. Virtually all of them are a form of communication intended to change the behaviour or attitudes of others. Political conflict is usually verbal, not physical.

In short, politics is talk. The name of our highest political institution, Parliament, means literally 'a government of talk.' When conflicts arise, we attempt to talk them through. When violence silences talk, we speak sadly of political *failure*, and wish for the reestablishment of politics through negotiation. The term applied to this process at the international level, diplomacy, literally means 'a letter folded double.' When diplomacy fails between nations, war often results. When politics fails within countries, internal war may follow.

Canada is facing the serious possibility of profound political failure. Our political institutions have proved incapable of resolving serious conflicts over Anglo-French relations, regionalism, native issues, ethnicity, environment, gender, and social class. Not all of these conflicts will lead to violence and national disintegration, but some might, and at least one is very likely to do so. Each of them can be understood in relation to our political culture.

The most important way in which political culture is transmitted is through language. To understand how political actors think, an observer must first learn their language. Assumptions about politics and the meanings of institutions and practices are always present in language, however hidden. Thus language serves to express and transmit, encode, and preserve culture. 'There are other modes of cultural expression, notably art and music, but even these . . . have been described and transmitted in part through the medium of words. In effect, language . . . is all pervasive.'[1] Yet the importance of language often goes unrecognized. Many, especially unilinguals, think language is a neutral medium of expression, free of any particular values or assumptions. Those who are untrained in examining language seem unaware that their words contain and preserve their culture, shaping their outlook and even colouring their sentiments.[2] By organizing the ways we see and make sense of things, language organizes our world. Many metaphors suggest themselves: language as map, language as lens, language as filter. When children are taught social behaviour, they learn to use words in particular ways: to accept only some of many possible meanings and to build their sentences according to a blueprint called 'grammar'. But vocabulary and grammar influence both logic and evaluation. So children learn to think about and react to the world around them in ways confined by their language; and all this without being aware of it.

When we think of language, we usually think of words. But in the most general sense, a language is simply a way of symbolizing the world. And words are only one type of symbol. The invention of the printing press made verbal texts the dominant form of communication and print the most important medium of culture. But we have moved beyond the print epoch. Our dominant medium is television and our new language is based on images as much as it is on words. By the time a child reaches adolescence, she or he will have spent more time in front of a television set than in a school classroom. Much of what we see on television consists of commercials. The vast majority of the remainder is American programming. Little wonder that Canadians lack a strong sense of national identity. Most of the images that are seared into our national consciousness originated in another country.

People who are deeply exposed to—or as they may feel, threatened by—a different culture understand implicitly the link between language and culture. Francophones have always felt that their language must be kept in common use if their culture is to survive. But anglophones react in similar ways. When a writer named Erna Paris moved from Canada to France with only a smattering of French, she experienced the heavy psychological costs of thinking in a second language. She found that as her opportunity to speak English diminished, she lost her English-Canadian identity, and acquired a new personality and outlook, as a francophone. She reports that 'The French "me" was far weightier and more serious than her English counterpart, for humour is so quick and so involved with culture that it is one of the last things a bilingual acquires, if she ever does.'³ Paris interviewed a number of others with similar experiences. Each agreed that living in two languages strains a person's identity: it forces the individual to take on a second complete set of values and assumptions. True bilingualism therefore implies biculturalism as well.⁴

For this reason minority groups concerned about the survival of their culture see language rights as the first line of defence against cultural assimilation. In most of Canada, anglophones enjoy the comfortable position of dominance. As a result they 'do not need to think about their language, they just simply speak it'.⁵ But when groups like francophones in Western Canada, or anglophones in Quebec feel their ability to work and play in their native tongues is threatened, they sense profoundly the links between language and cultural survival. For native people this awareness is expressed more as a lament than a complaint.

A language difference often keeps people from understanding one another. Even interpreters and translations cannot make up for what is, after all, a cultural difference. Occasionally, when speakers of different languages keep talking to one another over a long enough period of time, they start to think alike. For example, the Swiss people comprise three different language groups that appear to understand each other very well. They have worked out mutually acceptable meanings of political terms that are unique to Switzerland.⁶ But societies like Switzerland are unusual. More often one finds misunderstandings and conflict between speakers of different languages. In Canada the speakers of English and French have frequently misunderstood each other. In the 1960s when franco-phones insisted that they were a separate 'nation' in Canada confusion and disagreement followed. To anglophones, the term 'nation' implies an entire state apparatus, not merely a sense of tradition and identity. The concept of *deux nations* raised the red flag of separation before English-Canadian eyes. Consid-erable ink was spilled in subsequent efforts to communicate across this partic-ular linguistic barrier.⁷ A task force set up in 1977 to study problems of Canadian unity found it necessary to prepare a glossary of political terms to help all Cana-dians, particularly anglophones and francophones, understand each other better.

These differences became even more profound a decade later. Quebec 'nationalists' demanded that the new Constitution, adopted in 1982 without Quebec's assent, recognize Quebec as a 'distinct society' within Canada. Bitter wrangling over the implications of this designation contributed to the defeat of the Meech Lake Accord, and the onset of the most worrisome constitutional crisis in Canadian history. Meech Lake came to symbolize very different things to different Canadians. Quebec francophones interpreted its failure as a rejection of Quebec by the rest of Canada. Some anglophones saw it as a betrayal of the vision of a united Canada with a strong central government. Others bitterly denounced the process of closed decision-making by eleven white men. Native people made Meech into a verb which in the past tense passive voice meant 'cheated or betrayed' by powerful decision-makers.⁸

Another, even more profound, crisis. Another Task Force on Canadian unity. This one chaired by Keith Spicer, who defined its primary mission as one of listening rather than speaking. (The Commission called itself, 'Citizens' Forum: The People Speak.') Commissioners toured the country to hear the many different voices of concerned Canadians. They designed a process intended to allow people at the grass-roots level to meet in small groups and talk about the problems that threatened the continued survival of the nation. Although the Commission was given no authority to introduce changes in governmental structure or policy, it attempted to transform forever the process of closed executive federalism whereby 'eleven white men sitting in a room' had rewritten the Canadian constitution through the Meech Lake Accord. Further constitutional changes would be informed by a much more open process. Leaders would be required not simply to *tell* Canadians what arrangements had been reached, but first to *listen* to their concerns and hopes and visions. Groups previously excluded or ignored would insist on being included in this new process. In the words of native leader George Erasmus, 'We're not going to sit on the sidelines.... If you want to see violence, just try to keep us out.... There's no goddam way you're going to have another Meech Lake without us.'[9]

Symbols and slogans help preserve and express political culture. They catalyze sentiments and sound the depths of communal division, telling us how deeply the community feels about a problem and the various ways of solving it. Agencies as different as political parties, the mass media, large corporations, schools, and churches use symbols and slogans to carry their own points of view to other members of society, including new arrivals and new generations: immigrants and children. This process is 'socialization',[10] an apt name since it describes an important means by which people get tied to the social order, and are persuaded to think a certain way. Because symbols and slogans are promoted with some awareness of the end result, they can be thought of as instruments of social control that make up the political culture and keep it alive.

Social change and cultural change are obviously interrelated. Both entail changes in language. The process often begins with naming or renaming, which is intended to refocus public awareness and challenge hidden assumptions. As the civil rights movement progressed in the United States, the term 'coloured people' was replaced by 'Negro', then 'black', and finally 'African American', each a claim to higher status and greater recognition. Aware of the subtle but profound links between 'language and women's place', feminists have insisted that 'inclusive' language replace the patriarchal language of male-stream thought which accepted male pronouns and words like mankind as generic for both genders.

But the feminist project extends beyond changing the vocabulary of gender-biased language. It embraces as well structural relationships between men and women as they are embodied in language, particularly the 'public discourse' that expresses legal relationships and governmental policy. Feminists began by challenging the distinction between private and public that effectively removes the daily lives and struggles of women in the house from the eye and concern of government and the media. The slogan of the women's movement, 'the personal is political', allows a whole range of 'women's issues' legitimacy as public concerns that once 'named, articulated, represented and properly recognized within the public discourse...become subject to resolution in a similar manner to any other public or political issue'.[11]

Shifts in discourse reveal changing values and customs. They mark the infusions of new ideas, and the fading of old ones. Canadian political discourse in the 1990s features a vocabulary uncontemplated twenty or thirty years earlier:

- Meech Lake
- Sovereignty Association
- distinct society
- aboriginal rights
- women's issues
- gay rights
- multiculturalism
- environmentalism
- free trade

These are, to be sure, substantive policies or political issues. But they are more significantly emotion-laden symbols to be conjured with in political rhetoric. They are part of the 'political spectacle'.

What a nation remembers about itself, its history, is a major source of its political culture. History as *tradition* literally 'gives across' or hands down institutions, practices, symbols, and slogans from one generation to the next. History offers us 'myths' that make our values, beliefs, and assumptions clear, concrete. To change the present and define new directions for the future, one must know what has come before, and why historical forces have created the current situation. Ignoring history is like travelling without a map or compass. Canadians who do not know their own history are unprepared to understand their own politics.

For this reason, among others, Canadians are poorly equipped to respond to present political challenges. In 1970 the historian A.B. Hodgetts published a study of the history taught in Canadian high schools entitled *What Culture, What Heritage?* Professor Hodgetts found that high school history courses gave a great deal of attention to British and American history. The relatively little Canadian history being taught was bland and dull, almost sure to kill student interest. 'Never Heard of Them—They Must be Canadian' was the title Mel Hurtig gave to a pamphlet reporting the results of a 'student awareness survey' conducted in 1975 by the Committee for an Independent Canada. The study clearly showed that few Canadian high school students know anything about important Canadians, past or present. Among other results, Hurtig reported that of the final-year high school students surveyed:

- 68% were unable to name the Governor General;
- 63% were unable to name three Canadian Prime Ministers who had held office since the end of the Second World War;
- 61% failed to identify the BNA Act as Canada's constitution;
- 89% could not identify Gabriel Dumont;
- 69% could not identify René Lévesque;
- 96% could not identify Emily Murphy;
- 97% could not identify Norman Bethune;
- about 70% had little or no idea what percentage of Canada's population is French-Canadian.

Typical comments by the students included:

- 'I know more about American Presidents than Canadian Prime Ministers!'
- 'Most of the kids in my class will fail this test because the school system doesn't teach us this stuff. Who is at fault?'
- 'In this high school there are mostly American textbooks, so how am I supposed to know?'
- 'I don't take Canadian history!'

Troubled by those (and similar) findings, the Association of Universities and Colleges of Canada (AUCC) established a Commission on Canadian Studies to investigate and report on the state of research and teaching about Canada. Appalled by what they found, the Commissioners recommended that no student be allowed to graduate from high school or university without 'certain minimum levels of knowledge about the political institutions and political culture of their country'.[12]

This recommendation was not adopted and the general problem has not improved. A survey of 'above average' Ontario high school students conducted in the mid-1980s found equally depressing results. Of the grade 13 students surveyed:

- 31 of 70 knew the name of the Premier of Ontario
- 10 of 70 knew the name of the Lieutenant Governor
- 8 of 70 knew the name of the Premier of Quebec
- 2 of 70 knew the name of the Premier of British Columbia
- 30 of 70 thought that the Governor General...and Senate are elected
- 40 of 70 believe that Canada is a republic

In a humorous vein, *One Hundred Years of What?* is both the title and the message of a book on Canada's first century, by Eric Nicol and Peter Whalley. The authors begin by pointing out that:

the whole history of Canada since Confederation has been that of a nation deeply steeped in misgivings. No other nation in the world can boast such a long and continuous tradition of doubt about the validity of its existence.

Canada is history's foster child. Despite the comfortable circumstances of her homeland, she cannot shake off the suspicion that she does not know her real parents. . . .

The result is a young nation that refuses to become emotionally involved with herself in case she turns out to be somebody else.

The Nicol-Whalley solution to Canada's cultural crisis takes the form of a challenge: rewrite history, or at least present 'a judicious revision of certain events to give them the heroic aura presently minus'.[13]

This book does not attempt to rewrite Canadian history in response to their challenge. But only by turning to the historical record can we discover the unspoken assumptions and root meanings that hide beneath the great issues and debates of the day. This objective lies at the very heart of the study of Canadian political culture. To attain it we must be archaeologists and excavate the buried and sometimes mummified axioms of political behaviour.[14]

Social scientists have no patent on this undertaking. Important insights into political culture have come from novelists and poets, historians and politicians, no less than from carefully trained survey researchers. Indeed, the user of survey results must take care not to confuse a short-lived public opinion with the deep-seated, slow-changing political culture. In brief, the exploration of Canada's political culture will take us back into history, and through the maze of Canadian political life. Our guides will be many and varied.

Troubled by national disunity, in the past twenty-five years Canadian writers have described their society in the language of doubt, if not despair. A group of Western and Maritime Canadian intellectuals brooded over the 'burden of unity'; at the same time their colleagues from Ontario asked the ominous question, 'Must Canada fail?' A philosopher offered a 'lament' for Canada, an economist documented its 'silent surrender', and a political scientist called into 'question' Canada's continued existence. According to other writers, Canada is a 'nation unaware' of its past and uncertain of its future: Our legendary capacity for 'survival' stands threatened by internal strains, 'divided loyalties', and foreign 'dominance'.[15]

Each of these writers interpreted the problem of disunity in a slightly different way, but such diversity is inevitable. What one sees as a political problem (and its solution) depends largely on one's political values, beliefs, and assumptions. In short, the political culture affects even scholarly perceptions of politics.[16] Our concern is to examine the conceptual lenses that make up the political culture as much as it is to look through these lenses and understand the 'problems' facing Canada. Indeed the two activities are inseparable. The Canadian political culture is itself disunified, and what some Canadians regard with pride, others view with contempt. Beyond describing the major divisions in Canadian society,[17] we carefully examine people's thoughts and feelings about them.

What Canadians feel, think, and do politically—our political culture—has come down to us as a rich tradition with roots in the distant past. Therefore our study of present-day Canada begins by discussing Canada's founding and the early, formative events in its history. Just as etymology takes us back to the root meaning of words, so this exploration will examine the origins and root meaning of political actions and symbols.[18] We are explicating the etymology of Canadian political life.

Notes

[1] Raymond Gagné, 'French Canada: The Interrelationship Between Culture, Language and Personality', in Bruce Hodgins and Robert Page (eds), *Canadian History Since Confederation* (Georgetown: Irwin Dorsey, 1972): 526.

[2] 'Symbolic interactionists believe that the distinctive attributes of human behaviour grow from man's immersion in a cultural environment that depends upon the existence of language and the creation and manipulation of signs and symbols. Language is the vehicle by which culture is transmitted from generation to generation, and through it, individuals are able to organize their actions within a framework of mutual expectations.' Jack Haas and William Shaffir, *Shaping Identity in Canadian Society* (Scarborough: Prentice Hall, 1987): 5. See also the discussion of Alfred Schutz, 'Language as a Map', *ibid.*: 134 ff.

[3] Erna Paris, in Haas and Shaffir: 141. For a highly sensitive analysis of the implications of bilingualism for individuals, see Jean Laponce, *Languages and Their Territories* (Toronto: University of Toronto Press, 1989) Ch. 1.

[4] 'Culture is a way of being, thinking and feeling. It is a driving force animating a significant group of individuals united by a common tongue and sharing the same customs, habits, and experiences.' Royal Commission on Bilingualism and Biculturalism, *Report* (Ottawa: Queen's Printer, 1968). Curiously, their report led to the declaration that Canada had two official languages but no official culture. Instead, Canada would support a policy of multiculturalism. See below, Ch. 3.

[5] Gagné: 529.

[6] 'The word *liberté* to a French Swiss means much the same thing—local self-government—as *Freiheit* means to a German Swiss. But to a North German, *Freiheit* might easily mean subjection to a familiar tyranny, as in the days of the German emperor or of Hitler; and to a Frenchman, *liberté* might mean membership in a highly centralized republic governed by a charismatic general as president. What distinguishes the Genevois from the Parisian, and makes the Swiss a people, is the group with whom each shares the meaning of words rather than those with whom each shares the mechanics of grammar and vocabulary.' Karl W. Deutsch, *Politics and Government: How People Decide Their Fate* (Boston: Houghton Mifflin, 1974): 130.

[7] Under the intellectual guidance of Marcel Faribeault, the Conservative Party in 1968 endorsed the concept of *deux nations* and incorporated it into their campaign platform. While both the platform and party leader Robert Stanfield took great pains to explain the French connotations of the term, Pierre Trudeau exploited to its fullest the potential for miscommunication across the language barrier. For example he told an election audience in Winnipeg, 'If you start talking of two nations you start talking of two states and that's not the way we want to go.' Quoted in James Laxer and Robert Laxer, *The Liberal Idea of Canada* (Toronto: James Lorimer and Company, 1977): 177.

[8] See Tony Hall, 'What Are We? Chopped Liver? Aboriginal Affairs in the Constitutional Politics of Canada in the 1980's', in Michael D. Behiels (ed.) *The Meech Lake Primer* (Ottawa: University of Ottawa Press, 1989): 423.

[9] The *Toronto Star*, 21 April 1991: A12. The widespread anger and disgust over the 'closed' policy of constitutional reform epitomized by Meech Lake signals an important change in our political culture. The pattern of deference to 'élite accommodation' and 'executive federalism' has begun to evaporate in the internal heat of demands for more popular involvement in a more open process.

[10] See Jon Pammett and Michael Whittington (eds), *Political Socialization: Foundations of Political Culture* (Toronto: Macmillan, 1977). Note as well Murray Edelman's important work on symbolism in politics, particularly his *Symbolic Uses of Politics* (Urbana: University of Illinois Press, 1964), and *Political Language: Words that Succeed and Policies that Fail* (New York: Academic Press, 1977).

[11] Liora Salter, 'The Boundaries and Limitations of Electoral Reform. Reflections from Research on Inquiries and on the Interplinary of Language and Politics.' Unpublished paper prepared for the Royal Commission on Electoral Reform and Policy Financing, 1991: 11. Cf. Jane Jenson: 'the politics of struggles over meaning—the power to label social relations—[is] absolutely crucial'. 'Representations in Crisis...' *Canadian Journal of Political Science* XXIII:4 (Dec. 1990): 663.

[12] See T.H.B. Symons, *To Know Ourselves: The Report of the Commission on Canadian Studies* (Ottawa: The Association of Universities and Colleges of Canada, 1975). The quoted comment is from T.H.B. Symons in Jon Pammett and Jean Luc Pépin (eds) *Political Education in Canada.* (Montreal: Institute for Research on Public Policy, 1988: 126.

[13] Eric Nicol and Peter Whalley, *One Hundred Years of What?* (Toronto: Ryerson Press, 1966): vii-viii.

[14] 'Our political thought is implicit, not explicit. It must be inferred from what we do in and through governments rather than expounded from the texts of founding manifestos and revolutionary pronouncements.' Edwin R. Black, *Divided Loyalties* (Montreal: McGill-Queen's University Press, 1975): xi. Note as well, William T. Bluhm's distinction between 'forensic' and latent ideology in *Ideologies and Attitudes: Modern Political Culture* (Englewood Cliffs, NJ: Prentice-Hall, 1974): 10: 'Forensic ideology is explicit and easily recognized. It consists of elaborate often abstract expressions that typically appear in political discussion during periods of stress. Latent ideologies are implicit. They "are expressed in attitude and behaviour during more settled times", but they can be "excavated" by patient research.' Much of the present book consists of such 'ideological excavation'. In this respect it resembles Michel Foucault's project of genealogy and archaeology.

[15] Abraham Rotstein, *The Precarious Homestead: Essays in Economics, Technology, and Nationalism* (Toronto: New Press, 1973); David J. Bercuson (ed.), *Canada and the Burden of Unity* (Toronto: Macmillan, 1977); Richard Simeon (ed.), *Must Canada Fail?* (Montreal: McGill-Queen's, 1977); George Grant, *Lament for a Nation* (Toronto: McClelland & Stewart, 1970); Kari Levitt, *Silent Surrender* (Toronto: Macmillan, 1970); Donald Smiley, *Canada in Question*, 2nd ed. (Toronto: McGraw-Hill Ryerson, 1976); Herschel Hardin, *A Nation Unaware* (Vancouver: J.J. Douglas, 1974); Margaret Atwood, *Survival* (Toronto: Anansi, 1972); Edwin Black, *Divided Loyalties* (Montreal: McGill-Queen's, 1975); John Hutcheson, *Dominance and Dependency* (Toronto: McClelland & Stewart, 1978).

[16] See David V.J. Bell, *Power, Influence and Authority: An Essay on Political Linguistics* (New York: Oxford University Press, 1975), Introduction; and 'The Political Culture of Problem-Solving and Public Policy,' in David Shugarman and Reg Whitaker (eds), *Federalism and Political Community: Essays in Honour of Donald Smiley* (Peterborough: Broadview, 1989).

[17] Although a longer book than this one might address additional sources of conflict and disunity, no book on Canadian society could avoid the issues on which we have focused. Several of the works cited in note 15 (particularly those of Hardin, Hutcheson, and Black) identify roughly the same cleavages we examine.

[18] The word root has meanings that span half a dozen disciplines from botany through physiology, history, mathematics, and music. It is a complex term that implies origins, base, core, antecedent, support, nourishment, element, and source. As such it is ideally suited to this study of the complexities of political culture and Canadian disunity. Of all its meanings, its use in linguistics is most appropriate for this undertaking. The study of word roots is the concern of etymology, a word made up of the roots *etymon* and *logy*. The Latin root *etymon* is itself derived from the Greek *etumon*, which means 'true sense of a word'. Etymology is therefore the study of 'the origin and historical development of a word, as evidenced by the study of its basic elements, earliest known use, and changes in form and meaning'. Similarly, this book is about the root meanings of our political culture, and how they have changed over time.

1 | Perspectives on Political Culture

Many concepts used in social science have a long, cloudy history. By contrast, the history of the term *political culture* is short and clear. Gabriel Almond first introduced the term in his article 'Comparative Political Systems'.[1] Political culture, Almond argued, improved upon such earlier notions as 'national character', 'custom' and 'modal personality', whose meanings were 'diffuse and ambiguous'. These earlier terms had led to writings full of 'exaggeration and oversimplification', which failed to 'give proper weight to the cognitive and evaluative factors' in human behaviour.[2]

Among its other advantages, political culture helped explain 'why formally similar institutions operated in radically different ways'[3] in different societies. The term *ideology*, although related, is narrower in scope and refers to an 'explicit doctrinal structure characteristically borne by a minority of militants'. Political culture encompasses the 'vaguer and more implicit orientations which generally characterize political followers'.[4] Students of political culture would probe popular views and values, even questioning relatively inarticulate people who lacked an explicit, formal ideology.[5]

So broadly defined, a political culture might include more than one ideology and might even extend beyond the borders of a single society or self-governing state. With this in mind Almond spoke of the common culture of the 'Anglo-American democracies'. He allowed that views on politics in Britain, Canada, the United States, and other English-speaking countries would differ; but similarities would outnumber the differences. Also, Almond noted that a single state might contain several political cultures. If so, it would lack the uniform thinking of societies in which 'the great majority of the actors' generally agree on 'the ultimate goals of the political system'.[6] Thus the territorial base of a political culture could not be known in advance of a study. But the complexity only started here. To fully understand 'political culture' we must understand the terms 'political' and 'culture' that make it up.

In 1871, anthropologist Edmund V. Tylor put forward the first authoritative definition of *culture*: 'Culture...is that complex whole which includes knowledge, belief, art, morals, law, custom, and any other capabilities and habits acquired by man as a member of society.'[7] Anthropologists and other scholars have worked on Tylor's concept of culture for three-quarters of a century now and have changed it in a number of ways. Indeed, Almond's choice of a concept invented by anthropologists and modified by sociologists was deliberate. Because other social scientists commonly used the term, Almond could 'utilize the conceptual frameworks and approaches of anthropology, sociology, and psychology' in his discussions of political culture. This gave him access to such related concepts as 'socialization, culture conflict, and acculturation'.[8] Almond hoped in this way to inform political science of 'certain sociological and anthropological concepts' he thought would 'facilitate systematic comparison among the major types of political systems'.[9]

Tylor's definition of culture is so broad that it includes everything from a cooking pot to a Beethoven sonata. Given Almond's limited objectives, he had to choose a narrower formulation. From the hundreds of definitions of culture then available, Almond selected Talcott Parsons'[10] definition of culture as 'psychological orientations toward social objects', where 'orientation' in turn meant 'the internalized aspects of objects and relationships'.[11] Parsons identified three such orientations: cognitive (knowledge and belief), affective (the feelings and emotions), and evaluative (judgements and opinions that 'typically involve the combination of value standards and criteria with information and feelings'). By following Parsons, Almond narrowed the anthropologist's wide definition to something more manageable: to knowledge, beliefs, feelings, opinions, and judgement.

Next Almond took on the task of stating what he meant by 'political'. At first he tried to combine Parsons' concepts of 'system' and 'role' with Max Weber's definition of political authority (a 'legitimate monopoly of physical coercion over a given territory and population'). The result was muddled: a political system became 'the patterned interaction of roles affecting decisions backed up by the threat of physical compulsion'.[12] This was both too cumbersome and too vague. Unhappy with this result himself, Almond pointed out that a better job of defining politics in terms of system was 'still to be done'.

Almond and Verba's 'Civic Culture'

A short time later, Almond worked together with Sidney Verba on a major study of political culture in five countries: the United States, Britain, Germany, Italy, and Mexico. Here the 'political objects' of orientation were defined more clearly than before. Following an approach to political systems that David Easton had developed, the authors picked out four separate 'dimensions of political orientation'.[13]

1. *System as a general object*. ('We deal here with the system as a whole and include such feelings as patriotism or alienation.')
2. *Input objects*. (Those roles or structures, incumbents, and policies or decisions that 'are involved in the political or "input" process'.)
3. *Output objects*. (Those roles or structures, incumbents, and policies or decisions that 'are involved in the administrative or "output" process'.)
4. *Self as object*. ('The content and quality of the sense of personal competence

vis-à-vis the political system'; and 'the content and quality of norms of personal political obligation'.)

From this point of view, every political culture combined the four dimensions in a somewhat different way. But out of the dozens of possible permutations, three 'ideal typical' combinations could be isolated: these were called parochial, subject, and participant political cultures.

To use the political culture approach, researchers would draw samples of typical people in different societies, and then measure the distribution of political orientations in each sample. The data for measuring and comparing national orientations would come from survey questionnaires and personal interviews. The authors could then classify each society into one of the three ideal types, depending on how often each of the orientations appeared in the answers individuals gave.

Almond and Verba acknowledge that the three 'pure' types of political culture exist only in theory. Any society, indeed any given person, *combines* parochial, subject, and participant orientations. Even a primarily 'participant' political culture will contain some people whose approach to politics is 'subject' or 'parochial': people who are badly informed, passive, and unthinking when it comes to political matters. But as societies become 'modern', their institutions supposedly become more democratic, and their citizens learn to take a greater part in civic matters. To support a modern kind of democracy, developing nations must move toward a participant culture by fostering a 'sense of national identity, subject and participant competence, social trust, and civic co-operativeness'.[14]

The cultural mix of attitudes that best suits and supports democracy Almond and Verba called 'the civic culture'. The United States is the best example of this form of politics, they argued. It serves as a model for less developed societies to imitate. This view may raise some eyebrows today; but believing in it seemed especially vital to American social scientists during the Cold War period in which Almond and Verba worked. To find out the cultural basis of American-style democracy was, they supposed, to help fix the course of political development in Third World countries. This in turn would tip the global balance of power toward the United States and away from the Soviet Union. That they held this view, and believed so firmly in the importance of their mission, must be kept in mind when reading their work.

Almond and Verba describe the political cultures in the five particular countries they studied without paying much attention to the historical processes and events that created these cultures. They rely on data gathered at a single moment in time; this is a 'synchronic approach'. The alternative, a diachronic or historical approach, would use survey data gathered at different points in time, or other kinds of data entirely. The synchronic method has a limited value precisely because it ignores how something changes with the passage of time.

In summing up Almond and Verba's approach to political culture, several features should be noted. First, the authors define culture in terms of individuals' internalized, and therefore subjective, orientations to the outside world. They direct our interest to studying the ways political participants view the world, however right or wrong their views might be. Using a public survey the authors measure the variety of cultural orientations (or views) among a representative sample of members of a society. Thus, political culture is seen as belonging to the popular 'mass'. They did not bother to study separately the beliefs and attitudes of the top groups in society because Almond and Verba assumed that 'political élites share the political culture of the nonélite'.[15] Political beliefs and values are put into categories defined by a conception of politics drawn from 'systems theory'. Finally, though cultural change is part of their general concern, the authors study it in a peculiar, synchronic fashion: they try to understand change by looking at several political cultures at different stages of development, not at a single culture as it changes over time.

Many scholars have adopted Almond and Verba's approach. Almost every political survey carried out by academics in the past twenty-five years has included at least a few questions taken, with or without modification, from their pioneering study. This generalization applies as much to work in Canada as to work elsewhere.[16] Yet, for a variety of reasons, research into political cultures has moved outside of and beyond the Almond and Verba framework.

Some researchers have felt that their approach puts too much stress on invisible, internal aspects of culture. They argue that visible signs of culture—symbols, myths, policies, and more recently, language and discourse—must be examined also. For these scholars the opinion survey is only one tool among many, and perhaps not even the most trustworthy one, no matter what forms of culture are to be studied.[17] After all, survey interviews are not everyday events: in fact, they are contrived and sometimes tension-raising. What people say when interviewed may have little bearing on their actual behaviour or true feelings.

Critics also doubt that the political culture of ordinary people influences the political process very much at all. Far more significant is the élite culture, which may be quite different; certainly, understanding that culture requires different methods of study, such as looking at what members of the élite have said in their speeches and writings, or examining élite policies and groupings. Further, critics argue that political culture should be studied historically, as well as by comparing nations. Yet this is not within the means of Almond and Verba's 'synchronic method'. Nor, further, is it clear that American democracy should serve as a model for other societies to emulate, or as a standard for measuring the extent of political development, as Almond and Verba so fervently believed.[18]

In basing their conception of politics upon systems theory, Almond and Verba chose a theoretical framework that works best for a unitary, harmonious political system, but fits poorly the politics of a federal state like Canada, where the political culture varies from one region to another. Moreover the systems approach equates politics with government. But limiting our attention to government betrays an ideological preference for the 'establishment', and an inattention to countercultures.

Almond and Verba, amazingly, said little about the role of power in public affairs. They lumped together élite and mass, assuming that their ideas and interests were similar. What was needed was a theory about self-interested people wielding unequal amounts of power; and an explanation of how this inequality influences the style of political thinking that prevails. Karl Mannheim had already provided just this in his earlier analysis of ideology, published in 1936.

Ideology and Political Culture

Karl Mannheim acknowledged that 'we do not as yet possess an adequate historical treatment of the development of this concept of ideology'. But he finds its 'immediate precursor' in the suspicion and distrust conflicting groups invariably feel toward one another. Mutual accusations of distortion and untruthfulness give way finally to a more sophisticated understanding: namely, that the views of an adversary may have a social basis of which even he or she is unaware. 'We begin to treat our adversary's views as ideologies only when we no longer consider them as calculated lies and when we sense in his total behaviour an unreliability which we regard as a function of the social situation in which he finds himself.'[19]

Therefore the student of ideology looks behind the statements of social actors, and attempts to 'unmask' the deceptions they contain by discovering the economic and social interests from which they arose. 'The particular [Marxist] conception of ideology, therefore, signifies a phenomenon intermediate between a simple lie at one pole, and an error, which is the result of a distorted and faulty conceptual apparatus, at the other. It refers to a sphere of errors, psychological in nature, which unlike deliberate deception, are not intentional, but follow inevitably and unwittingly from certain causal determinants.'[20]

Mannheim accepted Karl Marx's view that thought mirrors the daily social and economic life: particularly, the process of production and the domination that arises from it. Ideology, indeed all culture, rests on this structural or material base. According to Marx, the ruling class wears ideology as a mask to hide its nature and true interests. Thus an ideology is made up of beliefs, values, and rules suited to keeping the status quo. It reflects a particular stage in the history of a society, a particular mode of production and style of control.

The ruling ideology of industrial society is capitalist, or bourgeois, according to Marx. To change such a society, to hasten its revolutionary transformation from bourgeois to socialist and finally communist social forms, requires that the working or proletarian class acquire radical self-consciousness. Proletarians must become aware of their interests and abilities to make the change. But to do this they must first break the hold that bourgeois ideology has over them. Thus, unmasking the disguises of the ruling class becomes a tactic in the class struggle. An important tool of oppression, the ruling bourgeois ideology must be replaced by a proletarian ideology if the revolution is to succeed.

Marx's attempt to relate ideology to social class and economic interests remained incomplete or 'particular' in Mannheim's view. A paradox had suggested itself. If the ruling ideology can be seen as little more than the adorned self-interest of the ruling class, can we not reduce *all* forms of thought to the underlying interests that produce them? By extending and refining Marx's partial insight, Mannheim hoped to construct a 'total' conception of ideology: a theory of knowledge that applied not only to Marx's enemies but even to Marx himself. The Marxist study of ideology had merely aimed to 'unmask...deceptions and disguises' of interest groups and political parties.[21] Mannheim's new approach, which he named the sociology of knowledge, would be less one-sided. Concerned with more than exposure of attempts to deceive the powerless, it would study all the 'varying ways in which objects present themselves to the subject according to differences in social settings'.[22]

The sociology-of-knowledge approach constituted a departure from earlier theories of knowledge. Epistemology, the branch of philosophy that studies the nature and origins of knowledge—how we know what we know—is concerned with the relationships between language and thought, observation and insight. But Mannheim was trying to understand knowledge by assessing how situation and environment shape what the 'knower' sees and judges through the 'social or existential determination of actual thinking'. Sociology of knowledge examines the ideological basis of knowledge. It attempts to show how 'knowledge' is full of unconscious bias arising from the social situation of the knower. Hence, the sociology of knowledge thoroughly examines the context within which people act. And because social settings change, we must pay attention to history. 'Every epoch has its fundamentally new approach and its characteristic point of view, and consequently sees the "same" object from a new perspective.'[23] The sociology of knowledge approach allows us to see the importance of what Mannheim calls 'perspective'. 'Perspective in this sense signifies the manner in which one views an object, what one perceives in it, how one construes it in his thinking.'[24]

In effect, Mannheim removed some of the radical element from the term *ideology*. For example, 'class interest', one of the important influences upon thought in Marx's analysis, was replaced by 'social setting'. Thought, both Marx and Mannheim believe, is never unique to the individual: it is shared and learned. People's thinking is influenced by the social activities of which their life is a part. For this reason a person's thoughts will show the imprint of his or her daily experience. Production and domination are considered the most basic conditions of social life, by Mannheim as by Marx. Hence the social outgrowths of these conditions, namely classes, are still, for Mannheim, the basic units of social organization. Yet one cannot hope to account for the rich 'variety of types of thought' without calling attention to other such 'highly differentiated social groupings' as 'generations, status groups, sects, occupational groups, schools, etc'.[25] Without these, explaining behaviour that ignores or even betrays class interests becomes very difficult. Here Mannheim and Marx come to a parting of the way, and Mannheim takes the right-hand fork in the road.

If Marx's understanding of ideology was based on a limited insight and therefore yielded only a 'partial' theory of the relationship between culture and social setting, both Marx and Mannheim can be faulted for failing to recognize a bias both of them shared. For Marx, the crucial material condition of life was *production*—the way in which a society goes about the task of providing the means of its subsistence. Marx devoted most of his scholarly career to exploring the important implications of this profound, but partial, insight. What he failed to recognize was the equally profound impact on culture of *reproduction*—the way in which a society goes about providing the means of its existence. From this insight equally profound analyses flow concerning the relationship of men and women in all places and all settings. On this point it is revealing and significant that Mannheim fails to include gender or women in his illustrative list of the 'highly differentiated social groupings' that deserve the attention of the sociology of knowledge. Fortunately a rich (though recent) tradition of feminist scholarship has opened our eyes to the importance of these matters (at the same time that gender and sex have emerged as critical issues in contemporary politics).[26]

Although Mannheim's concept of ideology is not identical to the notion of political culture, his work shows that a culture must be studied in relation to the social and economic structure with which it coexists. This is not to accept a simple one-way view that what we do determines what we think and feel. Rather the relationship between social structure and culture needs to be explored through observation. Likewise, the analysis in this book examines both the social and economic roots of culture, and the way culture influences society and economy.[27] The relationship is reciprocal; moreover, it is dialectical and self-changing. Thus Mannheim helps to correct one major weakness of the Almond and Verba approach: namely, its inattentiveness to power and class. The contributions of feminist scholars correct a defect in Mannheim's work itself: the failure to consider seriously gender. We turn now to two approaches to political culture that remedy another weakness of Almond and Verba: their failure to examine how political culture changes over time. We are referring to the work of Louis Hartz and of S.M. Lipset.

Hartz's Fragment Theory

In Almond and Verba's research, the answers individuals give in interviews are aggregated (literally, 'flocked together') to permit first a classification of the society into one of several 'types', then a comparison with other societies. Any two or more countries can be compared in this way if equivalent[28] survey questions are asked. But Louis Hartz rejects this 'aggregative' approach, using instead a comparative method that is both holistic and historical. Hartz compares 'fragment' societies that evolved from the same root or 'founding' society, and looks at the stages through which they passed. He believes that the colonial beginnings of New World societies shaped their political culture well into the twentieth century.

The 'fragment theory' emerged as a by-product of Hartz's famous book on the liberal tradition in America.[29] Written during the McCarthy era of fierce anti-communism, the book tried to explain (in part) how a 'liberal' society could prove so blindly intolerant.[30] Hartz studied the history that had led up to this apparent contradiction and, as he did so, found that other societies followed similar paths of development. Indeed the same pattern appeared wherever a part, or fragment, of European society had detached itself and migrated to the New World. Eleven years later, Hartz and four collaborators had fanned that flicker of light into burning controversy in their comparative[31] study of ex-colonies. The book applied 'fragment theory' to the United States, South Africa, Australia, Latin America, and—most important for our purposes—to Canada.

Hartz's 'fragment theory' is about development in both the New World and the Old. Explaining why socialism did not blossom in the United States, for example, entails his explanation of how it did arise in Europe. Both Hartz's method and his language differ from that of Almond and Verba. A student of classical political theory, Hartz thinks in the traditional terms of European political philosophy. Yet for all the differences, Hartz's conclusions complement rather than contradict their ideas, providing insights into precisely those matters on which Almond and Verba are deficient.

According to Hartz, societies of the New World base their political cultures on single European ideologies. In Europe, conservatism, socialism, and liberalism are merely parts of a varied political culture. But in the New World, the part often becomes the whole. Liberalism in America, for example, becomes a way of life; conservatism and socialism are excluded.

Ideologies normally develop, according to Hartz, in the dialectic of social conflict. Thus in Europe conservative thought was born when liberal capitalism attacked feudalism. The radical impulse of liberalism later combined with the organic or collectivist element of conservatism to produce socialism. Thus these three ideologies—conservatism, liberalism, and socialism—are related, by logic and history, at their inner core. But 'when a part of a European nation is detached from the whole of it, and hurled onto new soil, it loses the stimulus toward change that the whole provides.'[32] When one of the 'early' ideologies, liberalism or conservatism, is missing, the later one, socialism, cannot appear. Socialism cannot appear where liberalism is absent: it needs individualism to implant a concern with equality that can grow into socialism. Likewise, socialism cannot appear where conservatism is absent. Without conservatism there is no longing for community to which socialists can appeal with their offer of an organic, though classless, society.[33]

The 'fragmentation process' of which Hartz speaks is colonization. It allows the European ideologies carried in the 'cultural baggage' of each group of emigrants to escape the dialectical conflict in Europe and develop unhindered. Thus, the colonization of New France carried the political principles of the feudal *ancien régime* across the sea to a new setting. Here they were safeguarded from the attacks on feudalism that became ever more common in European politics. In the colonization of Anglo-America, by contrast, liberal bourgeois culture migrated to a part of the world where the feudal mentality had never been known.

The New World did not develop as Europe did. Yet we cannot make sense of either process except by comparing it with the other. Europe is a complex society that 'renews itself out of its own materials' through a dialectical process of 'contagion', involving attack and counter-attack, according to Hartz. Thus the 'feudal world' helps to generate the attack against itself by giving 'its own "class-consciousness" to every Enlightenment ideology,...but it holds out as well the memory of a corporate community which, in the midst of revolution, men seek to capture'.[34]

The New World societies are only partial embodiments of that complexity; there the 'contagion process' is interrupted through 'isolation'. In this way America is saved from a dose of socialism (the 'European disease'). But this very isolation permits the 'interior unfolding' of the fragment, which Europe's complexity and turmoil had prevented. Freed from the 'multiplying challenges' which an ideology like liberalism faces in Europe, this fragment, this 'embryonic telos' wins the day. Compare this victory of liberalism in the New World to a game in which the opposing team did not show up. 'The story is marvellous,' Hartz writes, 'like a succession of Cinderella dreams. Bossuet, Locke, and Cobbett, miserable men abroad, all wake up in worlds finer than they have known.'

Though it sometimes sounds otherwise, the process Hartz is describing is purely mechanical and not in the least mysterious. In his words, 'A part detaches itself from the whole, the whole fails to renew itself, and the part develops without inhibition.'[35] The unfolding of the fragment ideology, Hartz continues, proceeds through two basic 'stages': universalization and nationalization. When still a part of its parent culture, the fragment ideology is known 'mainly in terms of its enemies'. Detached, it becomes for the first time the 'master of a whole region'. Sinking deep beneath the surface of consciousness, it comes to enjoy universal validity. 'Then, almost instantly, it is reborn, transformed into a new nationalism arising out of *the necessities of fragmentation itself.*'[36]

The concept of 'necessity' steals into the argument here, without any immediate elaboration; yet it proves to be a major underpinning of Hartz's theory. Later, in explaining what he means by 'necessity', Hartz reveals a serious weakness in his argument. His explanation amounts to what might be called a 'postulate of psychic necessity'. Hartz argues that a fragment can *never* bear to think of itself as merely a part of a larger whole. This postulate seems to draw a general rule from a single case, namely that of the New England fragment. It seems almost certainly wrong when we consider some Eastern religions, whose members appear quite content to think themselves mere particles of the cosmos, hence merely part of a larger whole. Neither does the postulate describe the English-Canadian fragment adequately, for reasons that will become clear below.

Hartz gets into even more difficulty discussing the 'nationalization' of the fragment ideology: 'Universalism itself comes fairly easily. The fragmented British Puritan can make Calvin universal in New England simply by virtue of his migration. It is nationalism that is more difficult. What "nation" does the universal Puritan belong to? He is no longer completely "English". Being English means...being connected precisely to that totality, past and future, which the fragment has fled.'[37] The key word in this quotation is the last one, asserting the colonist has 'fled'. But has the colonist really fled? Migration is one thing, flight quite another.

In order for the 'laws of fragmentation' to work in the way Hartz describes, the fragment must be kept apart from the whole. Hartz believes emigration always brings isolation, for he has confused migration with flight. Yet migration does not inevitably lead to isolation. Emigrants may indeed isolate themselves; they occasionally choose to dissociate themselves from the parent culture. Sometimes, they are forced to do so. In any event, isolation requires an act of will, a conscious turning away, by someone; or a series of uncommon events that make isolation inevitable. Here too Hartz's theory fails to deal adequately with the English-Canadian fragment, as the following chapters will show.

Hartz's approach to political culture can be described as 'genetic'. It is concerned with origins: with the origins of the ideology and institutions of 'founder societies'. But also, like Darwin's theory of evolution, it speculates on the paths, stages, and forces of change. The 'fragment theory' sees the culture of founding groups as a kind of *genetic code* that does not determine but sets limits to later cultural developments. It selects the pathway of future change. In turn, the pathway chosen goes only so far, offers only some choices and not others.

As the example of Hartz's notion of 'psychic necessity' suggests, this theory moves between 'levels of analysis' with difficulty. Hartz tries to explain the development of a national political culture by referring to personal needs for an identity. But even if individuals or immigrant groups needed cultural stability as much as Hartz believes, could they get other members of society to think as they do? If everyone needed to keep his or her original identity, as many cultures would flower as there were distinct immigrant groups, or even individuals. A reduction to absurdity, perhaps, but too easily accomplished!

Hartz's theory fails to explain how fragment cultures keep themselves alive, by acculturating *new* immigrants and children, thereby surviving, passing the culture from one generation to the next.[38] In this respect, fragment theory resembles the theory of genetic transmission before the structure of DNA was discovered.[39] It requires a complementary theory that explains the learning and modification of culture in simple, unmysterious terms. The ideology of the founding groups may indeed contain the genetic code of political culture, as Hartz suggests. But this insight alone is not enough. For besides the values inherited from founding groups, later events visibly influence the way a culture develops. Such 'formative events' can even cause a culture to shift directions. An important insight into this kind of change appears in the work of Seymour Martin Lipset.

Lipset's Theory of Formative Events

The contrast between Lipset and Hartz shows up clearly in the following passage from Lipset's book, *The First New Nation*: 'Countries, like people, are not handed identities at birth [as Hartz's genetic theory contends], but acquire them through the arduous process of "growing up", a process which is a notoriously painful affair.'[40] Lipset's comparison of countries to people may not be prudent. But still, his book tries to describe the 'growing up' of the American people, and we may learn something by considering the metaphor.

Hartz, a student of political theory, applies European ideological categories (conservatism, liberalism, socialism) to what he calls 'fragment cultures'. A student of political sociology, Lipset instead analyses cultural values using general categories called 'pattern variables', developed by Talcott Parsons. These categories comprise the major ways in which people are expected to interact with one another. The four sets of dimensions, or 'pattern variables', describing a society's 'core' value system Lipset calls achievement-ascription, universalism-particularism, self-orientation-collectivity-orientation, and egalitarianism-élitism. (He added the last dimension to Parsons' three.) According to Lipset,

> a society's value system may emphasize that a person in his orientation to others:
> (1) treats them in terms of their abilities and performances or in terms of inherited qualities (achievement-ascription); (2) applies a general standard or responds to some personal attribute or relationship (universalism-particularism); (3) perceives the separate needs of others or subordinates the individual's needs to the interests of the larger group (self-orientation-collectivity-orientation); and (4) stresses that all persons must be respected because they are human beings or emphasizes the general superiority of those who hold élite positions (egalitarianism-élitism).[41]

The special features of a value system are seen most readily when it is compared with another value system. Thus a comparison of societies is implied by this approach, as by Hartz's (and Almond's). But which comparison is the most revealing? Some might think that comparing two vastly different societies—for example, Canada and Albania—would reveal the most about Canada's character;

and in some cases it might do so. But Lipset chooses instead to compare two similar societies, Canada and the United States. This has the effect of holding constant many common features. The influence of *remaining* differences, for instance, differences in formative events, then becomes all the more evident. In this sense Lipset's method purposely exaggerates the differences between similar cultures, since he wants to show the importance of formative events, one of the 'remaining' differences.

In his search for national differences, he examines a great range of institutions and practices, including education. Lipset points out that 'in Canada education has had a more élitist and ascriptive import than in the U.S.'[42] To support his claim, Lipset compares college enrolment figures, and finds that (in 1960) the proportion of persons aged 20 to 24 enrolled in institutions of higher learning was three times greater in the United States than in Canada. The proportions enrolled in secondary school were similar in both countries, but the United States came out somewhere ahead again. Lipset says these data show that Americans believe that all who are qualified should get a college education, while Canadians believe college should be reserved for the 'intellectual élite—and for children of the well-to-do'.[43]

Lipset finds further support for this judgement 'in the content of the education curricula'. He claims that Canadian educators pay less attention than Americans to 'vocational and professional curricula, especially in institutions of higher learning'. 'Canadians, therefore, differ from Americans in being more eager to maintain the humanist emphasis in the curricula, a point of view which seems to accompany ascriptive values in other societies as well. So we find that Latin is still taught in most Canadian secondary schools.'[44]

Finally, Lipset reports the results of a survey concerned with the purposes of education, which compared the beliefs of both educators and citizens in the two countries. The survey suggested that 'Canadians as a group assigned considerably higher priority than did Americans to knowledge, scholarly attitudes, creative skills, aesthetic appreciation and morality, as outcomes of schooling. Americans emphasized physical development, citizenship, patriotism, social skills and family living...'.[45]

Lipset also compared national attitudes to figures of authority, including political leaders, in the two countries, contending that Americans believe in the equality and dignity of all people more than Canadians do. For example, all free men got the right to vote in the United States in 1845; they did not get the same privilege in Canada until 1898. Thus property qualifications (i.e., unequal wealth) limited the number of voters for a half-century longer in Canada than in the United States. Lipset also examined the ratio of police to population, and the ratio of lawyers in private practice to total population in the two countries. The Canadian ratio is lower in each case. This suggests that Canadians obey the law more readily and do not press their interests in court as often. In leaving the law to law-makers and law-enforcers, Canadians are élitist, he surmises.

The pioneer experience in the two countries yields further symbolic contrasts. In popular mythology the American West was full of rugged individuals—free-spirited, gun-slinging cowboys. Canadians do not imagine such wildness, if they think about their historical frontier at all. The Canadian West was dominated by that red-coated enforcer of laws, the Mountie. Indeed, the purpose of the British North America Act, is to secure the blessing of 'Peace, Order, and Good Government',[46] not liberty and the pursuit of happiness. Accordingly, data show that Canada has had a much lower crime rate than the United States. Crime of all kinds, including criminal homicide, burglary, forgery and counterfeiting, fraud and embezzlement, and larceny, has been less common in Canada.

Data on political protest movements led Lipset to similar conclusions. For example, conservative 'right-wing' anti-communists like Joseph McCarthy were able to win a considerable following in the United States a few decades ago. To Lipset this kind of movement indicates the strength of American support for populism and grass roots democracy. Lipset further argues that people with élitist views, including Canadians, respect figures of public authority more than people who, like Americans, favour equality. For this reason Canadian élites are better able than their counterparts in the United States to protect the civil liberties of unpopular groups. Indeed, values favouring equality encourage people to criticize politicians and public administrators. Election is yet another means of speaking out. Not by chance, the United States fills many more administrative offices by popular election than Canada does.

Lipset believes that even political corruption, which many think is more common in the United States than in Canada, has its sunny side. It shows the strength of the American people's wish to achieve and succeed. So much stress is placed on success that any resolve to follow the rules, which may slow the attainment of success, is relatively weak. Thus, Lipset's value analysis ends up glossing over much of what is worst in American society and, like the legendary philosopher's stone, manages to turn dross into gold. By the same token Lipset portrays Canada as a country that is sadly lacking.

Canada's labour legislation, Lipset continues, is more restrictive than that of the United States because it limits the right to strike to formally organized unions. Canadians are slower to invest in the economy or start a new business. They have less faith in free enterprise. Generally, Canadians are quicker to ask the government for help in achieving their collective goals. 'In recent years, proposals for medicare, grants for large families, government intervention in the economy, public ownership of major enterprises have encountered much less opposition north of the border than south of it.'[47] These examples are supposed to show that Canadians have less desire to achieve or to realize their personal potential.

Another built-in restraint is the 'vertical mosaic', Canada's continuing commitment to ethnic separation and inequality. This value compares poorly, in Lipset's eyes, to the 'melting pot' ideology of the United States. In this connection, Lipset points out that the Canadian census and, until recently, Canadian passports, have documented each person's ethnic origin. But ethnic (and religious and regional) distinctiveness has taken its toll. Politically, the 'third parties' that have appeared have tended, in his view, to represent narrow sectional interests. They have fostered neither progress nor unity.

In yet another area of investigation Lipset compares our religious traditions with American ones; and he assumes customs in marriage and divorce grow out of these traditions. Religion in Canada has been much more conservative than in the United States; also, more sympathetic to inequality, and more strongly supported by the state, he contends. Lipset compared divorce rates per thousand marriages in the two countries in various years between 1891 and 1960; the consistently higher rate in the United States he took to mean that the United States is less tradition-bound than Canada.

Origin and Impact of Value Differences

From all of these and other similar data Lipset concludes that Canadians have a greater respect for tradition of all kinds: for tradition in social life (like permanent marriage), for traditional loyalties (like ethnic solidarity), and for traditional forms of deference (to traditional élites). Canadians seem to like law and order better than freedom and equality. In terms of the pattern variables, Canadians are more particularistic, diffuse, collectivity-oriented, and élitist than Americans: in a word, less modern. What, Lipset asks, caused this difference; and how has this difference influenced the course of national development in each country?

Underlying Lipset's analysis of value systems as 'causal factors' is the notion 'that a complex society is under constant pressure to adjust its institutions to its central value system, in order to alleviate strains created by changes in social relations'.[48] But if value systems are not handed to a society at the moment of its birth, where do they come from?

To deal with this question, Lipset 'assumes a perspective taken by Max Weber'. Using Weber's metaphor of 'loaded dice',[49] Lipset argues that early events favour some outcomes over others: 'The key historical events set one process in motion in one country and a second in another.... [O]nce the dice come up with a certain number, they would tend to come up with the same number again. In other words, historical events establish values and predispositions, and these in turn determine later events.'[50] Restated, Lipset is arguing that certain historical 'formative' events serve to fix certain values in the public mind, largely by embodying these values in institutions that endure. Lipset's writing, therefore, stresses 'continuities in the essential values of...society'[51] and the ability of institutions to direct change into the channels cut by these essential values.

According to Lipset's theory, Canada's major formative event turns out to be the flip side of America's. America's was the revolution, Canada's the *counter-*

revolution and the movement of anti-revolutionary Loyalists to Canada from the United States. Thus 'two disparate founding ethos' account for the observed contrast between American and Canadian society. In Lipset's words:

> once these events have formed the structure of the two nations, their institutional characters were set. Subsequent events tended to enforce 'leftist' values in the south and 'rightist' ones in the north. The success of the Revolutionary ideology, the defeat of the Tories, and the emigration of many of them north to Canada or across the ocean to Britain—all served to enhance the strength of the forces favouring egalitarian democratic principles in the new nation and to weaken conservative tendencies. On the other hand, the failure of Canada to have a revolution of its own, the immigration of conservative elements, and the emigration of radical ones—all contributed to make Canada a more conservative and more rigidly stratified society.[52]

Thus the two societies differ today because their historical experience has not only been different but opposite. The difference has since been regularized and stabilized—in short, institutionalized—in religion, family life, class relations, and education within each country. These institutions, in turn, channelled social and economic change, and thus channelled the political development of the two societies, in customary ways.

Lipset's approach and his conclusions have been criticized from every imaginable standpoint. Many have doubted Lipset's interpretation of the data he collected. In some cases, they argue, Lipset might have drawn the very opposite conclusions from these same data.[53] A few attack his way of explaining the observed value differences, arguing that these differences can be explained by 'cultural lag' if one assumes that Canada is very similar to the United States, but lags behind it culturally by twenty, thirty, or forty years. If so, current Canadian data should be compared with American data from the 1940s or 1950s to measure the true depth of cultural similarity.[54] Others have asked Lipset to state clearly which Canada, French or English, he is analyzing. In one of his articles, Lipset admitted he was ignoring the francophone subculture. But in most of his work he has failed to make this distinction. Often Lipset's data measuring national rates of behaviour (rates of crime or divorce, for example) lump together anglophones and francophones. Another critic attacks the analysis of values itself, asking: what really are values, and whose values are we discussing? Is the description of American values meant to describe every single American, the statistically modal American, or only American institutions? Lipset doesn't say.[55]

Similarly Lipset's discussion of 'formative events' has failed to specify which kinds of events are formative and which are not. This lapse makes identifying formative events in other countries uncertain, and comparing nations difficult. Yet, if we extrapolate Lipset's meaning, we can possibly bring Lipset's work together with Hartz's. Let us begin by supposing that, by formative events, Lipset meant those historical events that leave their mark upon (a) the 'national memory' through the medium of language, myths, symbols, or sagas; (b) basic institutions and structures, perhaps set up or modified in response to these events; and (c) political alliances, especially among minority groups.[56]

In applying the notion of 'formative events', however, we must also examine the 'cultural baggage' immigrants brought to these societies, particularly during the 'founding' periods. True, culture in the New World may feature 'new learning', as the 'frontier theorists' (e.g., Turner) as well as Lipset, have argued. But immigrants often keep their native culture and attempt (even unconsciously) to adapt their new society to the culture they knew at home. And as Hartz points out, the founders of a country, by arriving first, start with a relatively blank slate, free of opposing cultures or social institutions.[57] Indeed, in a country as large as Canada, there is a 'new beginning' each time settlers move into an area where few live, such as the Canadian West or, more recently, the North. Hartz's fragment theory can help us understand the effect of many such new beginnings, which may constitute a form of 'subfragmentation'.

Hartz's theory has difficulty explaining the rise to dominance of a single national culture amidst competing immigrant traditions. The formative events and historical residues of which Lipset has written play an important role here. Thus Lipset and Hartz come together in complementary fashion. Still, many problems remain in Lipset's analysis. But rather than dealing with them at some remove from the real world I shall try, by synthesizing the two theories, to apply what is useful and ignore what is not.

Conclusion

This chapter has reviewed the history of the concept 'political culture'. The term was invented to substitute for 'ideology', which some felt reflected the Marxist viewpoint too strongly and underestimated the role of ideas in political affairs.

A culture—a set of ways of thinking about the world—means nothing, however, outside the material circumstances of its birth and development and the social arrangements that keep it alive. Culture is no Olympian or exotic thing. A people's culture reflects and guides the daily way of life. To ensure that our study would not ignore the 'structural underpinnings' that shore up a political culture, this chapter introduced the ideas of Karl Mannheim. As in Mannheim's 'ideology', so too in dealing with 'political culture', a student must approach any situation through what Weber called *verstehen* ('understanding'): we must penetrate the minds of our actors, learn their language, listen to them speak, and understand the world as they understand it. We must try to hear all the voices, and not ignore those of the minorities and the disadvantaged who too often are muted by the loud talk of the strong and powerful. Then, we must go one step beyond and understand the ways a culture relates to the economic and social relations in which it is embedded. Even the way communication is organized plays a key role.[58]

Finally, this chapter examined Louis Hartz's theory of fragmentation, and Seymour Lipset's notion of formative events.[59] The next chapter will draw out these ideas in more detail, raising new questions. So, like a flower opening outward, the range of discourse will get progressively wider. We shall discuss many of the issues that surface in any good analysis of Canadian society: the problematic relations between English and French Canadians, regional disparity, the absence of class consciousness, the elusive Canadian identity, and so on.

Increasingly, in tracing the ideas of Lipset and Hartz and others to their logical conclusion, we shall discover that Canada has no single political culture. This very complexity at the level of political culture simply demonstrates Canada's disunity at other levels. Cultural disunity represents the problem of national disunity in miniature, it is true; but perhaps it is also a root *cause* of national disunity. One cannot imagine Canada's various subgroups co-operating to build the nation, or even sharing a common purpose, when they lack a common political culture: a shared view of the illnesses afflicting the political order and the remedies likely to make it healthier.

Notes

[1] Gabriel Almond, 'Comparative Political Systems', *World Politics* (1956). Reprinted in Almond, *Political Development* (Boston: Little, Brown, 1970).

[2] *Ibid.*: 35.

[3] *Ibid.*: 19.

[4] *Ibid.*: 36.

[5] See Richard M. Merelman, 'The Development of Political Ideology: A Framework for the Analysis of Political Socialization', *American Political Science Review* 63 (September 1969): 75-93.

[6] Almond: 37.

[7] Quoted in Anthony Walker, *Culture and Personality* (New York: Random House, 1961): 6.

[8] Gabriel Almond and Sidney Verba, *The Civic Culture* (Boston: Little, Brown, 1965): 12.

[9] Almond: 29.

[10] Professor Samuel Beer also credits Parsons' formulation with providing an important 'American starting point' for the construction of the concept of political culture (personal communication to the author, 14 February 1977).

[11] Almond and Verba: 14. Glenda Patrick complains that Almond overemphasizes the subjective internalized considerations to the exclusion of an equally significant component of Parsons' concept of culture: its objective manifestations in symbols, language, and other 'cultural objects'. She then proffers an alternative definition of culture that takes into account these 'objective' considerations: 'political culture refers to the particular pattern of authoritative standards that defines the range of acceptable behaviour for actors within any political system; it consists of the total constellation of beliefs or ideas about the structure of authority, norms (rules and laws), values (goals and purposes), and symbols embodied in the formal constitution or lodged in a set of informal customs and habits, deviation from which evokes authoritative sanctions.' The objective definition of political culture requires research techniques that go beyond survey research, and takes as acceptable evidence institutional practices in addition to stated beliefs and values. In this respect, the objective definition is quite compatible with the approach to political culture of both Lipset and Hartz, who look at many kinds of evidence in assessing political culture. See Patrick, 'The Concept Political Culture', unpub-

lished monograph, Committee on Conceptual and Terminological Analysis, 1976. Note as well the discussion of culture as both 'extériorité' and 'intériorité' in Léon Dion and Micheline de Sève, 'Cultures politiques au Québec', mimeo., n.d.

[12] Almond and Verba: 34.

[13] *Ibid.*: 14. Inexplicably, the authors nowhere acknowledge their intellectual debt to Easton.

[14] *Ibid.*: 373.

[15] *Ibid.*: 352.

[16] See for example the work of John Meisel, Richard Simeon, David Ekins, Michael Whittington, Jon Pammett, and others cited elsewhere in this book. The most thorough critique appears in Dion and de Sève.

[17] See for example Gad Horowitz, 'Notes on "Conservatism, Liberalism, and Socialism in Canada" ', *Canadian Journal of Political Science* 11,2 (June 1978): 383-99, particularly 396 ff.

[18] For a brilliant critique of political development scholars' presumptions about the modernity of the American political system, see Samuel P. Huntington, 'Modernity: America vs. Europe' in his book *Political Order in Changing Societies* (New Haven: Yale University Press, 1968). A thorough assessment of the use of the political culture approach in political development appears in Ali Banuazizi, 'Social-Psychological Approaches to Political Development' in Myron Weiner and S.P. Huntington (eds) *Understanding Political Development* (Boston: Little Brown, 1987).

[19] Karl Mannheim, *Ideology and Utopia* (New York: Harvest Book, 1958): 60, 61.

[20] *Ibid.*: 61.

[21] *Ibid.*: 265.

[22] *Ibid.* For two excellent studies of Marxist theories of ideology, see Jorge Lorrain, *The Concept of Ideology* (London: Hutchinson, 1979); and *Marxism and Ideology* (London: Macmillan, 1983).

[23] Mannheim: 271.

[24] *Ibid.*: 272.

[25] *Ibid.*: 276.

[26] According to Bonnie Fox the nature of feminist scholarship varies across a wide ideological spectrum, ranging from *liberal feminists*, who assume that men and women are basically equal and therefore women deserve 'equal opportunity'; through *radical feminists*, who believe that women's and men's nature differ essentially, that male oppression of women is universal, and that feminists should strive to create 'a positive assessment of feminine characteristics, if not a wholly separate women's culture'; to *Marxist feminists*, who emphasize the different roles males and females play in economic production and use class analysis to analyze the oppression of women; to *socialist feminists* who attempt to synthesize radical and Marxist feminism. See 'The Feminist Challenge: A Reconsideration of Social Inequality and Economics Development' in Robert Brym and Bonnie J. Fox, *From Culture to Power: The Sociology of English Canada* (Toronto: Oxford University Press, 1989): 176. The importance of reproduction as an underpinning of culture is the basis of Mary O'Brien's innovative book, *The Politics of Reproduction* (London: Routledge, 1981).

[27] Clearly, there are many theoretical and common-sense similarities between *ideology* and *political culture*. The popularity of the term *political culture* points, however, to a major split within the social sciences. Professor Samuel Beer claims that *political culture* was introduced a generation ago partly in reaction to the 'exceptionally hard-nosed economic determinism that infused the Marxism of that day'. Marxists' inflexibility limited the usefulness of the concept *ideology* for non-Marxists. A new term was needed if non-Marxists were to discuss 'the role of ideas in history', whose importance had been clearly shown by 'the evident power of ideologies in the tortured world of the 1930s and 1940s'. But because ideology had been largely claimed by the Marxists, a new term, *political culture*, seemed necessary (personal communication to the author, 14 February 1977).

Different groups in the social sciences still prefer one term over the other. Some, like Almond, adopt a 'functionalist' or systems approach to the study of society. Their style of thinking goes back through Talcott Parsons and Max Weber to German idealism, and they usually prefer the term *political culture*. More radical social scientists, whose thinking descends from Mannheim and Marx, usually speak of *ideology*. In a few instances, both terms are used (somewhat along the lines proposed by Almond). Then, political culture is considered the broader term and ideology appears as a variant (or subculture) within a larger culture.

The use of the term *political culture* in this book does not reflect an assumption that values rule over the material world, or that agreement about values is more common than disagreement, or that we should ignore the role of power in human affairs. Rather I wish to to avoid too-narrow Marxist connotations of class conflict and the weight of intellectual baggage that an old term, like ideology, is always made to carry. This decision might have been different if Mannheim's 'total conception' of ideology had gotten wider recognition, for my understanding of 'political culture' is similar to Mannheim's conception of 'ideology'.

[28] Some scholars emphatically deny that equivalence is attainable. Even the identically worded question, properly translated, may take on an entirely different meaning in moving from one culture to another. Thus, Alisdair MacIntyre criticizes Almond and Verba for an insensitivity to cultural nuances that virtually invalidate comparability of many of their findings. Similarly, Irwin Deutscher questions the assumption that survey responses provide valid, reliable clues to behaviour: 'There is adequate reason to suspect that . . . responses to questions may not provide an adequate basis for imputing behaviour toward the objects themselves (i.e., responses to the people or situation to which the words [in the questions] refer)' ('Words and Deeds: Social Science and Social Policy', in W.J. Filstead, ed., *Qualitative Methodology* [Chicago: Rand McNally, 1970]: 31). See Alisdair MacIntyre, 'Is a Science of Comparative Politics Possible?' in Alan Ryan, ed., *The Philosophy of Social Explanation* (London: Oxford University Press, 1973).

[29] Louis Hartz, *The Liberal Tradition in America* (New York: Harcourt Brace, 1953).

[30] Cf. Kenneth D. McRae, 'Louis Hartz's Concept of the Fragment Society and Its Applications to Canada', *Etudes Canadiennes* 5 (1978): 17-30. See also H.D. Forbes, 'Hartz-Horowitz at Twenty: Nationalism, Toryism and Socialism in Canada and the United States', *Canadian Journal of Political Science* 20,2 (June, 1987): 287-316.

[31] Thus for Hartz as for Almond, cross-national comparison is indispensable to understanding political culture.

[32] Louis Hartz et al., *The Founding of New Societies* (New York: Harcourt Brace, 1964): 3.

[33] Note, for example, the nostalgic tone of Marx and Engels' attack on the bourgeoisie which 'has put an end to all feudal, patriarchal, idyllic relations. It has pitilessly torn asunder the motley feudal ties that bound man to his "natural superiors", and has left remaining no other nexus between man and man than naked self-interest, than callous "cash payment".' *Manifesto of the Communist Party*, reprinted in Lewis S. Feuer, ed., *Marx and Engels: Basic Writings on Politics and Philosophy* (New York: Anchor Books, 1959): 9.

[34] Hartz et al.: 7 et passim.

[35] Ibid.: 9.

[36] Ibid.: 5.

[37] Ibid.: 11.

[38] Hartz argues that immigrants are resocialized by the 'new nationalism' to accept the 'fragment ethic', but he acknowledges that cultural conflicts posed by immigrants dilute the 'purity' of fragment culture. For this reason societies like Afrikaner South Africa, and French Canada, which 'tended to renew themselves from within' rather than by immigration, present 'the purest cases of fragment traditionalism' (ibid.: 14.).

[39] Cf. Thomas Thorson, *Biopolitics* (New York: Holt, Rinehart and Winston, 1970). Note as well David V.J. Bell, 'Methodological Problems in the Study of Canadian Political Culture', unpublished CPSA paper, 1974.

40 Seymour Martin Lipset, *The First New Nation* (New York: Basic Books, 1963).

41 S.M. Lipset, *Revolution and Counterrevolution* (New York: Anchor Books, 1970): 38.

42 *Ibid.*: 40. Although his point is confirmed by John Porter, it was probably more true prior to the rapid expansion of Canadian higher education in the 1960s. Porter's data were drawn from the 1950s.

43 *Ibid.*: 41 (Lipset quoting Woodside).

44 *Ibid.* Latin has become almost extinct in the Canadian high school curriculum since Lipset published that statement. In his most recent comparative analysis of Canada and the U.S., Lipset modifies his earlier views, pointing out that Canada is 'moving away from an élitist emphasis,' particularly in higher education. Nevertheless, he insists that the two countries still 'differ somewhat' in the predicted directions. See S.M. Lipset, *Continental Divide* (New York: Routledge, 1990): 217-18.

45 *Ibid.*: 42 (Lipset quoting Downy).

46 In a fascinating attempt to identify cultural factors associated with the 'myth of the peaceable kingdom' (a prominent literary allusion in Canada), Judith Torrance speaks about the 'high value placed on peace and its enshrinement as a national attribute'. Taken in conjunction with two other cultural themes ('a low assessment of the natural sociability and benevolence of mankind', and 'an élitist preconception of the role of government in society'), this belief has contributed to a unique pattern of response to incidents of political violence. Her research shows commonalities of response that recur over time and cut across party lines, therefore suggesting a widespread, enduring political culture of violence perception, at least among the élite. See Judith Torrance, 'The Response of Canadian Governments to Violence', *Canadian Journal of Political Science* 10,3 (September 1977): 473-96. Quoted passages appear on pp. 494, 495. See also Judy H. Torrance, *Public Violence in Canada* (Kingston and Montreal: McGill-Queen's University Press, 1986).

47 Lipset, *Revolution and Counterrevolution*: 52-3.

48 Lipset, *The First New Nation*: 7-8.

49 Lipset's interpretation of the loaded-dice analogy takes great liberties with Weber's use of the example. Weber's concern in 'The Logic of the Cultural Science' was to deal with the problem of 'Objective Possibility and Adequate Causation in Historical Explanation'. Faced with the difficulty of singling out a few 'essential' components from 'among the infinity of determining factors' (Max Weber, *The Methodology of the Social Sciences* [Glencoe, Ill.: The Free Press, 1949]: 171), one begins by postulating a 'law of events' or 'empirical rule' which allows us to arrive at 'judgements of possibility—i.e., ...what would happen in the event of the exclusion or modification of certain conditions' (p. 173). But to convert such judgements of possibility to a more elaborate 'calculus of probability' (i.e., to be able to assign numerical values to various 'possible' outcomes) would necessarily require that historical situations follow the laws of 'absolute chance' to the extent that 'given a very large number of cases, certain simple and unambiguous conditions remain absolutely the same' (p. 182). But Weber insists that absolute chance is an unrealistic application of probability theory to historical causation; instead we must develop a notion of 'favoured' outcomes analogous to the outcomes of repeated throws of 'loaded dice'.

Entirely absent from this discussion, however, is any suggestion that the historical dice are loaded because of the interplay of historical events and values. This interpretation appears to have been 'read in' to Weber's discussion by Lipset.

50 Lipset, *First New Nation*: 7.

51 *Ibid.*: 139.

52 *Revolution and Counterrevolution*: 60-1.

53 See for example Tom Truman, 'A Critique of Seymour M. Lipset's article, "Value differences, absolute or relative. The English-speaking democracies" ', *Canadian Journal of Political Science* 4,4 (December 1971).

54 See for example James Curtis, 'Canada as a Nation of Joiners: Evidence from National Surveys',

in J.E. Gallagher and R.D. Lambert, *Social Process and Institution: The Canadian Case* (Toronto: Holt, Rinehart, Winston, 1971). See also Craig Crawford and James Curtis, 'English Canadian-American Differences in Value Orientations: Survey Comparisons Bearing on Lipset's Thesis', *Studies in Comparative International Development* (Summer, 1979). See also I.L. Horowitz, 'The Hemispheric Connection', *Queen's Quarterly* 80,3 (Autumn, 1973): 327-59.

[55] Fred Matthews, 'The "Myth" and "Value" Approaches to American Studies', *Canadian Review of American Studies* 3,2 (Fall, 1972). Note that Lipset has refined his analysis in the many different versions he has presented. The most sophisticated, and most recent, is *Continental Divide* (*op.cit.*).

[56] Seymour Martin Lipset and Stein Rokkan, eds, *Party Systems and Voter Alignments* (New York: Free Press, 1967). Lipset works this idea out in detail in his study (with Rokkan) of political parties and cleavages. There he uses the term 'historical residue' to refer to the legacy of formative events, that is, of dramatic or prolonged conflict. For some fascinating research on historical events, heroes, and memories see J.A. Laponce, 'The heroes' trade: a contribution to a geography of culture'. *Social Science Information* 29, 2 (1990); and Howard Schuman and Jacqueline Scott, 'Generations and Collective Memories', *American Sociological Review* 54 (June 1989)

[57] Hartz is not oblivious to the pre-founding presence of aboriginal peoples. Indeed he discusses the pattern of European-aboriginal contact in each of the 'new societies'.

[58] For a discussion of the contributions Harold Innis made to understanding transportation and communication as the 'material base' of culture, see Bell, 'Methodological Problems' and the literature cited therein; and David V.J. Bell, 'Political Culture in Canada' in Michael Whittington and Glen Williams (eds), *Canadian Politics in the 1990s* (Toronto: Methuen, 1989).

[59] A note on methodology is required here. At first reading both Lipset and Hartz appear to be writing in the 'idealist' mode, which places primary emphasis on values and ideas as causal factors in explaining action. The contrasting 'materialist' mode of explanation emphasizes instead aspects of the social structure and economy as primary factors.

Certainly Lipset criticizes what might be called vulgar materialism. In a section of *First New Nation* entitled 'The Inadequacy of a Materialist Interpretation of Change', he criticizes William Whyte and David Riesman for implying that 'the economy, in order to be productive, requires certain types of individuals, and requires that they hold certain values' (p. 122). Lipset easily demolishes such a 'materialist interpretation' with a simple demonstration from comparative analysis: since Britain industrialized earlier than the U.S., 'If the causal connection between technology and social character were direct, then the patterns described as typical of "other direction" or "the organization man" should have occurred in Great Britain prior to their occurrence in the European nations. Yet [these] appear to be preeminently American traits' (p. 123). But Lipset is really calling for a balanced approach that examines both culture and structure, or in his words 'work[s] out the implications of the value system within a given material setting—while always observing, of course, the gradual, cumulative effect that technological change has upon values' (p. 123).

Similarly, Hartz's entire approach to fragmentation appears to some critics hopelessly idealistic. Gad Horowitz helps correct that distortion, first, by pointing out that Hartz is well aware of ' "environmental" factors (such as the continuing tie with the mother country, and the interaction of the fragment culture with native peoples)' that prevent the fragment from evolving according to the genetic blueprint embedded in fragment culture; second, by showing that Marx and Engels themselves were well aware of the impact of values and ideology on the course of political development. Horowitz opens his article with a quote that could have been written by Louis Hartz, but instead came from the pen of Friedrich Engels: 'A durable reign of the bourgeoisie has been possible only in countries like America, where feudalism was unknown and society at the very beginning started from a bourgeois base.' See Gad Horowitz, 'Notes on "Conservatism, Liberalism and Socialism in Canada" ': 383, 384. Note as well S.M. Lipset, 'Radicalism in North America: A Comparative View of the Party Systems in Canada and the United States', *Proceedings of the Royal Society of Canada,* 1976.

2 | Founding Fragments and Formative Events

Building on Louis Hartz's interpretation of societies founded by European immigrants as 'fragments' of European political culture, Kenneth McRae has pointed out that 'Canada offers almost a classic instance of a two-fragment society'. The older fragment broke off from France in the early seventeenth century, when Champlain first settled Quebec permanently in 1608. But, according to McRae, the sparsely populated colony did not take on its enduring character until nearly sixty years later, when it came under direct royal control. From 1663 onwards, French-style absolutism dominated the political development of the colony: 'New France was a projection—a deliberate and official projection—into the New World of a dynamic, authoritarian society at the zenith of its power.'[1]

Geography kept the 'absolutists' from completely realizing their plan. Lying on the other side of an ocean, the colony was months away from the royal officials in France who tried to govern its affairs. The unsettled frontier offered a place of refuge to those *habitants* who found the European social order too limiting. Certain feudal customs failed to survive the transatlantic voyage without change; the social distance between *habitant* and *seigneur* in New France did not approach the immense gap in wealth and refinement that in France separated the nobility from the peasantry.[2] Within these limitations, the French fragment of Canada evolved according to the political culture of modified absolutism, adapting the social, political, and religious institutions of seventeenth-century feudal France to its own needs.

Yet colonial departures from the French model were neither accidental nor determined by the environment. In many cases colonial officials consciously sought to institute a different kind of feudalism in the New World, partly to avoid some of the abuses that troubled the Old. 'Feudalism in France was an organic growth; in Canada it was a transplanted institution, and French administration saw to it that in the transplanting it was pruned of less desirable characteristics. The French monarchy had established itself in the teeth of feudal opposition and was in no mood now to offer the seigniors [*sic*] sufficient independence and power so as to require repetition of the experience.'[3] Thus the French crown deliberately denied the *seigneurs* important political, judicial, and military rights enjoyed by the French nobility.[4] Likewise, steps were taken to protect the welfare of the peasants. Even their new name, *habitant*, indicated a better status than the Old World *paysan*.

According to the governors of New France, agriculture and settlement were the primary activities. Trade and missionary work disrupted them. A thriving fur trade that allowed men to flee into the woods and 'escape the discipline of society' challenged the feudal institutions despite their modifications and improvements. Yet the fur trade was controlled from France, so it produced only a group of romantic outsiders—the *coureurs de bois*—and not a class of prosperous local merchants who might have fought the feudal ideology and its institutions.[5] The few capitalists who had gained a foothold in New France fell as the first victims of the British conquest in 1759.

Referred to by francophones as *la cession* (a term that reveals their sense of betrayal), the end of French rule removed many non-feudal elements and strengthened tradition at the expense of modernity. It 'purified' the French fragment. The British took control of the fur trade, and local francophone merchants and entrepreneurs returned to France. The new rulers disbanded the militia, which had provided a countervailing power for the *habitants*, from whose ranks the militia captain was always chosen. Many of the civil authorities dismissed by the British had also been aggressive businessmen. In the words of historian John Bosher: 'There was an ambiguity in the royal financial administration of New France, indeed of the entire French kingdom. The system was almost as much a private enterprise as a public function.'[6] Now the French merchants and officials were gone, and the impulse of bourgeois modernization deadened.

The only institutions surviving the conquest were the Catholic church (whose power eventually expanded to fill the vacuum), the feudal landholders, and French language and civil law. Thus the dynamic forces for change were destroyed, while the traditional institutions were strengthened, with British colonial institutions superimposed on them.

At first no Assembly was elected; an Assembly was only granted later when the newly arrived anglophone colonists demanded it. But the Assembly became almost immediately the crucible of Anglo-French conflict. Ultimately French leaders used it to save rural tradition from the English impulse to change and modernize. Pierre Trudeau wrote that the francophones 'had but one desire—to survive as a nation; and it became apparent that parliamentary government might turn out to be a useful tool for that purpose. [In 1837, the] Canadians fought at Saint-Denis and Saint-Eustache as they would eventually rally for electoral battles or parliamentary debates whenever their ethnic survival seemed to be imperilled, as men in an army whose sole purpose is to drive the *Anglais* back.'[7]

No one can guess with any certainty the kind of society that might have evolved in Quebec if the British had not conquered New France. But it certainly would have been quite different. Quebec would probably have progressed and become cosmopolitan more quickly than it did. Perhaps it would have been clerical and feudal for a shorter time. The conquest was survived by a group of traditional people sensitive to the threat posed by alien rulers and led by a clerical élite committed almost fanatically to guarding their people against the twin dangers of dispersal and absorption. 'Therefore it was that the Church, profoundly convinced that to keep the race French was to keep it Catholic, came to look upon isolation as the chief safeguard for a racial individuality threatened on all sides by the advances of the New World.'[8]

The Canadian French proved remarkably ingrown. Efforts to attract emigrants from France had never enjoyed much success, despite offers of assistance that sometimes amounted to bribery. In order to encourage marriage, the authorities had to increase the supply of girls and young women. This they accomplished by 'shipping from France "demoiselles" for the military officers and what pious Mother Marie de l'Incarnation called "une merchandise mêlée"—mixed goods— for the ordinary settlers, something more than a thousand altogether.'[9] To encourage large families, bonuses were given to those who had at least ten living legitimate children (not in religious orders) and fines to those whose children delayed marriage beyond age 20 for males and age 16 for females! Almost the entire francophone population of Quebec has therefore descended from about 10,000 original colonists who arrived between 1608 and 1760.[10] Even today relatively few surnames are to be found amongst the francophone Québécois.[11] The high rate of population growth this group achieved through natural increase alone averaged about two and a quarter per cent a year for three centuries. This demographic feat, known as 'the revenge of the cradle', has rarely been equalled in the world.[12]

An almost total absence of francophone immigrants after 1763 meant a very low level of 'population turnover'. Without 'fresh blood', new ideas were few, and tradition was able to keep its grip on the population. No revolutions or upheavals broke the existing pattern. As the present century dawned André Siegfried observed that French Canada avoided the French Revolution, 'never went through its 1789': 'All the old beliefs have been preserved as it were in ice among the French of Canada, and it would seem that the great stream of modern thought has as yet failed, with them, to shake the rock of Catholic belief.'[13] Indeed, some church leaders thought the Conquest was a godsend: it insulated New France from the sacrilegious turmoil of the French Revolution and allowed the church to propagate Catholicism of the unreformed variety in the New World. Tradition started to break down only in the middle of the present century when it had to contend with life in large cities, the growth of bureaucracies, and the spread of modern mass media: the so-called Quiet Revolution.

In contrast, Canada's anglophone society began as a more open, fluid fragment and has ever since been changed and enlivened by newcomers. These immigrants have come first from the United States, then from Britain, later from Europe, and most recently from Asia and the Caribbean. Anglophones and English-learning newcomers have dispersed into all regions. Yet from among the many anglophone groups that have come to settle in Canada, attention has been focused especially on the earliest settlers, the Loyalists. Unfortunately, scholars studying early English-Canadian history have disagreed more sharply over the Loyalists than over any other single issue or group.

Origins of Loyalism

One could say that the process that produced loyalism really began when the British acquired Quebec in 1763. During negotiations leading up to the Treaty of Paris, which ended the Seven Years' War, Britain was sorely tempted to let France keep this area. Instead, Britain would have taken Guadeloupe, whose potential contribution to the English economy appeared more valuable than the 'acres of snow' in continental North America. Finally, however, concerned about security and wishing to eliminate the French threat to the Thirteen Colonies, Britain passed up the chance to add the Sugar Island to its empire, and kept New France instead.

Defending this new territory meant spending more on weapons and supplies. The British decided that the American colonies ought to shoulder at least a part of the war debt and the added costs of policing the new lands. Removing the French threat to the Thirteen Colonies had, however, cut the bonds holding in check the colonists' ambitions for land. But for the moment Britain wished to keep American colonists from spreading into this wilderness that so invited settlement. Efforts to keep settlers out of this area, coupled with repeated attempts to tax the colonies to help pay for their own defence and administration, led inexorably to the Declaration of Independence in 1776, and then to the American Revolutionary War. This war, in turn, produced the Loyalists who sought refuge in English Canada. But we must not rush ahead too quickly.

In the years between 1763 and 1776, one thousand British military officers and merchants replaced the French fur traders and political officials in Quebec, settling mainly in Montreal and Quebec City. The élite of the Catholic church were allowed to keep their privileges. They even strengthened their hold over the francophone population. With help from the clergy, a tiny British ruling class balanced itself at the apex of a francophone society now numbering about 80,000 persons. Under British military rule, Quebec lacked entirely those institutions of representative government found in all the English-speaking colonies of North America.

Nova Scotia was another recent British acquisition, also taken from France around the middle of the eighteenth century.[14] In 1755, many French-speaking Acadians were rounded up and exiled, the unlucky victims of a colonial policy of expulsion and resettlement. Some Acadians managed to remain in Canada by disappearing into the back country of what is now New Brunswick and Prince Edward Island.[15] Prior to the American Revolution, however, the officially recognized population of Nova Scotia consisted largely of transplanted New Englanders, later dubbed by J.E. Brebner 'neutral Yankees'.[16]

These settlers were Yankees by birth and inclination, neutral by common sense and often reluctant choice. They probably would have preferred to join with their cousins in Massachusetts who had declared themselves independent from Britain. But for a variety of reasons Nova Scotia, the Fourteenth Colony, did not join the other thirteen. Nova Scotia's economy was not developed enough to support a drive to independence. Besides, the powerful naval garrison situated at Halifax made rebellion very risky. The relatively young colony also lacked a network of transportation and communication links that might have enabled nationalist anti-British feeling to spread and take hold. For all these reasons, Nova Scotia was destined to remain under British rule. During and after the American Revolution, about one-third of Nova Scotia's 14,000 inhabitants left to rejoin their relatives in New England; but most stayed behind.[17]

To sum up, the major formative events of this period were three: the acquisition of Nova Scotia from France in the mid-eighteenth century, the acquisition of New France in 1763, and the American Revolution. And of these three events, the last is the most important. Americans may recall it as the time the Thirteen Colonies threw off British rule. In fact, the American Revolution was a struggle to control all of the east coast of North America north of Florida (which was then a Spanish possession).

For Canada it signifies, first of all, the *failure* of the revolutionaries to conquer Quebec and bring it under American rule; and the parallel failure to bring Nova Scotia into the Revolution. Perhaps most important of all, the struggle produced the Loyalists of the American Revolution: colonists who opposed the Revolution and decided to leave rather than help build the new American nation.

The Loyalists were to play a major part in helping Canada to emerge as a separate nation on the northern half of this continent. In most important respects, the Loyalists founded English Canada. Depending on the sources one cites and how a Loyalist is defined, between 30,000 and 60,000 Loyalists emigrated to the Maritimes and to what are now Ontario and Quebec after the Revolution. At the time, the European population of these regions comprised fewer than 15,000 Anglophones altogether. Thus English Canada came into being as a by-product of the American Revolution.

For an internal war to produce two countries may seem unusual, but it has happened before. Such an outcome depends largely on the fate befalling the losers of the internal war. Sometimes the losers are exterminated; many Russian and French anti-revolutionaries met such an end. At other times losers are absorbed into a strong neighbouring society, just as many Cuban refugees were absorbed by the United States after Castro's revolution. But sometimes losers move to a weak underpopulated area nearby and start a new society. Many losers in the Chinese Revolution moved to Taiwan (Formosa) and Hong Kong; most losers in the American Revolution moved to Canada.

Both Lipset's and Hartz's analyses of Canadian political culture start with the

Loyalist migration. For Louis Hartz, Canada's political culture is rooted in a 'liberal' fragment 'etched with a Tory streak coming out of the American Revolution'.[18] For S.M. Lipset the American Revolution produced its counterpart in the Canadian 'counter-revolution' which, he says, dedicated itself to keeping Canada different from the United States.

The Anglophone Fragment

Who were the Loyalists, a people who rejected—or, depending on one's point of view, were rejected by—the American Revolution? The answer obviously depends on how the Revolution itself is interpreted. Those who believe that the Revolution was class-based tend to think that colonial American society was made up of two social classes, the privileged and the rest. The privileged favoured a social hierarchy, an established church, passive obedience to superiors, and government by an aristocracy. The underprivileged wanted universal equality (at least among white men), the separation of church and state, freedom from foreign domination, and representative government.

During the American Revolution, this interpretation argues, the underprivileged threw out their oppressors. The defeated Tory group then moved north to Canada, where it attempted to create another society based on hierarchy, the 'establishment', and so on. W.S. MacNutt has called this attempt the Loyalist dream of 'Elysium'. A.R.M. Lower puts it this way: '[The] loyalist movement withdrew a class concept of life from the south, moved up north and gave it a second chance. . . .'[19] If this interpretation is correct, early English Canada might be characterized in Hartz's terms as a pure Tory conservative fragment. This interpretation contains enough truth to prevent us from dismissing it out of hand. Yet it obscures far more than it reveals, resting as it does upon three erroneous assumptions: assumptions about colonial American society, the Revolution, and the Loyalist migration itself.

Although interpretations of the American Revolution vary on this point,[20] one important school denies that an aristocracy of inherited wealth ever dominated colonial society. A leading proponent of this view is Bernard Bailyn. After carefully analyzing American colonial society in Virginia, Bailyn concludes that the attempt to create an English type class-based society in America failed after one generation. A ruling group did, of course, emerge but 'their political dominance was a continuous achievement'. Since the 'apex' of this social structure lay in England, the colonial portion was delicate and fragile. The top local élite was always in flux. 'There was continuity in public office,' Bailyn continued, 'but at the highest level it was uncertain, the result of place-hunting rather than of absolute prerogative at birth.'[21]

Nor did an aristocracy of birth establish itself later on in colonial history. If anything, the forces opposing such a development became stronger. Elsewhere Bailyn writes, 'There were no "classes" in colonial politics, in the sense of economic or occupational groups whose political interests were entirely stable, clear and consistent through substantial periods of time. More important, there was not sufficient stability in the economic groupings . . . to recreate in America the kind of stable interest politics that found in England so effective an expression in "virtual" representation.'[22]

The comparison with England is worth pursuing. There, a partly modernized form of medieval corporatism survived throughout the eighteenth century largely because an entire class of people (labourers and peasants) lacked political awareness and a role in politics. America, however, did not enjoy this rather dubious advantage. The forty-shilling freehold test, which enfranchised only a few in England, permitted most of the adult white males in the colonies to participate fully in politics.

Underlying this wider political participation was a surprisingly modern political mentality. For example, colonial America, with a population a fraction as large as England's, had almost as many bookstores and newspapers as the mother country.[23] American colonists were, on average, much better informed about politics than their British counterparts. Migrants from Europe to colonial America had been primarily members of the urban middle and lower-middle classes. These were spirited bourgeois activists, not a traditionally docile European peasantry. No wonder, then, the term 'peasant' disappeared in favour of 'farmer', suggesting the bourgeois character of American agriculture.[24] America, to paraphrase de Tocqueville, had the good fortune to be 'born modern' without having to become so.

By the time of the Revolution, American society was still amazingly fluid. Any aristocracy that existed at all was an aristocracy of merit, based more than anything upon entrepreneurial skill. As Carl Bridenbaugh has commented, élite positions were 'accessible': '[After the Seven Years' War] many new faces appeared at genteel balls, around festive boards, and at meetings of fashionable clubs and fine societies, for since wealth was the measure of all things, no possessor of it remained long outside of charmed circles.'[25] An unpredictable colonial economy dictated the rules of the game. No one could afford to feel comfortable: old fortunes were wiped out as often and as swiftly as new ones were made. Even in the South, where a feudal landed aristocracy might have been expected, one finds instead the 'bourgeois' plantation capitalist, working ceaselessly to stay ahead in an incredibly complex and unstable tobacco market.[26]

If we take 'aristocracy' to imply an inherited status based on land ownership, the term fails to apply in colonial America. There was far too much social mobility both up and down the hierarchy of wealth and power. The American Revolutionaries did not attack a firmly established land-based aristocracy. None existed. There was however a colonial élite. Some had more money and power than others. But their status was not based on land ownership, nor was it a function of noble birth. This image of colonial society is false.

Even more to the point, the American Revolution did not split colonial society along class lines. Members of the élite fought on both sides. Whether a colonist supported or opposed the Revolution was not determined by membership or exclusion from this élite, but rather by how much of the colonist's wealth and power depended on the colonial connection. According to William Nelson, 'What distinguished the Tory from the Whig oligarchs was that the former needed, and the latter did not need, support from Britain, since the Whig oligarchs could, and the Tories could not, gain sufficient support in America to hold power.'[27]

As the Revolution progressed, the colonial society split apart, not 'horizontally', along class lines, but rather 'vertically', between those in each class who stood to gain and those who stood to lose by cutting ties with Britain. Nor did loyalty to Britain vary in any simple way according to religious affiliation, degrees of political influence, or amounts of wealth. The determining factor was whether one belonged to a religious group that dominated or was subordinate; whether one took part in the political or in the bureaucratic institutions of the colony (of which more will be said later); and whether one's wealth came from trade inside or outside of the British mercantile system. These considerations cannot be reduced to any single element. As a result, the Loyalist élite cannot be distinguished from the Revolutionary élite on the basis of the usual categories of socio-economic or 'class' analysis.

When contrasting the Loyalist and Revolutionary masses, the differences become even smaller.[28] In effect élite members were *pulled* into the Revolution by the various kinds of interest and dependency mentioned above. The masses, by contrast, were almost entirely *pushed* to participate, by force of group pressure and the example set by their leaders. On which side they ended up was largely a matter of chance. How the masses affiliated themselves depended chiefly on which political/military organization, Revolutionary or Loyalist, was stronger in the immediate area.

The Counter-revolution and Ideology

The counter-revolution did not, therefore, transfer north a pure, pre-modern Tory ideology, opposed to liberal values and nostalgic for the return to a feudal aristocracy. In my view, Lipset, Lower, and others are simply wrong on this point. Indeed, to some extent, Lipset has misread his own sources, in particular William Nelson's book, *The American Tory*. From this book Lipset quotes a passage suggesting that as a result of the Revolution 'the Tories' organic conservatism' disappeared from America and was exported to Canada. But Nelson sandwiches this quoted passage between statements omitted by Lipset arguing that 'organic conservatism' made up a very small part of Tory philosophy. Nelson writes, 'between the extreme, logical and perhaps foolish conviction of, say, Boucher [representing the organic conservative outlook] on one side, and Paine on the other, were men of all conceivable subtleties of outlook.' The passage Lipset quoted comes shortly thereafter, and it is followed immediately by this statement: 'But it would be a mistake to attribute the absence of a conservative tradition in America to the suppression of the Tories. For their exclusion was not so much a cause as a confirmation and an illustration of an alarming uniformity of outlook in America.'[29]

Indeed most of the Tories were just as sympathetic to John Locke as were their opponents. Besides, they found in Locke an entire arsenal of counter-revolutionary arguments to hurl against the supporters of Independence. Locke is well known for the passages, paraphrased in the Declaration of Independence, justifying revolution in the face of tyranny, 'a long train of abuses and prevarications' that indicate the ruler's intention to enact a 'system of slavery' against the people. The Tories were fully familiar with this side of Locke. Some of them even issued their own Declaration of Independence against the Revolutionary Congress, complete with a word-for-word preamble, naming George Washington the tyrant in place of George III and bitterly attacking his, rather than Congress's, tyrannical acts.[30]

However, the Tories took much more comfort from the passages of Locke's *Second Treatise* that propose a counter-argument to the revolutionary doctrine. Locke distinguished between a tyranny that tried to impose a system of slavery on the people, and a government that was basically 'just' but merely guilty of mistakes, even 'Great Mistakes' resulting from 'human frailty' rather than 'evil design'. Against tyranny violent revolution is amply justified. But anyone who attempts to use violence against a just government, said Locke, is himself 'guilty of the greatest Crime, I think, a Man is capable of, being to answer for all those mischiefs of Blood, Rapine, and Desolation, which the breaking to pieces of Governments brings on a Country.'

Any such 'common pest of mankind' is for Locke the moral opposite of a 'revolutionary'; he is instead a 'rebel'. He commits the crime of *re-bellare*, causing a return to the dreaded 'state of war'. Rebellion is quite different from the morally justified act of revolution, which literally means to 'revolve back' to the time of good government that preceded tyranny.[31]

Colonists were able, therefore, to subscribe to most of John Locke's principles and yet oppose the call to arms against Britain. Everything turned on deciding which George, George Washington or George III, was the *true* 'tyrant'. One clever Tory, distressed to see the 'rebels' distorting Locke's doctrines, offered an ode to the 'immortal sage'.[32]

Alike in subscribing to Locke's writings, the Whigs and Tories arrived at radically different conclusions. Contrary to Lipset's view, the debate that raged before and during the Revolution did not pit democracy against aristocracy, equality against hierarchy, liberty against privilege, or new against old. The debaters disagreed about independence and national unification. The Whigs eventually argued that the colonies formed a nation; the Tories, that they did not, and that independence was impossible, even disastrous. The Tory counter-revolution was not based, therefore, in organic conservatism but in the timidity of colonial thinking, what some have called a 'colonial mentality'.[33]

The American Revolution and Native Peoples

To this point our discussion of the historical origins of Canadian political culture has ignored the aboriginal inhabitants of North America, the real 'first nations' of North America. Their role in the American Revolution had a formative impact on their later involvement in both Canada and the United States.

The pattern of social cleavage in the American Revolution cut across classes rather than following class lines. This vertical split in the top groups was driven deep into the masses of colonial society as the contending élites vied for popular support. The military struggle took the form of a 'civil war for Independence', even splitting parents from children and pitting siblings against each other. As with other wars of this kind, the fighting sometimes assumed ferocious intensity, and acts of barbarism were perpetrated by both sides.

The nature of the terrain, the stage of socio-economic development, and the initial formal superiority of the British in terms of weaponry and training forced the revolutionaries to resort to guerrilla war tactics. (Indeed it is said that both Mao Tse Tung and Ho Chi Minh read George Washington's diaries for hints about how to conduct guerrilla warfare in their own Civil Wars for Independence.) In this struggle, the military skills and knowledge of native peoples were valuable resources which, however, the revolutionaries largely failed to tap. At least two considerations account for their failure. First, one of the major bones of contention between the British and the revolutionaries was the Proclamation of 1763, which forbade further settlement west of the Appalachians. Intended by the British to ease relations with the Indians and facilitate supervision of the vast territory acquired from the French by the Treaty of Paris, this prohibition angered colonists, some of whom had already staked out claims in the rich new territory. Second, the officials charged with handling relations with the Indians were appointed by, and remained loyal to, the British. Particularly in New York, the Indian Agent Sir William Johnson enjoyed excellent working relations with the Mohawk Indians. His leadership, exercised through Chief Joseph Brant who served as his Secretary, ensured strong Mohawk support for the British cause. Moreover, other agencies contributed to this close bond. According to Lydekker, even the Anglican Society for the Propagation of the Gospel (SPG) had played a dual role, helping not only in 'evangelizing' with the Indians but also in 'establishing and cementing the English alliance with the Mohawks'.[34]

Despite the strong influence of Johnson and Brant, the Six Nations Indians hesitated before choosing sides. Some leaders wanted to remain neutral; a few counselled support for the revolutionaries. Ultimately in 1775 the Great Council in Oswega decided to support Britain because 'The King was rich and powerful both in money and subjects. His rum was as plenty as the water in Lake Ontario and his men as numerous as the sands upon its shore; And the Indians were assured, that if they would assist in the war, and persevere in their friendship for the King until its close, "they should never want for goods or money".'[35]

The British took care throughout the war not to encroach on the land of the Six Nations. Indeed they reminded the Six Nations leaders that 'the great king never deprived them of an acre since 1759 when he drove the French away'.[36] The Americans tried their hand at persuasion and propaganda as well. Notwithstanding the Treaty of Alliance with Great Britain approved in principle at the Oswega Great Council two years earlier, Congress in 1777 despatched a lengthy Address to the Six Nations, flattering the Oneidas and Tuscaroras for staying out of the war but chiding the other tribes for their involvement. The Address described the British as 'cruel oppressors' and appealed to North American solidarity in an effort to attract Six Nations support: 'Let us who are born on the same great continent love one another. What are the people who are born on the other side of the great waters to either of us?'

The appeal failed. The Americans quickly declared the Six Nations Indians prime enemies, and moved against them accordingly. In 1778, George Washington instructed an army to invade and devastate Six Nations settlements capturing 'as many prisoners of every age and sex as possible. The country must not be merely over run, but destroyed.'[37] The negative image of the Indian in American culture, the view of native peoples as hostile enemies, in large part traces back to the alignment of the political forces during the American Revolution. (A decade after the war, the American Indian Chief Cornplanter confided, in a letter to Joseph Brant, that 'We are despised by the whites on both sides . . . because they both want to be the greatest people.'[38])

Naturally, the British sought allies and supporters wherever they could find them, not only among native groups. As part of the inducements offered colonists, the British promised to safeguard their well-being and ensure them a means of livelihood after the war. Despite British efforts to include in the Treaty of Versailles articles that would guarantee the rights of the loyalists to obtain compensation for losses inflicted by the states, no such assurances were secured. The bitterness engendered during the struggle lived on long afterwards, making it impossible for most British supporters to continue living in their old homes. Deserters from regular (European) regiments were welcomed by the revolutionaries; those who deserted from loyalist regiments such as Butler's Rangers and Sir John Johnson's corps were sent back. The British authorities had to devise a plan for relocating the thousands of loyalists who were expelled as a result of their participation in the war on the losing side. The Loyalist migration constituted a true diaspora, as colonists fled to England, the Bahamas, Florida, and in largest numbers to what is now Canada. Included in this migration were members of the Six Nations, particularly the fierce Mohawks, who had fought for the British under the leadership of Johnson and Brant (and to a lesser extent of Colonel Butler).

The Mohawks were the most disciplined warriors of the Six Nations, and it seems they were also the most Europeanized. They were excellent farmers, and had adopted many European customs (dress, housing, etc.). A number of them had received formal education: Joseph Brant and his sister Molly attended a 'grammar school' run by Jonathan Edwards, and Joseph took further studies at the missionary school which later became Dartmouth College. Several of the Mohawk leaders (including Joseph's grandfather and Joseph himself) had visited England and been received by the King.

The Mohawks were close to the whites in other ways as well. Many of them had white blood in their veins. The entire Brant family for example descended from a Briton who had arrived in Albany around 1665, and whose descendants had intermarried with both Mohawks and Dutch.[39] Sir William Johnson is said to have fathered more than a hundred children of various Indian women, the most famous and influential of whom was Joseph's sister Molly. In 1759, at the age of about 23, she took over management of his household and stayed with him until his death in 1774. During that period she bore Sir William nine children, several of whom married influential white colonists. Herself of mixed blood, Molly effected a unique synthesis of European and Mohawk culture, for example dressing in Iroquoian fashion but using European materials. 'Her children, however, she dressed in European style to protect them from inquisitive eyes.'[40] Later she, like her brother, played an important role facilitating relations between Indians and whites, interpreting one group to the other on the basis of her intimate familiarity with each.

With Sir William's death, leadership passed to Sir John Johnson, Joseph Brant, and Molly. Given the Six Nations' matrilineal traditions and Molly's extraordinary personal charm, initially she probably exercised the most influence. In 1779, Daniel Claus (a brother-in-law) informed Governor Haldimand that '. . . one word from her is taken more notice of by the Five Nations than a thousand from any white man without exception'. A year later Captain Alexander Fraser reported that '. . . Miss Molly Brant's influence over them is far superior to that of all the Chiefs put together.'[41]

The years of bitter border skirmishes that followed took a heavy toll. Of the approximately 5000 Mohawks living in Upper New York, only about 2500 arrived in Upper Canada during and shortly after the War. The entire region of what is now Southern Ontario was sparsely inhabited at the time. There was no significant European settlement, and only a total of 1000 Mississauga Indians who had gradually drifted south into the area, which had earlier been Iroquois territory. Refugees began to collect in two places—near Fort Niagara, and at the eastern end of Lake Ontario near Fort Cataraqui (Kingston). Most Indians went to the Niagara region but about 150 headed for the Kingston area. Wherever they settled, the Indians brought with them shock and disappointment.

The Indian tribes which supported the British viewed themselves as independent nations, without lords or masters, who had chosen to ally themselves with the British monarch as equals, not subjects. For them, the war between America and Britain was not of their making, nor should its outcome have any direct bearing on their own territory, over which neither side exercised legitimate control. A prime motive for participating in the War was to protect their land against any incursions. Upon learning that the peace negotiations excluded them from any form of participation and, worse, that the terms of the treaty included ceding their land to the victorious Americans, the Indians felt a deep sense of betrayal. In a report to Sir Frederick Haldimand dated 18 May 1783, Brigadier Allan Maclean reported the Six Nations' disbelief that the English could have 'pretended' to 'give up their country to the Americans without their consent, or consulting them'. They could not understand how 'our King could pretend to cede to America what was not his own to give; or that the Americans would accept from him what he had no right to grant'.[42] Were such stories true, the English were guilty of 'an act of cruelty and injustice that Christians only were capable of doing, that the Indians were incapable to acting as to friends and allies'.[43] The Indians had hoped and believed that they would continue 'to live on their own lands as good and free neighbours of the Americans'.[44]

Incredible as it seemed (then and now), the Peace of Paris of 1783 included not a single mention of the Indians. Ignoring their legitimate claims to the Ohio country, the peace treaty carved up the territory of North America like a slaughtered animal. The Six Nations Indians became refugees, driven out of the 'lands of their fathers', victims of the vagaries of international power politics, and of what one commentator has charitably described as 'profound administrative amnesia' on the part of the British.

Like thousands of colonists expatriated by the American Revolutionary War, many of the Six Nations sought refuge further north, in territory destined to remain under British control. Although they were later treated as second-class citizens, initially the Six Nations had a formal guarantee of British support. In April 1779, Frederick Haldimand, then British Governor of Quebec, renewed a pledge made by his predecessor Sir Guy Carleton that the Indians would be restored to lands as suitable as those they held in New York. The pledge was honoured in 1784 when the British purchased (for 1,180 pounds sterling) 2,842,840 acres in the Grand River region from the Mississauga Indians, and granted a portion of this (786,000 acres) by deed to the Six Nations Indians 'and their posterity . . . for ever' to serve as a 'safe and comfortable retreat for them'. This land was granted en bloc to the Six Nations. Subdivision for further sale was explicitly forbidden except under strict conditions involving a public meeting of the 'Chiefs, Warriors and People' of the tribe called to approve sale of the land back to the Crown. These provisions stood in contrast to the arrangements made for distributing land to non-Indian loyalists in several ways. Land grants to whites were made to individuals or families; furthermore, the size of these individual grants varied according to the grantee's rank in the colonial fighting forces and/or number of dependents. Grants usually carried some stipulations requiring improvement of the land, building of a road, or construction of a house. At the same time, grants to whites were made in fee simple giving the grantee full title to dispose of the land as he or she wished.

Land grant terms were hotly disputed in later years, particularly by Joseph Brant, who served as main liaison between the Six Nations and the British authorities. For example, in a letter dated 10 December 1798 Brant complained bitterly of the 'long difficulties we had concerning the lands on this [Grand] river—these difficulties we had not the least idea of when we first settled here, looking on them as granted us to be indisputably our own, otherwise we would never have accepted the lands . . . .' In several earlier letters Brant had stressed the theme of betrayal, warning that the 'covenant chain' of mutual understanding linking Six Nations with the British, was 'in danger of getting rusty', not through breach of promise by Indians but rather as a result of British duplicity. In this 1798 letter, Brant goes on to point out that the 'real intentions' of the Ministry appear evident: 'to tie us down in such a manner, as to have us entirely at their disposal for whatever vices they may in future want from us'. The Six Nations were caught in a painful bind. The development of lands bordering on the reserve, and changes in the local economy, meant that now 'hunting is of very little account to the young and robust' Indians. This put pressure on the Indian community, and made it 'necessary to sell some land, that we may have an income, the hunting being entirely destroyed'. But the terms of the grant, and interpretation given thereafter, virtually precluded sale: 'We now learn that the ministry never intended we should alienate the lands.'[45]

Later generations may have been grateful that the Six Nations Reserve was protected in this way, but Brant felt cheated. Although his numerous complaints and petitions met very little success, by 1914 the Six Nations reserve had shrunk to 43,000 acres through sale of the lands back to the Crown in return for various forms of compensation, including a per capita annuity. Similarly, his efforts to receive compensation from the U.S. government for lands taken after the Revolutionary War met very little success.[46] Thus despite Britain's oft-professed appreciation of Indian support during the war, the Indians were not treated identically to non-Indian loyalists. Moreover, the 'mark of honour' (U.E.) awarded to bona fide white loyalists was apparently not extended to most Indians. One exception in this regard, however, was Molly Brant. Because of her valued services as a 'diplomat' during the War, and in view of the discontent among Indians afterwards, she was regarded as a valuable asset. The colonial authorities, eager to gratify her, provided Molly with a house at Kingston and an annual pension of £100. Her children were educated at government expense, and Molly was granted several tracts of land near Kingston, Fredericksburg and Niagara.[47]

> On the official Loyalist Returns, Molly was listed as Mrs Molly Brant and the children as Johnsons. Her decision for this distinction of names grew from her position as link between two cultures which were in military alliance. By keeping her matronymic of Brant, she held her status in the matriarchal order of the

Iroquois. By allowing her children to use the patronymic of Johnson, she gave them their place in the patriarchal order of the British.[48]

This passage is important for several reasons. First, it indicates clearly that Molly Brant was highly conscious of her mixed blood status, of having a foot in both cultural camps. In fact she and her brother had always 'believed they could introduce their people to the best of the White man's ways, the best of Christianity, the best of agriculture, good housing, good schooling, without loss of Iroquois identity'.[49] But to do so would require a synthesis, in effect creating a new mixed identity, and this achievement remained beyond her. Although her children felt comfortable in both cultures, and were strikingly capable of combining them in manners of dress for example, the legal/political structure of colonial Upper Canada was binary. One was either Indian or white. Molly Brant received land as if she were white. Other mixed bloods faced a similar choice. Some lived as white persons, others as Indians. None of them apparently succeeded in staking out a third option.

Not until much later would the categories of Métis and Non-Status Indian receive clarification or even recognition. This development followed from the 'wardship' relations which ultimately characterized the status of Indians in Canada. In a sense, therefore, problems of 'Indian identity' emerged in response to complex arrangements for the administration of Indian land and other related issues.[50] These problems existed only in embryo during the post-Revolutionary period.

The long-standing controversy over title to, and encroachment upon, Indian lands was but part of Indian-white relationships which ran the gamut of friendship and hostility, co-operation and conflict. Important contrasts emerged when one compares British North America with the United States. American attitudes were made a matter of permanent record in a much neglected section of the Declaration of Independence which grimly prefigured the genocidal violence of later decades. In the inventory of indictments against George III appeared this remarkable statement: 'He has excited domestic insurrections amongst us and has endeavoured to bring on the inhabitants of our frontiers the merciless Indian savages, whose known rule of warfare is an undistinguished destruction of all ages, sexes and conditions.' The Indians' plight north of the border was never idyllic, but it is less than coincidental that while American frontiersmen were slaughtering these 'merciless savages', Canada avoided a major Indian war. Part of the explanation surely lies in the fact that the Indians too were 'Loyalists', as their descendants proudly reminded the celebrants of the centennial of the U.E.L. settlement of Upper Canada. A grandson of Joseph Brant, Chief Hill of the Mohawks, uttered a statement inconceivable in the American setting:

> Red and White fought side by side in the Revolutionary war. The blood of the red man and that of his white brother mixed together to uphold the Loyalists' cause. . . . Now after a hundred years of friendship and many changes, we are

still brothers, and I feel happy, as the descendent of one who proved himself a loyal man, to meet so many white Loyalists.

It is impossible to know how warmly the 'White Loyalists' received this expression of fraternity,[51] but Chief Hill was not the only Indian to proffer it. Chief A.G. Smith declared that 'there is a very large representation of my people, the Six Nations Indians, of Grand River, who are today as anxious to be identified with the descendants of the United Empire Loyalists of Canada, as their forefathers were one hundred years ago'. On the whole, Chief Smith continued, 'relations with the government of the country' have always been 'attended with the happiest results'. His people had 'few reasons to complain' because the government 'has in general kept faith with us . . .'. The only exceptions in his view were the failure to grant Indians representation in Parliament, and the Loyalists' inattention to the 'dear old historical landmarks' of the United Empire Loyalists' ordeal! Few if any of Smith's later descendants would express much positive sentiment about their later treatment.[52] But let us return to some other aspects of the legacy of the loyalist experience.

The Counter-revolution and Feelings about Bureaucracy

Because the Loyalists had strong political and economic relationships to the mother country, their northward migration was bound to have 'conservative' results. In attempting to recreate the pre-revolutionary Thirteen Colonies in Canada, the Loyalists would strengthen traditional ties with the mother country. They would seek justification of their authority not from fellow colonists but from the mother country. This choice would animate a debate about political legitimacy in North America, as between the principles of democratic election and administrative appointment.

In one sense, the American Revolution had been a war between politicians and administrators. The politicians, by and large, were elected to represent the people, and they sat in the colonial assemblies. By contrast the administrators, who included minor customs officials, judges, and (in all colonies but one) the governor himself, were appointed. Most colonial officials had been appointed by the king or the governor, and were directly or indirectly controlled by Britain. Thus they drew their authority from across the sea. The politicians on the other hand were elected locally; the local people gave them authority.

From the beginning of colonial history, the interests of London-oriented administrators and locally oriented politicians conflicted. Britain's policy of stepping up the administrative 'outputs' of the colonial system after 1763—what has elsewhere been described as the 'new imperialism'—merely heated up this conflict.[53] One historian has insisted that 'the causes of the Revolution stem . . . from the effort of the British Government . . . to organize a more efficient administration in North America . . .'.[54] Years of conflict and controversy passed, further dividing politician from administrator, and the Revolution merely brought this drama to an explosive end. Then, each member of the political and administrative élite was forced to choose sides for the last time.

Most politicians understandably sided with the forces of revolution. Equally understandably, most administrators stayed loyal to the colonial power that had elevated and rewarded them. D.P. Coke, one of the commissioners who invest-igated Loyalist claims for compensation after the Revolution, observed that the expatriates included '. . . a long procession of officials, from those who were a power in the land to the humble tide-water and lowest custom-house official. The interests of all these were inextricably bound up with the past system of government, and it was inevitable that they should feel the first shock of the earthquake.'[55]

After the Revolution, most of the administrative élite fled from America. Though many returned to Britain or were posted in various parts of the Empire, a few prominent officials and many lesser ones settled in Canada. There, ac-cording to some critics, the Loyalists 'indulged their lust for bureaucratic office'.

This exodus had important but different effects on the political cultures of both countries. In the United States, according to Carl Friedrich, the Revolution 'created a permanent suspicion of executive power which has stood ever since in the way of developing responsible government'.[56] In attempting to bring the bureaucracy firmly and finally under their control, many of the revolutionaries went to almost absurd extremes. Finally, instead of merely controlling the ad-ministration, they managed to politicize it! In the immediate post-Independence phase, under the Articles of Confederation, the Americans wanted to have elected politicians directly responsible for supervising the work of governmental administrators. According to Merrill Jensen, 'The more democratic revolution-aries distrusted executive power of any kind and insisted that members of Congress themselves, acting in committees, should directly control all depart-ments where permanent employees carried on routine business.'[57] Here is the historic root of American distrust of the bureaucracy. Andrew Jackson, trium-phantly proclaiming the 'spoils system', George Wallace, smugly threatening to 'throw the bureaucrats' briefcases into the Potomac River', and the Reagan/Bush penchant to reduce government through privatization and deregulation, all follow in a tradition as American as the Revolution itself. California's controver-sial Proposition 13, designed to limit drastically the money government spends on services, and the Gramm/Rudman amendments to limit deficit spending, further exemplify this tradition.

In America, the Revolution helped to politicize the bureaucracy. The counter-revolution might be expected, therefore, to have affected Canada in the opposite way, making Canadian government and politics more bureaucratic. To some extent this is precisely what happened. In the mid-nineteenth century, the British North American colonies were governed very much like the Thirteen

Colonies before the Revolution. For example, no neutral civil service existed yet. The British-appointed governor and the locally elected Assembly shared control of the administration, with the governor clearly dominating through appointments to the Legislative and Executive Councils. Further, within the governing Executive Council administrative responsibility was not divided among departments; the Council reported as a group. But by the late nineteenth century, an American-style 'spoils system' operated in Canada too. Indeed, Canada did not adopt British administration practices of a merit-based neutral civil service until the beginning of this century.

Several factors had served to 'Americanize' Canadian government in the course of the nineteenth century despite the best intentions of our loyalist founders. The counter-revolutionary forces were neither so numerous, nor so luminous, as some have said. Many of the *top* Loyalist élite in the Thirteen Colonies chose to be posted in Britain or elsewhere in the Empire instead of Canada. There were, of course, some exceptions, of whom William Smith is a notable example.[58] Most Loyalist immigrants to Canada, however, were unremarkable and, indeed, totally illiterate. Of the former bureaucrats who did end up in Canada, many had served only as petty functionaries before the Revolution.

Yet finally, Canadian politics were largely 'bureaucratized'. The Loyalists who settled in Canada demanded the same institutions that they had known in the Thirteen Colonies. Thus when British North American society began to modernize, politicians and administrators began to struggle just as they had, for similar reasons, before the American Revolution. But in Canada the administrators fought off the challenge of the politicians far better than their predecessors had done in the Thirteen Colonies. Unlike Sam Adams, the Canadian rebels William Lyon Mackenzie and Louis Joseph Papineau were defeated. Why?

Loyalist sentiment was at least partly responsible. As one historian pointed out, 'in a dependency a desire for political progress can always be interpreted by opponents as disaffection. . . . A suspicion of disloyalty was the most potent influence [used by the Family Compact] against reformers in the [eighteen] thirties.'[59] The British distrusted demands for representative government, indeed all political change; such demands renewed much of the pre-Revolutionary tension in North America, this time in British North America. In every colony, appointment, not election, brought a similar small élite into power.[60] (The derogatory term 'Family Compact', however, appeared only *after* the Assembly had begun to compete for power and criticize the bureaucracy more loudly than it had before.)

During the early years of the American Republic, a key problem for political development was how to create a bureaucracy strong enough to keep the already powerful legislature from interfering with administration. However, in the first half of the nineteenth century, this problem was reversed in British North America. Here elected representatives needed to wrest power from an entrenched group of administrators (the Family Compact) and lodge it instead in the popularly elected Assembly. The resolution of this problem is commonly described as 'the struggle for responsible government'.

While American politicians debated how much to limit their own government's administrators, Canadian administrators were busy developing the colonies of British North America despite opposition from a few, weak, elected politicians. Even though all the colonies had elected an Assembly by 1791, decades passed before any Assembly had garnered enough power to challenge the Executive and bureaucracy successfully. Up to about 1840 the Assembly suffered from an unclear definition of its authority in relation to that of the executive.

But even if the Assembly *had* possessed the right in law to take control of the state, the hard facts of early colonial life would have made exercising this authority difficult. The Assembly met rarely, for surprisingly short periods (perhaps a few weeks to a month each year). In the early years many representatives felt they had far more pressing duties to attend to and, in any event, lacked the information and time needed to review executive decisions. For these reasons the colonies in the early nineteenth century were ruled by a largely appointed, somewhat secretive government.

Keeping this system stable demanded the Assembly's passive agreement, which was forthcoming only so long as pioneer conditions prevailed. As transportation and communications improved, however, more citizens interested themselves in the kinds of decisions bureaucratic élites were taking. These decisions were becoming more expensive and more important; and people were becoming more aware of politics. Inevitably government by an unharnessed executive came, in some cases violently,[61] to an unlamented end.

Responsible Government

In each colony the change-over from administrative to political control of public policy followed a slightly different pattern; but the problems encountered were remarkably similar. For by the 1830s, in all four colonies of British North America—Upper and Lower Canada, New Brunswick, Nova Scotia—assemblies were made up of politicians bent on winning the 'power of the purse'. Historians and political scientists have paid an extraordinary amount of attention to this so-called 'struggle for responsible government'. Yet they have often misinterpreted it. Even Norman Ward's description of this struggle, which is otherwise excellent, is incomplete; for it ignores the period of irresponsible Assembly control that followed the victory over the Executive.

Ward identifies three phases in the struggle for responsible government. Their respective goals were to (a) 'make the executive at least partially dependent on the assembly for its income', (b) 'make it wholly so', and (c) 'insist on some sort of detailed public accounting of expenditures after they were made'.[62] Ward seems to imply that the politicians were inspired primarily by a desire for 'good government'. In fact, they were at least as interested in the immense opportunities for patronage that the 'power of the purse' can bestow. Hence between phases (b) and (c) there occurred a period of 'fiscal irresponsibility' reminiscent of the American system's worst abuses. J.E. Hodgetts speaks of that period's 'free-for-all system still peculiar to the United States, whereby any private member of the legislature had the right to introduce his own measure calling for the expenditure of public funds'.[63] Even during phase (a) in Ward's model, other American practices such as the use of legislative committees to control executive action became popular in British North America. As J.R. Mallory has shown: 'Before the days of responsible government the committee system flowered, as it does generally under a system of separation of powers. A legislative majority unable to control the strings of power will naturally resort to every parliamentary device at hand to harass and contain the government. One of the most obvious of these is the committee system.'[64]

Despite themselves the Loyalists, founders of British North America, had created a political system more American than British. It even included an American-style separation of powers. Ahead lay the two tasks of improving co-operation between institutions, especially between the Executive and the legislature; and making the bureaucracy responsible, through the Cabinet, to the legislature.[65] Many strands are interwoven in these twin processes of reform; untangling them is not easy. Yet one can safely say that the progression from this phase to the next began when Lord Durham recommended reforms in his famous *Report* to the British Parliament.

Durham found the colonial administration in chaos. The Executive Council displayed 'neither unity nor responsibility'. The governor himself was but 'slightly responsible', and rarely bothered to distinguish between 'political' appointments and 'civil' or merit appointments.[66] In the years following the *Report* the Colonial Office often sent despatches praising the British parliamentary system and roundly condemning the vices of the American system which had been transported to Canada. In a despatch to Lord Mulgrave in Nova Scotia in 1862, the Duke of Newcastle darkly alluded to the spoils system as 'an evil which is so notorious in a neighbouring country that it may serve as a warning to the public men of the British Provinces in North America . . .'.[67]

This and similar evidence suggests that modern British institutions, such as cabinet government, were imposed upon Canada and did not come about through natural evolution. Had the early nineteenth-century political institutions of British North America been allowed to evolve without British intervention in the form of Durham's recommendations and subsequent policy changes adopted by the Colonial Office, Canadian political institutions undoubtedly would have ended up more American than British.[68] By the time of Confederation, the British had guided through reforms that introduced a British-style parliamentary system to replace the earlier American hybrid. But this alone did not put an end to the modified spoils system. Although unified and responsible to Parliament now, the Executive still appointed people to the bureaucracy on almost purely 'political' grounds. As in the United States, this practice ended only after statutory legislation.

A Civil Service Act was passed in 1868, almost coincident with Confederation; but it affected patronage appointments only slightly. In the dozen years that followed, patronage thrived as never before, owing largely to the growth of the new 'national' political parties. The Canadian style of patronage was by now neither American nor British. As Dawson has noted, it lacked the self-confident vigour of the Jacksonian spoils system. On the other hand patronage was much more common here than in Britain, where the civil service had been fully re-formed by 1870. Several inquiries all revealed the same dismal fact: patronage was the 'guiding principle' of civil service appointments in Canada.

In 1880, a Royal Commission was appointed 'to make a 'full, intelligent and painstaking inquiry' into the condition of the [Canadian civil] service, and to suggest suitable remedies'.[69] According to Dawson, the Commission's resulting proposals were 'weak in many respects', especially insofar as they relied on competitive examinations, which selected people more fairly but did nothing to protect already appointed civil servants against political pressures. The Act, finally passed in 1882, weakened the Commission's proposals even further. Now, 'Political patronage was as powerful as ever, except that the illiterate and hopelessly incompetent were excluded. Before the passage of the Act a Minister could give office to any of his supporters; after the Act he was limited to those who could pass an elementary test.'[70]

After another Royal Commission, appointed by Laurier in 1907, found that corrupt practices had continued, the Civil Service Amendment Act of 1908 introduced the first really effective reforms. The Act also set up an agency, the Civil Service Commission, to enforce the law. Though these measures applied almost entirely to the 'inside' civil service (i.e., those employees posted in Ottawa), the Act's provisions could be extended by Orders-in-Council.

By 1917, in part because of the war, further reforms were badly needed. The new Union government moved quickly, first by Order-in-Council, soon afterward (1918) by statutory legislation, to keep its pledge to clean up the civil service. From that point on, both 'inside' and 'outside' Ottawa, the grossest forms of patronage virtually disappeared from the Canadian federal civil service, more than two decades before comparable legislation in the United States. More significantly, the civil service legislation in Canada covered both top-level personnel and a wide range of provincial and local officials—judges, prosecutors, and others—whose position in the United States is secured through election on the 'long ballot'.[71]

Recently the old problem of responsible government has arisen in a new way. Government grew tenfold between 1950 and 1975. Agencies and administrators proliferated, and major policy decisions were increasingly made by appointed officials rather than elected representatives. Indeed, legislatures and Parliament lost much of their prestige and influence. Thus the 'administrative culture' in Canada and in other affluent societies features a new brand of almost invisible, if not irresponsible, government. Finding ways to make the complex administrative machine responsive and responsible at all levels of government will prove a major challenge for the future.[72] This quest is the animating principle of the theory and practice of 'democratic administration.'

Canada's experience with bureaucrats after the American Revolution profoundly influenced the way our political and bureaucratic institutions developed. These institutions, in turn, came to embody a certain political culture which survived for nearly two centuries. Moreover, the counter-revolution also shaped our attitudes toward these institutions, which likewise became part of the political culture.

The Counter-revolution and Attitudes toward the Political System

Like all revolutions, the American Revolution resulted from a crisis of legitimacy. The policies Britain pursued after 1763 were widely opposed, in part because important groups in the Thirteen Colonies no longer regarded those policies as legitimate. To explain why requires a short general discussion of the bases of legitimacy.

Broadly speaking, legitimacy can be established in either of two ways, hence giving rise to two types of legitimacy: substantive and procedural. *Substantive* legitimacy accepts a ruler not on the basis of the way he or she was chosen, nor the way the ruler arrives at or carries out decisions. Rather it is the quality of the ruler's decisions that confers the right to rule. Thus, for example, rulers who abuse this right by serving their own private ends instead of the public good are considered tyrants, illegitimate rulers. A ruler's actions are legitimate only so long as they are not tyrannical in substance.

Notions of *procedural* legitimacy substitute the idea that laws and actions get their legitimacy from the way in which decisions are reached. As democratic notions came to replace earlier theories of monarchy and aristocracy, doctrines of procedural legitimacy took the place of ideas of substantive legitimacy. Eventually, modern democratic theory reduced or eliminated limits to the exercise of authority on substantive grounds. Any decision the properly elected representatives of the people reached in proper ways was viewed as legitimate.

The leaders of the American Revolution opposed British policies on substantive grounds: recent Acts, they argued, amounted to a 'system of slavery'. But in the revolutionary slogan 'No taxation without representation' also rested an embryonic theory of procedural legitimacy. Thus, the philosophy behind the American Revolution included notions of *both* substantive and procedural legitimacy.

After the Declaration of Independence nullified British authority in the Thirteen Colonies, a new basis for governmental legitimacy was needed. Strict conformity to a democratic model would have required endorsing procedural legitimacy alone. But for a variety of reasons the American revolutionaries were unwilling to abandon all of their traditional notions. They distrusted purely procedural limits, and insisted on putting into the Bill of Rights strong substantive limits to the exercise of power.[73]

In the post-Revolution period, the Assembly in the British North American colonies (like its forerunner in the Thirteen Colonies) became a 'negative' body. It merely acted to oppose executive actions that it considered illegitimate. Since, however, the authority of the British crown was still intact, Canadians did not have to decide immediately whether a procedural concept, such as democratic election, was needed in order to enhance governmental legitimacy.

So, Canada moved toward procedural legitimacy slowly and gradually. Canada did not introduce 'constitutional government',[74] but rather 'responsible government' in which the exercise of authority is legitimated by subordinating executive and administrative activities to an elected body (i.e., Parliament). By contrast, American government, through its Constitution, retained a mediaeval notion of substantive limits embodied in 'higher law' and 'judicial review'.[75] The American Constitution sets out a number of absolute limitations on governmental power. With the introduction of the Charter of Rights in 1982, Canada moved towards the American practice and expanded the role of the courts (through 'judicial review') dramatically.

Much of this analysis can be translated into the language of systems theory, thus linking it to the concepts such as 'civic culture' and 'political development'. Peaceful modernization requires that the political system increase its 'outputs' of legislation and administration. But no such increase can occur unless the system widens its base of popular support by finding new sources of legitimation. Otherwise instability and protest will result, as they often do in today's modernizing countries.

In liberal democracies the additional legitimacy needed is attained by increasing 'inputs' into the system through greater public participation. But when people participate more, they demand more of the system. Such demands for greater output argue for the elimination of all substantive limitations on power. In theory at least, there comes a time when all outputs are presumed to originate from procedurally legitimate inputs, and those alone. Then whatever the duly constituted government decides through 'proper procedure' is deemed legitimate.

Systems theory links changes in the bases of legitimacy to changing general orientations toward the political system. There are at least two such orientations defined by Almond and Verba's theoretical scheme. The first, 'citizen competence', refers to the individual's sense that he or she can influence the decisions the political system is making. Where citizen competence is great, people believe strongly that a citizen's wishes influence what the system does. 'Subject competence', on the other hand, refers to the people's feeling that they will be treated fairly by the system: that decisions the system makes are equitable.

Where subject competence is great, people will accept readily whatever the system's administrators decide. Both citizen competence and subject competence are sources of procedural legitimacy.

What impact did the American Revolution have on these two aspects of political culture? In the United States the Revolution brought together previously isolated groups and heightened the general awareness of politics. In this way it helped to build up a high degree of citizen competence that has lasted to this day.[76] But another result, already noted, was the widespread distrust of 'output' institutions, especially the bureaucracy. Thus, although the Revolution raised citizen competence, it lowered subject competence.[77] Moreover, the Revolution seemed to aggravate an underlying fear of government (*cratophobia*) particularly directed toward a central government that might recreate the tyranny of British rule. Feelings of this kind survive today; they are responsible for much of the continuing opposition in the United States to governmental initiatives in health, education, and welfare, to regulation of the economy, and other issues where the common good is at stake.

One might expect counter-revolution to have the opposite result. Thus, all other things being equal, in Canada citizen competence would be less and subject competence greater than in the United States. The actual outcome is somewhat more subtle and complex than this, for all other things are rarely equal. The Loyalists and their descendants did not become self-satisfied, docile subjects who neglected their rights as citizens. Not at all; they too began to demand certain rights, even though less vigorously than their American cousins.[78] They too had been fired up by the Revolutionaries. Some Loyalists, especially members of the élite, did not come to fear government, but to love it (*cratophilia*). In this regard, European, American, and 'Canadian' liberals of the eighteenth century are found to contrast in an interesting way. According to Louis Hartz, European liberals were torn between 'hating [political] power, but loving it also'.[79] American liberals, instead, had fought the Revolution against 'tyranny'. So strongly did they hate tyrants that they scarcely experienced the European liberals' dilemma, for the American liberals hated power more than they loved it.[80]

The Canadian—properly the British North American—liberals had fought to defend government. They did not despise it; government had been good to them. If they had been part of the élite, they were welcomed by the governor, especially if they expressed aristocratic sentiments. Loyalism effectively disguised an underlying liberalism.[81]

The Canadian liberals loved government with a passion equal (but opposite) to that of their American counterparts. Even the Loyalist masses became fond of government; after all, they received favours for having defended it. During the Revolution the British encouraged them to expect rewards; they were assured that they would never be asked for anything but their present support. So, after the war the Royalist expatriates brought many demands before the

British, who responded with reparations of war losses, free grants of land, tools for farming and pioneering, pensions and grants of half-pay, and even, in some instances, several years' food supplies.[82] The Loyalists benefited from Canada's first hand-out scheme; they were our first 'welfare bums'.[83] Little wonder, then, that Canadian political culture traditionally permitted a wider range of state interventions in the economy and other forms of 'positive government' that were anathema in the United States.

Conclusion

The previous chapter argued for an historical (instead of a synchronic or cross-sectional) analysis on the grounds that past developments help to explain the present. This chapter has applied certain key theoretical concepts—'founding fragments' and 'formative events'—to show that on a very general level of analysis, some elements of the Canadian political culture have remained unchanged for centuries.

Besides showing continuity, history shows origins, hence meanings. Now it is true that the original meaning of a cultural object may not be the present meaning. Indeed the very opposite may be true, at least on a conscious level. Each generation changes its 'perspective', the grounds upon which people rationalize or justify their social institutions. In an important sense, much history-writing has been therapeutic mythology, an invention of useful new 'meanings'. The presentation of a people to itself, by historians and other social scientists, as by artists and politicians, often helps to change a society. For 'situations defined as real are real in their consequences.'[84] Historians vie to persuade us to accept as correct the way they have defined a situation that extends across time. Accepting such a definition may shape our future actions.

This chapter has reconciled the implications, for Canada, that Hartz and Lipset have drawn from their separate theories. One theory sees francophone society originating in a colonial fragment that stops receiving new ideas from abroad. The other sees a 'nation' whose surrender to a foreign power effectively closes the door to modern influence for two centuries. The result of each process is the same; a hermetically sealed culture founded upon seventeenth- or eighteenth-century French absolutist thinking.

Likewise Hartz's and Lipset's analyses of the origins of anglophone society appear similar. In each the founders are Loyalists, fleeing north with an incomplete political philosophy but a strong sense of self-righteous resentment against the American revolutionaries. Is this not the ultimate source of Canada's almost legendary anti-Americanism? We may find new ways every generation to justify our disdain, fear, and envy; but the sheer continuity of these feelings suggests a simpler explanation. English Canadians are a bourgeois people situated next to the most powerful capitalist nation that ever existed. Though we speak the same language, indeed partake of the same food, wear similar clothes, share many mass media, adopt similar life styles, and so on, we protest that we are different. Yet we seemingly want to be different only to the extent of being called Canadians. In photographic terms, we are merely the 'negative'.

Another legacy of the loyalist tradition was the development of a psychological dependence upon Britain. Loyalism was supposed to help keep Canada from being swallowed up by the United States. Instead it perpetuated a colonial mentality, an artificial loyalty to the Crown that grew ever more strained as new Canadians without British origins poured into the population. It delayed unifying the nation, perhaps forever.

These are a few of the symptoms of Canada's national problem that can easily be traced back to the country's founding. The next chapter, about the English-Canadian identity, will probe this question further. The present chapter has also examined a few other Canadian traits that will get further attention below: traits like the support given for strong governmental intervention in the economy and society; a relative lack of substantive limits on government power (until the Charter); and a tendency to accept official decisions with little hesitation, even when we have felt powerless to affect the course politics have taken.

What bears mention is that this development of opposite Canadian and American political cultures is not all bad. On the matter of bureaucracies, our system may be less democratic, but it is also less erratic and less corruptible. Our willingness to accept authority may seem craven to some. But, on the other hand, it does keep our society clean and orderly, as we have boasted so often to visitors from south of the border.

A number of recent changes introduced into Canadian politics suggest that the differences between Canadian and American political culture are receding. Some of these changes, such as the introduction of the Charter, are the legacy of the Liberal government of Pierre Trudeau. Other changes such as the move toward privatization of crown corporations, deregulation of the economy, and a general reaction against government interference (extending even to a questioning of social programs) have been championed by the Mulroney Conservatives in explicit emulation of Reaganism. All of these changes undoubtedly reflect the impact of American mass media on the Canadian consciousness. They complicate further our endless quest for a sense of identity and national purpose.

Notes

[1] Kenneth McRae, 'The Structure of Canadian History' in Louis Hartz, et al., The Founding of New Societies. For a critical review of the relevant literature, see Roberta Hamilton, Feudal Society and Colonization: The Historiography of New France (Gananoque: Langdale Press, 1988).

[2] Sigmund Diamond, 'An Experiment in "Feudalism": French Canada in the 17th Century', in J.M. Bumsted (ed.), Canadian History before Confederation (Georgetown: Irwin Dorsey, 1972): 92, et passim.

[3] Ibid.

[4] S.D. Clark, *The Developing Canadian Community* (Toronto: University of Toronto Press, 1968): 32, *et passim*.

[5] Historians have hotly debated the character of New France. Some have argued that prior to the conquest a thriving entrepreneurial spirit dominated the colony, but all was lost with the conquest. For a brief account of this debate see the articles reprinted in Bumsted, *op. cit.*

In a very sophisticated study of the historical development of ideologies in Quebec, Denis Monière challenges much of the historiography of the period around the Conquest. Too little attention has been paid to the importance of what Monière, following Marx, calls 'petty producers'—those who owned their own tools of production and were independent of the control of the bourgeoisie, the Church, or the state. By the mid-eighteenth century, New France had entered an early stage of preindustrial commercial capitalism, and this, not feudalism, was the driving force in that society. Indeed, Monière contends that 'the seigniorial system in Canada was no more than a feudal crust over the petty producers' mode of production . . .'. The most dynamic economic sector was of course the fur trade, but the conquest wreaked devastating effects on New France 'by eliminating its dynamic class layer, breaking the rhythm of its development, removing it from the intellectual source that was natural to it, and allowing a reactionary, regressive ideology to become first entrenched and later dominant' (p. 80).

This latter development was not completed for nearly three quarters of a century. Despite the conquest a new leadership based in the 'petty bourgeoisie of the professions' played a very significant role leading up to the rebellions in 1837-38. According to Denis Monière, their defeat 'marked the end of a century of development for the French Canadian nation'. In place of the ideology of nationalism which they proposed, the ideology of collaboration took hold, and thus what had been a 'dynamic and progressive nationalism became defensive and conservative'. *Ideologies in Quebec: The Historical Development* (tr. by Richard Howard), (Toronto: University of Toronto Press, 1981): 119, 120.

[6] J.F. Bosher, 'Governments and Private Interests in New France', in Bumsted, ed.: 116.

[7] Pierre E. Trudeau, *Federalism and the French Canadians* (Toronto: Macmillan, 1968): 105.

[8] André Siegfried, *The Race Question in Canada* (Toronto: McClelland & Stewart, 1966): 25. See also Denis Monière, *Ideologies in Quebec: The Historical Development* (Toronto: University of Toronto Press, 1981): 80-82.

[9] Diamond, *op. cit.*: 89

[10] Jacques Henripin, *Tendances et Facteurs de la Fécondité au Canada* (Ottawa: Dominion Bureau of Statistics, 1968); also Jacques Henripin and Yves Peron, 'The Demographic Transition in the Province of Quebec', in D.V. Glass and Roger Revelle (eds), *Population and Social Change* (London: Edward Arnold, 1972): 213-31.

[11] Even this figure under-represents the number of descendants produced by this incredibly prolific society. Including francophone progeny who left Quebec to move to other parts of Canada and the U.S., the total might approach ten million.

[12] Louis Henry, 'Some Data on Natural Fertility', in *Eugenics Quarterly* 8 (June 1961): 81-91.

[13] Siegfried: 22, 25.

[14] France had ceded Acadia (present-day New Brunswick and Nova Scotia) to Britain in 1713 but maintained a strong military presence in the area based in the garrison and naval fortress of Louisbourg, on what became Cape Breton Island. Louisbourg fell to the British in 1758 shortly after the Seven Years' War began. See S.D. Clark, *Movements of Political Protest in Canada, 1640-1840* (Toronto: University of Toronto Press, 1959), chs 1 and 2. For an assessment of historical differences in outlook between them see Mason Wade, 'Québécois and Acadien', *Journal of Canadian Studies* 2,2 (May 1974): 47-53.

[15] A.R.M. Lower, *Colony to Nation* (Toronto: McClelland & Stewart, 1977): 104 n. P.E.I. was then called Isle St-Jean.

[16] J.B. Brebner, *The Neutral Yankees of Nova Scotia* (Toronto: McClelland & Stewart, 1969. First published in 1937).

[17] David V.J. Bell, 'Nation and Non-Nation: A New Analysis of the Loyalists and the American Revolution' (unpublished PhD dissertation, Harvard University, 1969), ch. 6.

[18] Hartz: 34.

[19] W.S. MacNutt, *New Brunswick: A History: 1784-1867* (Toronto: Macmillan, 1963): 92; and Lower: 118; also 113, 114.

[20] For a good review see Joseph Ernst, 'Political Economy and Reality: Problems in the Interpretation of the American Revolution', *Canadian Review of American Studies* 7,2 (Fall, 1976).

[21] Bernard Bailyn, 'Politics and Social Structure in Virginia', in James Morton Smith (ed.), *Seventeenth-Century America* (published for the Institute of Early American History and Culture at Williamsburg, VA, by the University of North Carolina Press, 1959): 95, 112.

[22] Bernard Bailyn, 'The Origins of American Politics', in D. Fleming and B. Bailyn (eds), *Perspectives in American History* 1,1 (1968): 75.

[23] At the time of the Revolution, the five leading cities in the Colonies had 151 bookstores, compared with only 104 in the sixteen leading cities in England (see Carl Bridenbaugh, *Cities in Revolt* [New York: Capricorn, 1955]: 381).

[24] For a general discussion of the character and background of colonial immigrants, see Marcus Lee Hansen, *The Atlantic Migration* (New York: Harper Torchbooks, 1961): ch. 2.

[25] Bridenbaugh: 335.

[26] Obviously, these generalizations about the liberal 'market mentality' of the bulk of the colonists do not apply to the black slaves. But it would be a great mistake to liken the latter to mediaeval peasants, or even serfs. Culturally, they were clearly from a different tradition. More importantly, virtually none of the reciprocal rights and duties that characterize feudal society operated in the South. The bourgeois rather than feudal outlook of the plantation owner is nakedly revealed in his continued assertion that the slave is property, a view upheld as late as 1857 by the Supreme Court in the *Dred Scott* decision.

It is worth noting in this regard that the British had reasonable success attracting the support of slaves by offering to grant them freedom in return for their support. Approximately 2,000 blacks migrated with the Loyalists to Nova Scotia.

[27] William Nelson, *The American Tory* (Boston: Beacon, 1961): 3.

[28] It is often forgotten that nearly as many people fought for the British as fought against them. According to Wallace Brown, 'Between 30,000 and 50,000 Loyalists fought in the regular army for the king at some time between 1775 and 1783, and many more served in the militia or engaged in guerrilla warfare. In 1780, 8,000 Loyalists were in the regular army, at a time when Washington's army numbered only about 9,000' (*The King's Friends*: 249). These facts are borne out by the findings of Esther Wright (*The Loyalists of New Brunswick* [Fredericton: 1955]) and other students of the Loyalist colonial 'masses'.

[29] Nelson: 189, 190. Even Jonathan Boucher was more liberal than Tory in outlook. See Bell, *op. cit.* (1969).

[30] The Loyalist Declaration of Independence is reprinted as Appendix A in C.H. Van Tyne, *The Loyalists in the American Revolution* (Gloucester, Mass.: Peter Smith, 1959).

[31] John Locke, *Two Treatises on Government*, Peter Laslett (ed.) (New York: Mentor Books, 1965): 446-67.

[32] Great shade of Locke, immortal Sage

. . . .

Look down with Pity from the Skies!
Behold a vain deluded Race,
Thy venerable name, disgrace;
As Casuists pale, as Savage Rude,
With Glosses weak, with Comments crude,

Pervert thy fair, instructive Page
To sanctify, licentious Rage;
To form some wild ideal Plan,
And Break the Laws of God and Man.

The Patriots of North America: A Sketch (New York: 1775): 21, 22.

[33] See Bell, chs 3 and 4, for a fuller statement of this argument.

[34] J. W. Lydekker, *The Faithful Mohawks* (u.p.: Friedman, 1968. First published in 1938): xi.

[35] Wm. L. Stone, *Life of Joseph Brant-Theyandanezea* (New York: Blake, 1838 [reprinted in 1969]): 138.

[36] Col. Bolton to General Haldimand, quoted in E. Cruickshank, *Butler's Rangers* (1893; reprinted in 1975 by Richardson, Bond & Wright): 59.

[37] *Ibid.*: 68.

[38] Harvey Chalmers and Ethel Brant Monture, *Joseph Brant: Mohawk* (Toronto: Ryerson, 1955): 252.

[39] Jean Johnston, *Wilderness Women: Canada's Forgotten History* (Toronto: Peter Martin, 1973): 77.

[40] *Ibid.*: 87.

[41] *Ibid.*: 95.

[42] Roman N. Komar, 'The History of the Legal Status of the Canadian Indians to 1867' (unpublished paper, 1971): 998. See also Peter Marshall, 'First Americans and Last Loyalists: An Indian Dilemma in War and Peace' in E. Wright (ed.), *Red, White and True Blue* (New York: AMS Press, 1976): 39.

[43] *Ibid.* See also Sir John Johnson, *The North American Johnsons* (London: PRM, 1963): 87. See also Earle Thomas, *Sir John Johnson Loyalist Baronet* (Toronto: Dundurn, 1986).

[44] Johnson, *op. cit.*: 37.

[45] *Ibid.*

[46] This story is fully explained in Komar, ch. 8.

[47] Johnson: 107.

[48] *Ibid.*: 101-2.

[49] *Ibid.*: 111.

[50] One could argue that the Métis/Non-Status category emerged from the efforts of white administrators to impose a binary (White-Indian) framework on a complex set of interrelationships. Although the binary system had its origins in the eighteenth century, its effects were not felt until much later.

[51] Wm. Hamilton Merritt referred sincerely to 'our brave allies—the Six Nation Indians'. These quotations appear in the *Centennial of the Settlement of Upper Canada by the United States Empire Loyalists, 1784-1884* (Toronto: Rose, 1885): 116 ff.

[52] Despite the absence of 'Indian wars' in Canadian history, the recent American experience served as a model for armed confrontations between native peoples and police. The siege at Oka in the summer of 1990 consciously drew inspiration from a similar event that took place 20 years earlier at Wounded Knee, North Dakota. A few warriors who had participated there joined the Mohawks at Oka.

[53] See Bell.

[54] Lawrence Henry Gipson, *The Coming of the Revolution: 1763-1775* (New York: Harper Torchbooks, 1962).

[55] D.P. Coke, *Notes on Royal Commission on Losses and Services of American Loyalists*, H.E. Egerton (ed.) (1915).

[56] Carl J. Friedrich, *Constitutional Government Democracy*, 4th ed. (Waltham, Mass.: Blaisdell, 1968).

[57] Merrill Jensen, *The New Nation* (New York: Knopf, 1950): 360-1.

[58] Smith became chief justice of Quebec, a post similar to the one he enjoyed in New York. See L.F.S.

Upton, *The Loyal Whig: William Smith of New York and Quebec* (Toronto: University of Toronto Press, 1969).

[59] Aileen Dunham, *Political Unrest in Upper Canada* (Toronto: McClelland & Stewart, 1963): 138, 141.

[60] See *inter alia*, Gerald Craig, *Upper Canada: The Formative Years* (Toronto: McClelland & Stewart, 1963); D.W. Earl, *The Family Compact: Aristocracy or Oligarchy?* (Toronto: Copp Clark, 1967); and Gordon Stewart, *The Origins of Canadian Politics: A Comparative Approach* (Vancouver: University of British Columbia Press, 1986). Stewart's analysis of this entire period is excellent.

[61] Rebellions over the issue of responsible government occurred in both Upper and Lower Canada in 1837-38. Canadian developments during the nineteenth century resembled fairly closely American developments during the eighteenth century, giving some credence to the 'culture lag' theory of Canadian-American differences.

[62] Norman Ward, *The Power of the Purse* (Toronto: University of Toronto Press, 1962): 12.

[63] J.E. Hodgetts, *Pioneer Public Service* (Toronto: University of Toronto Press, 1956): 14. See also Hugh Thorburn, *Politics in New Brunswick* (Toronto: University of Toronto Press, 1961), *passim*. Twentieth-century reforms of U.S. practices greatly reduced the scope of Representatives in introducing such bills.

[64] J.R. Mallory, 'The Uses of Legislative Committees', *Canadian Public Administration* 6,1 (March 1963): 1-15.

[65] In the course of dealing with these two tasks, the reformers created another: making the bureaucracy, which although not responsible had been fairly well insulated from politics, neutral again.

[66] Gerald M. Craig, ed., *Lord Durham's Report* (Toronto: McClelland & Stewart, 1963): 64 *et passim*. See also R. MacGregor Dawson, *The Civil Service of Canada* (Toronto: Oxford University Press, 1928). For a critical assessment of the Report from the perpective of a Quebec nationalist, see Monière, *op. cit.*: 116 ff. A more complimentary appraisal appears in Janet Ajzenstat, *The Political Theory of Lord Durham*.

[67] *Lord Durham's Report* (Craig edition): 17.

[68] To a lesser extent, the same is true of educational and religious institutions. All these curiosities illustrate the 'Paradox of the Anti-American Yankee', discussed below.

[69] Dawson: 45.

[70] *Ibid.*: 51. See also J.E. Hodgetts *et al.*, *The Biography of an Institution* (Montreal: McGill-Queen's University Press, 1972), ch. 1.

[71] Several political scientists have outspokenly criticized this practice. Robert Lane, for example, asked 'Should the people elect administrators (as opposed to executive)? Today the long ballot everywhere attests to the strength of this misguided belief' (*Political Life* [New York: Free Press, 1959]: 35). A more trenchant comment was made by Dawson: 'Nor can the civil servant be adequately chosen by election, nor will he do the best work if his term of office is limited to five years, nor should he try to reflect public opinion. He belongs to an organization primarily concerned with thought rather than will', (p. 258).

[72] See P.K. Kuruvilla, 'Administrative Culture in Canada: Some Perspectives', *Canadian Public Administration* 16,2 (Summer 1973): 284-97.

[73] In at least this one respect, the American Founding Fathers showed they distrusted democracy. Their actions later had important effects that they had not anticipated. Some current observers argue that precisely because the United States constitution contains substantive limitations on power, the American political system has had problems in adapting a rapid social and economic change. For example, during the Great Depression the Supreme Court ruled many of President Roosevelt's New Deal measures unconstitutional (i.e., 'illegitimate'), since they differed so radically in substance from earlier legislation. But the contrasts between Canada and the United States on this issue are easily overstated. Some Canadian 'New Deal' type legislation was also overturned by the Judicial Committee

of the Privy Council on grounds that it lay outside the authority (*ultra vires*) of the federal government. Amendment to the BNA Act eventually permitted federal involvement in these areas.

[74] In contrast to the American Constitution, the British North America Act contains no substantive limitations on the exercise of power. The 'residual power', for example, is retained not by 'the people' but the federal government. With the adoption of the Charter, the Canadian constitution was Americanized, but with some important limitations on the constraining effect of the various rights it embraced.

[75] Bertrand de Jouvenel vigorously criticizes the decline of substantive limitations on authority in his book *Sovereignty: An Inquiry into the Political Good*, J.F. Huntington, tr. (Chicago: University of Chicago Press, 1957). In his view other states should emulate American practices.

[76] These observations, drawn from the historical record of the two countries, find some confirmation in survey findings. Comparing data from the 1960s and early 1970s, Nathaniel Beck and John Pierce discovered that Canadian political participation measured in terms of 'voting' and 'campaigning', was as high as or higher than that reported by Americans. Beck and Pierce also compared scores on 'political efficacy' and political trust, the results of which indicate that Americans and Canadian show similar scores on efficacy, with Americans less likely to agree that 'people like me don't have any say about what the government does'. By 1972, Americans had become more cynical than Canadians, but consistently more Americans felt that 'government wastes money'. This question gets closer to the cratophobia-cratophilia distinction than any other. See Nathaniel Beck and John Pierce, 'Political Involvement and Party Allegiance in Canada and the United States', *International Journal of Comparative Sociology* 18 (March-June 1979): 29.

See also Sidney Verba and Gabriel Almond, 'National Revolutions and Political Commitment', in Harry Eckstein (ed)., *Internal War* (New York: Free Press, 1964). Note, however, that high citizen competence refers only to American whites, not to blacks. The Revolution did little or nothing to mobilize the blacks; indeed in some respects they were worse off after the Revolution than before it.

[77] See Bell, ch. 5.

[78] *Ibid*., ch. 6. See also George Rawlyk (ed.), *Historical Essays on the Atlantic Provinces* (Toronto: McClelland & Stewart, 1967).

[79] Hartz, *Liberal Tradition*.

[80] Bailyn, *Ideological Origins*, ch. 2.

[81] Bell, ch. 7. There the terms 'cratophobia' and 'cratophilia' are introduced to refer to the respective tendencies in American and Canadian political culture.

[82] For a catalogue of the assistance given Loyalists by the British government, see Wright, *The Settlement of the United Empire Loyalists* (Toronto, 1934): 41 ff. The extent of financial assistance awarded through the 'Loyalist Claims Commission' is discussed in Coke.

[83] The designation 'corporate welfare bums' helped NDP leader David Lewis focus national attention on government subsidies to big business in the 1974 federal election. Herschel Hardin offers more benevolent views of this and related practices in his discussion of Canada's 'public enterprise culture'. See Herschel Hardin, *A Nation Unaware: The Canadian Economic Culture*. Note that the practice of state assistance to immigrants continued well into the present century.

[84] W.I. Thomas, with Dorothy Swaine Thomas, *The Child in America* (New York: Alfred A. Knopf, 1928); widely paraphrased and known as the 'Thomas Theorem'. See for example, Robert Merton (ed.), *Social Theory and Social Structure*, rev. ed. (New York: Free Press, 1957), ch. 11 on the 'self-fulfilling prophecy'.

3 | The English-Canadian Identity Puzzle

'Canadians are the only people in the world who continually pull themselves up by the roots to see if they are still growing.' This aphorism captures a widely expressed belief that Canadians examine themselves to a degree that is unhealthy and out of control. The political scientist Donald Smiley, for example, pointed out during the 1970s that 'some of us who have been on the Confederation circuit of forums and seminars and conferences on "defining the Canadian identity" have felt from time to time that this interminable self-questioning was dangerously close to collective masochism.'[1]

In a similar vein, novelist Hugh MacLennan exclaimed 'has Canada got an identity—this everlasting, frustrating question! It is like asking a person to state his reason for being alive, the assumption being that if he cannot explain why he is alive, he must be presumed dead.'[2] Extending the medical metaphor, Margaret Atwood acidly remarked, 'Canadians are forever taking the national pulse like doctors at a sickbed: the aim is not to see whether the patient will live well but simply whether he will live at all.'[3]

Canadian intellectuals frequently talk about Canadian identity in the language of irony. This trope is peculiarly appropriate according to Linda Hutcheon. It yields several dialects of emphases and interpretation that 'fit' the many paradoxes of the Canadian identity. Because it always invokes at least a double message, it allows the speaker simultaneously 'to work *within* a dominant tradition but also to challenge it.'[4] The harshness, tone, and humour of this double message can range across a broad spectrum of meaning, from self-deception to self-protection, from élitism through demystification, from opposition through correction to corrosion. In describing themselves, Canadians show a great penchant for self-deprecation that verges on self-mockery. This irony pervades their political humour and thus extends beyond intellectual cocktail conversation to touch the self-consciousness of those who listen to such programs as the 'Royal Canadian Air Farce' and 'Double Exposure' (both on CBC radio) or enjoy the hilarious stand-up comedy of Dave Broadfoot. It infects our poetry (as represented in such collections as *The Maple Laugh Forever*) and inspires countless jokes and phrases about the Canadian identity—for example the gastronomic observation that 'In any world menu, Canada must be considered the vichyssoise of nations—it's cold, half-French and difficult to stir.'[5] During the recent Free Trade debate Margaret Atwood, one of its most articulate critics, revisited the theme of our own elusive identity with the observation that we were 'doing the same old Canadian tango, which is: do we exist? don't we exist? except that we have gone around a couple of more times. We've established the fact of our own existence and now we are prepared to abolish ourselves . . . '.[6] But it is not at all clear that Canadians ever did fully 'establish this fact of our own existence'. Despite the flowering of English Canadian literature, poetry, scholarship, art, and music over the past 30 years, Canadians have been plagued by what one wag called the American occupation of the Canadian imagination. Our communications system, especially television, is dominated by American programming. Even our formal educational system has done a poor job of making Canadians aware of our own culture and heritage, and especially of our history. When it comes to this kind of self-knowledge, however, many Canadians have suffered from a kind of national amnesia.[7] As we noted in the Introduction to this book, some are bored by what little Canadian history they know, so they do not trouble to learn more. Others think it lacks importance, because the decisions that have changed Canada most have been made elsewhere. Still others have preferred the images and myths of other societies, particularly those of Britain and the United States. Historically Canada's population has grown as much through immigration as through natural increase. Immigrants come to this country largely lacking any knowledge of Canadian society. Efforts to teach them the national values and culture have succeeded less in Canada than in the United States, for reasons we shall explore later. This, too, keeps Canadian history from reaching a wider audience.

A study prepared under the auspices of the Association of Universities and Colleges of Canada (AUCC) reported that even universities, the citadels of higher learning, have failed miserably to 'meet the research needs of this country and its citizens'. The report, entitled *To Know Ourselves*, boldly stated that 'there is no developed country in the world with comparable resources that devotes as little attention [as does Canada] to the support of its own culture and of education relating to itself'.[8]

But doesn't this contradict the commentators mentioned above, including Smiley, MacLennan, and Atwood, who depict Canadians as compulsive examiners of their identity? Hodgetts, Hurtig, Symons, and many others have shown how poorly informed Canadians really are about their own society and history. It seems clear that even compulsive concern doesn't do away with ignorance; but why not? The balance of the present chapter looks at three pieces of this identity puzzle: Canada's inability to create an ideologically based nationalism, as other fragment societies have done; the resulting substitution of colonial symbols for indigenous symbols; and finally, the complicating effect of a high rate of turnover in the population.

Once again, we must turn to the formative experiences of Canadian history for help in fitting these pieces together. Though our analysis begins in the eighteenth century, we do not mean to imply that a national identity never changes. Nevertheless, certain elements are included and others left out of the picture from the very beginning. The truth of this becomes more evident when we compare Canada with the United States.

In the United States, where national identity was based on liberalism, ideological battles were bound to break out over the adoption of socialistic welfare measures, and over the issue of peaceful coexistence with communist countries. Neither of these issues was very inflammatory in Canada. Canadians accepted socialistic measures fairly easily; even during the Cold War, Prime Minister Lester Pearson expressed Canadians' mood concerning coexistence with communism with his comment 'Better red than dead'. No career in American politics would have survived such a remark.

Canada's current identity problems reflect the unique way the country developed. Because Canadian identity was closely tied to symbols of Britain and the Empire, Canada had difficulty adjusting to the eclipse of Britain as a major power and the concomitant demise of the British Empire/Commonwealth as Britain turned to Europe and away from her former colonies. Adjustment meant changing the most evocative symbols of national existence (flag, anthem, coat of arms, and others), and fuelling a continuing debate over the role of the monarchy in Canadian affairs.[9] Nor (until recently) have we known how to present the world with a national image appropriate to the country's bilingual reality. Finally, though both Canada and the United States have had to adjust to the presence of an aboriginal population and to racial and ethnic diversity, each society has handled diversity quite differently. Each has viewed it through a distinct cultural lens. We must return to examining each country's formative events to understand why.

Revolution Makes Loyalists

The American Revolution gave America, the 'first new nation' as Lipset has called it, a set of national symbols, a gallery of heroes, and sacred documents that enshrined the nation's ideals. These symbols and ideals helped to define membership in the American community. Citizenship meant accepting the 'self evident' truths on which the new nation had been founded. Later called the American creed or the American way of life, the national ideology of the United States embodied many of the principles of English liberal thought.

In effect, the American Revolution helped to make early liberalism the basis for an American national identity. Like other fragment cultures, America took upon itself a national orthodoxy: to be American meant to hold liberal ideals. So important was this single-minded fidelity to liberal philosophers like John Locke that rival ideological gods, like the graven images Moses smashed, could not be tolerated. Other ideologies posed a threat: they were branded and dismissed as 'un-American'.[10]

But where the successful revolutionaries felt convinced and self-assured, the Loyalists experienced ideological confusion and profound uncertainty about their own identity. When a revolution is won, the successful revolutionaries tend to forget the names they were called in the heat of battle. After the revolution, no one read or ever remembered 18th-century Boston Tory Peter Oliver's corrosive portraits of the men who had emerged as the hallowed 'Founding Fathers', for example. (No American edition of his work appeared until 1961!) The victors celebrate their success; after all, they are the winners, triumphant and confident. But the losers' fate is quite different.

The losers find it difficult to forget the names they were called. The epithets of revolutionary propaganda are, for them, reinforced in the most vivid way imaginable—by exclusion from the new society. The Loyalists were violently expelled, they were told, because they did not belong; they were traitors to America. But the Loyalists could not understand this. America was their home. The principles of John Locke were their principles. We can certainly sympathize with the Loyalists on this account, for they had good reason to be baffled. They were expelled as political exiles, but on false testimony that they were also ideological outsiders. Yet the facts that we have today do not support this accusation.

The Tories, many of whom later became Loyalists, rejected the plan to seize independence from Britain for two different but complementary reasons. Neither had to do with ideology *per se*. Some Tories felt America was not a separate entity, a whole unto itself. It was merely a part of a larger entity, the 'British Empire'. Others thought America did not exist as a whole because the many parts that it comprised could never unite in a common purpose.

Sometimes these two views coincided. For example, Peter Oliver coupled his praise of the British Empire and the kindness of its sovereign with doubts that the colonies were able to co-operate. 'The colonies', he wrote, 'are too jealous of each other to remain long in a state of friendship.' In the relationship between Massachusetts and the Southern colonies, Oliver saw Southern double-dealing and opportunism. The Southerners have cunningly reasoned, he declared, that the people of Massachusetts, 'a sett of brave hardy dogs', can be tricked into shouldering the main burdens of the war for Independence, making them 'easy prey' for Southern expansion after independence has been won. Similarly, Daniel Leonard of Massachusetts warned would-be revolutionaries that they would 'find no reason to expect any assistance outside of New England'. Speaking from the South, on the other hand, Maryland Tory Jonathan Boucher referred to new Englanders as 'the Goths and Vandals of America'.[11]

The Tories' suspiciousness and fierce loyalty help to explain why they failed to oppose the revolutionaries more effectively and doubted that a new, independent nation could survive in North America. To the Tories, the link with Britain provided invaluable benefits in trade and defence that would be lost with independence. But independence would also harm them more directly. They feared that government would fall apart and 'the mob' would come to rule. The colonies would fall to rivalry and conflict, and the nation to domestic unrest, even if the Revolution succeeded. And if the Revolution failed, the British would punish the rebels terribly. They thought the Revolution a great mistake, in every possible respect. But still, these Tories had not rejected John Locke and showed no lack of love for America.[12]

Forced to leave their country, the Tories, or Loyalists, suffered profound doubts. Expulsion kept the Loyalists from basing a fragment identity on the liberal principles of John Locke. Made to give up their real identity, the Canadian Loyalists invented a new one. As a substitute, it was not quite good enough, of course. How could it be, when they had continuously to deny its true nature, liberalism? 'The typical Canadian', an Englishman observed a hundred years ago, 'tells you that he is not, but he is a Yankee—a Yankee in the sense in which we use the term at home, as synonymous with everything that smacks of democracy.' The Loyalists in Canada were thereafter always a paradox, 'anti-American Yankee.' Only one path leads out of the dilemma: creating a myth that helps them survive. In this myth, they insist that they are British.[13]

Loyalist Myths and Their Makers

Throughout the nineteenth century, the most prominent anglophone historians were themselves Loyalists or descended from Loyalist ancestors. Along with others, they portrayed Canadian history in ways that glorified the Loyalists' aims and actions. They gave Canadians myth and rhetoric.[14] Opening the ceremonies held to mark the centennial of the Loyalists' arrival in Upper Canada, R.N. Ball called upon his countrymen to 'do honour to the memory of those noble men and women who, rather than live under an alien rule, left all the comforts and luxuries of their well-filled homes that they might found in the then wilderness of Canada a new home, where the British flag might still wave over, and British laws still govern them.' Later in the same ceremony, Lieutenant-Governor Robinson spoke passionately of the 'bravery and loyalty of the U.E. Loyalists, who have saved to the British Crown this finest unoccupied part of the world'.[15]

From these promising beginnings, the Loyalist saga of courage and resolve continued to unfold. Next came the War of 1812: 'the Canadian War of Independence' (from the United States). A glorious 'War of National Defence', Loyalist historiography has likened it to Thermopylae and other classic exhibitions of military skill. According to this myth, winning the war depended upon the resolve of thousands upon thousands of Loyalist sons and daughters, who almost without help threw back the waves of American invaders.

In fact, almost all the important battles of this war were fought by British regulars. The local citizenry, including even some Loyalist descendants, were divided in their loyalties. They supported both sides, although this fact is not part of the myth. Instead distortion has glamorized the event, as we see in the following passage written in 1871 by Loyalist descendant William Foster: 'We need not ransack foreign romance for valorous deeds. . . . [In 1812, a] call to arms ran throughout the country, echoing from lake to river, and piercing the inmost recesses of the forest. How the eyes of the old refugee loyalists must have flashed as the rusty flintlock was taken from the rack above the fireplace. . . . How must the pulses of the young men have throbbed as they grasped the trusty rifle.'[16]

Next in the catalogue of fables came the defeat of William Lyon Mackenzie's 1837 uprising in Upper Canada. Those who knew the cruelties arising out of rebellion simply turned their backs on violence, the story goes. (This telling of the story has entirely overlooked the evidence of Loyalist support for Macken-zie.) In the Loyalist version, Confederation in 1867 fulfilled a people's dream by uniting the *British* North American colonies into a single dominion still within the arms of the Empire. Later, Canadians participated in the Boer War and the 'Great World War', further demonstrating their loyalty and devotion to Britain. Canada had set a splendid example for other members of the Empire to follow.[17]

What pride the Loyalist descendants felt when they gathered in 1884 to cele-brate the great deeds of their ancestors! No stronger love of empire was bathed by the Thames than took the breezes of Lake Ontario that day. One speaker, A.L. Morden, assured his audience that

> It is ours today to be able in saying, 'I am a British subject' to utter a prouder boast than the Romans. . . . I have not read of any country which, during the last 100 years, has a more glorious history. If our forefathers for their fervent loyalty to Britain, lost everything but their honour, and bravely bore the hardships and privations of first settlers, what feeling should animate our breath today, when with our attachment to British laws, institutions, traditions, rights and liberties, there is added the intensity of our attachment to the Sovereign.

He closed his address with a prayer, attributed to Dr Ryerson: 'May Loyalty ever be the characteristic trait of Canadians, may freedom ever be our possession, may we ever have cause and heart to say, God Save The Queen.' Even Sir Richard Cartwright, whose friendly references to the United States had angered many Loyalists, declaimed that, 'We are here for the purpose of doing what honour we can to the memory of men to whom we owe it that not merely Ontario, but one-half the continent of North America remains today under British rule.'[18]

When they have been taken seriously, the Loyalist myths and the Loyalist pantheon have done great harm. They have encouraged us Canadians to honour colonial symbols instead of adopting our own, and to substitute for nationalism a peculiar form of coat-tails imperialism.[19] Loyalist myth-makers seemed incap-able of imagining a Canada disentangled from Britain. Perhaps this is why, for a long time after Confederation, few Canadians could think of Canada as a nation, and no longer a mere colony. Nowhere is the confusion more evident than in the words spoken by George Ross, Ontario's Minister of Education, in 1896: 'As Canadians, we should teach more of Canada and in teaching Canada we should teach it as only one colony of the vast British Empire on whose dominion the sun never sets. We should have a Canadian history fearless in exalting the great actions of Canada's great men. . . . We should honour our country's flag [i.e., the Union Jack] and know its significance.'[20]

The schools fed generations of Canadian children a steady diet of such nostalgia for the British Empire; they made almost everyone homesick for England. (No matter that an ever-declining portion of the Canadian people had any historic connection with this magical, decaying British Empire.) Who can forget the beloved regions of Imperial pink on Canadian globes and maps of the world?[21] Of course the Loyalist vision of Canada always had its critics, especially in Quebec. Yet pro-British sentiment remained strong in English Canada at least throughout the first half of the present century. It was particularly vital in Ontario, Canada's wealthiest and most powerful province.

By the contemporary period (post 1945), the Loyalist myth had been transformed into a 'new realism' devoid of romantic content; or, worse, it had been forgotten entirely. Because Loyalism no longer seems to bear directly on the Canadian self-image, it also has fallen prey to the national amnesia referred to earlier. As Dennis Duffy points out, 'our artists present images of the Bush, Native Peoples, Animals' but ignore the Loyalist contribution.[22] Loyalist history, once distorted, is largely just forgotten now. Its demise may have resulted from the ironic pervasiveness in Canada today of the culture of the very country from which the Loyalists fled. But it has not gone without leaving a legacy in the form of a particular view of the United States.

Loyalist Attitudes to the United States

Besides glorifying Britain and the 'United Empire', the Loyalist myth promoted a disdain for Americans and the American Republic. That scorn, however, has masked a thorough ambivalence, a dislike mixed with admiration, even envy, that appeared even before the Loyalists arrived in Canada. Edward Winslow, a prominent New Brunswick Loyalist, epitomized the Loyalist outlook when he vowed, 'By heaven, we will be the envy of the American states.'[23] That the United States would forever hold a special place in the Canadian consciousness was almost assured by the Loyalist experience.

Like other political refugees, the Loyalists kept hoping that a change of fortune would permit them to return successful, if not triumphant. But unlike their Cuban counterparts in the twentieth century, the Loyalist expatriates never tried to invade their former homeland. (No one offered to assist or guide them in such an attempt.) Perhaps because the Loyalists were not forced to fit into an already established society, they felt little compulsion to invade their former homeland. In Canada, however, they kept up a lively scepticism about the experiment that the United States represented. To their descendants and to all Canadians the Loyalists handed down the conviction that time would prove them right to have rejected the 'first new nation'. This belief in later vindication has influenced a very wide range of Canadian thinking, even including economic policy. According to Harry Johnson, 'Canadian economic policy has historically been dominated by the ambition to create a country rival in power to the United States, and so to prove that the Americans were wrong to revolt from colonial rule in 1776.'[24]

Such sentiments were more vigorous in Upper Canada than elsewhere, partly because of settlement patterns.[25] Few Americans emigrated to New Brunswick and Nova Scotia after 1790, but Upper Canada served as one more western frontier to the ever-increasing American population. Up to 1812, Americans were almost as free to settle in what is now southern Ontario as in Ohio and Michigan. New American settlers quickly swamped the original Loyalist population. Some of the new settlers were even given special land grants after claiming to be 'late Loyalists'.

The 'late Loyalists' of Upper Canada were suspected of wanting nothing but land and economic fortune. Some local citizens rightly questioned the purity of their motives and their authenticity as Loyalists. But Governor Simcoe was so eager to populate the fledgling colony of Upper Canada that he published invitations in Pennsylvania newspapers asking those whose fidelity to Britain had been dormant for some years to show their true loyalty and move to Upper Canada. Once there they would be granted land on terms similar to those offered the early Loyalists. This practice continued until about 1797.

With scarcely any settlement more than a few dozen miles from the American border, Upper Canada was vulnerable to invasion. The colony's entire population was strung out along the Great Lakes system, which makes travelling north and south just as easy as travelling east and west.[26] By 1791, the élite of Upper Canada saw a need to prepare against possible attack. Governor Simcoe hurried to build a system of fortifications and communications; and before 1812, conflict nearly erupted into war at several times (for example, in 1793 and 1807). Thus from the very beginning of its history Upper Canada feared for its ability to survive.

For the first three decades almost all Upper Canadians were Americans by birth or earlier residence. Yet after the War of 1812, the colonial élite began a very conscious, sustained effort to remove the American influence from every sphere of life including politics, religion, and education. Laws attempted, though with little success, to keep American immigrants from owning land, voting, and exercising other privileges for seven years. Perhaps more important, British immigrants were sought to offset the weight of American numbers in Upper Canada.

Accordingly, from 1815 to 1837, almost half a million immigrants poured into Canada from Great Britain, while settlers from the American Republic were limited to a mere handful. Politicians in the local communities and in the Assembly tried time and again to get rid of American teachers and American textbooks. Religious groups (especially Methodists) suspected of keeping too closely connected with their American counterparts were strongly urged, even forced on occasion, to align themselves with British groups instead.[27]

The colony fought frantically to keep the values of Loyalism safe from harm by Americanization. Yet the threat to Upper Canada was primarily political, despite the fears that American values would pervert education and religion. For, in a sense, American values had already been absorbed. One could find very little cultural difference between Upper Canada and the Northern United States before the 1830s. In his book on the social history of western Ontario, Fred Landon pointed out that British travellers who entered Upper Canada after journeying in the United States were 'struck by the similarity between the ways of living, the manners, and the speech of the neighbouring peoples'. The travel literature in this period is full of remarks about the 'Yankee' ways of the Canadians, as the following quotation by a visitor suggests: 'I shall renounce all pretensions to discernment if the inhabitants of Upper Canada are not the most accomplished Yankees on the other side of the Atlantic.'[28]

Could a society peopled almost entirely by Americans (Loyalists, late Loyalists, and non-Loyalists) be anything but American in its point of view? The paradox is fully captured by historian A.G. Bradley who described the Loyalist as 'a unique figure in history. So far as I know you may look in vain elsewhere for a truculently anti-republican democrat.'[29] The Loyalists were, in short, anti-American Yankees. Perhaps they were not so different in that respect from the thousands of Americans who later came to Canada protesting American activities in Vietnam. Like the Loyalists and despite themselves, these expatriates have probably made Canada somewhat more American in its thinking than it might otherwise have been.

Nevertheless, anti-Americanism became a Loyalist article of faith closely linked to, and often mistaken for, pro-British sentiment. Sydney Wise aptly describes the connection of these two views:

> Negative criticisms of American institutions, drawn from classical sources, were generally part of a comparison, stated or implied, with colonial and British institutions, and with the guarantee which the latter gave for 'firm and well established government' and 'for the repose and security which it is the object of every well formed system to provide'. Such comparisons and the positive values they upheld, were psychologically vital to the Loyalist population of British North America. How could this émigré people deny their history, or the choice they had made? Already, then, it was essential for Canadians not to believe in the United States and to assume that the country they lived in was not a kind of subarctic, second-best America, but rather a genuine alternative to this revolution-born democracy and organized upon principles and for purposes quite different from it.[30]

Given time and a bit of luck, Canada's success would indeed prove the superiority of the Loyalist 'race'. A stalwart Loyalist and major figure in the Imperial Federation League, Col. George T. Denison assured his compatriots that expansion into the North West would fulfil the Loyalists' most fervent hopes: 'I am very glad to hear such good accounts of the resources and fertility of the great

North-West. When filled up with a loyal population and a prosperous one, I have every confidence that in time it would prove a great source of strength to the Dominion and together we men of the North . . . will be able to teach the Yankees that we will be as our ancestors always have been, the dominant race.'[31]

Assessing Loyalist Myths

However understandable, Loyalism's combination of anti-Americanism and pro-British sentiment has its unhealthy side. In the first place, Canadians have gotten into the habit of comparing themselves with Americans at every opportunity, and almost always judging themselves the better. Smugness, though not a deadly sin, is no virtue either.[32]

Smugness smothers critical inquiry and creative thinking. Sometimes, convinced that Canadian institutions must be good because they originated in Britain, Canadians are blinded to the fact that some of these institutions are not very British, and some are not very good either. From watching too much American television many Canadians came to imagine that the rights granted to Americans by the Bill of Rights and the Constitution applied to them. Until the adoption of the Canadian Charter of Rights in 1982, however, the citizens' rights and privileges before Canadian law were comparatively few.[33] The criminal law, for example, has changed little since the nineteenth century. Americans have often debated the basic issues of political life, beginning in the Constitutional period and ever since then. But Canadians have seldom done this. When Prime Minister Trudeau invoked the War Measures Act during the so-called October Crisis, most Canadians simply accepted this suspension of their civil and political rights without alarm, and many applauded the government's efforts. A similar action in the United States would have been criticized and opposed much more vigorously, given the traditional American concern with protecting civil rights.[34]

The love of things British has proven even more harmful to Canada than anti-Americanism. Many early Canadians saw the British connection as the 'umbilical cord' through which 'the life blood has flowed into the province'. For this reason Canada achieved dominion status (with full sovereignty coming nearly sixty years later) not heroically, not defiantly, but by working along with the mother country. Of course, defiance and heroism are virtues only in the last resort, and when the prize that is sought is a virtuous one. Yet haven't we lost out on something by backing into nationhood so undramatically?[35]

Instead of a bold Declaration of Independence, Canada got the *British* North America Act, an act passed not on Parliament Hill but in Westminster. There was no stirring start. Unlike the ringing 'We the People of the (United States)', Canada's constitution begins with a lame and legalistic 'Whereas. . . '. So eager were Canadians to affirm this Britishness that until 1947 they were content to be known simply as 'British subjects'. Until recently, all Canadian passports carried this designation, and not 'Canadian citizen'. Until the middle of the

1960s, Canada's official flag was Britain's Union Jack, her national anthem 'God Save the Queen'!

In failing to create her own symbols of identity Canada failed to bridge the chasm between francophone and anglophone cultures. For it is precisely by building such bridges that a nation unifies its people. The unending celebration of loyalty to Britain had served to remind most French Canadians of the conquest, the outstanding 'catastrophe' in French Canada's history. Until well after the Second World War, francophone requests to abandon imperial symbols fell on stubbornly deaf ears. Not until the 1960s and 1970s (following the recommendations of the Royal Commission on Bilingualism and Biculturalism) were federal agencies and departments renamed in an effort to reflect official bilingualism (e.g., Air Canada, Transport Canada) or to remove the symbols of British monarchy that had proved so offensive in Quebec. Loyalism as the romanticization of the British connection has been anything but helpful in building a strong over-arching Canadian identity that could unite English and French. Are there any Loyalist traditions that might have contributed positively to making a viable Canadian identity? Perhaps so.

The Canadian Mosaic

No simple generalization can sum up the reasons why American colonists and not others emigrated to Canada. However, William Nelson has noted that the Loyalists (earlier called Tories) included a number of minority groups who felt threatened by the nationalistic ambitions of the American revolutionaries. 'It was in the patchwork societies of Pennsylvania and New York that the Tories were strongest.' Precisely those ethnic groups that had most strongly retained their ethnic culture supported the British cause. 'The Dutch and Germans seemed to have inclined towards supporting the Revolution where they were already Anglicized, but not where they had kept their language and separate identity.'[36]

Thus, the much noted Canadian ethnic mosaic got its start with the Loyalist migration. In Upper Canada, for example, the lively Loyalist mosaic included Highland Scots who settled in Glengarry County near Ottawa; French Huguenots, Palatinate and Swiss Germans, Pennsylvania Dutch who settled the Kingston area (hence the original German county names of Ontario); and Mennonites and Quakers who settled between Toronto and Niagara.[37] The Mohawk Indians who had helped Sir John Johnson in New York were given a large tract of land, and the town nearby was named Brantford, after their leader Joseph Brant. Loyalism was able to tolerate diversity because all ethnic groups and individuals, whatever their background, could join together in loyalty to the Empire. Beyond loyalty itself, there were no ideological requirements that might threaten their own culture and values. Being loyal proved to be in their own interest.

Loyalism's ability to tolerate cultural diversity may be traceable, ultimately, to

British imperial practice. Though inconsistent in this respect, British colonial administrators tended to follow the Roman example of taking from their imperial subjects only what was 'due Caesar', while leaving the rest alone. This reluctance to interfere in domestic, especially cultural, affairs contributed significantly to the lifespan of both Empires, and simplified the task of economic exploitation. Typically, imperial attempts to take over 'hearts and minds' have failed disastrously. The British in North America got an unusual boost, however, from the myth of Loyalism.

The Loyalist Centennial Celebrations held in Adolphustown, Toronto, and Niagara-on-the-Lake in 1885 took in a wide ethnic variety, even including Indians in full headdress.[38] Speakers praised the strength of diversity and stated their firm commitment to the common ideals and memories of Empire. Without ever using the term 'mosaic', they exemplified its most attractive features, celebrating the lore, food, and culture of many ethnic groups, and embracing them all as co-equal participants in the loyalist tradition.

The Canadian concept of 'mosaic' has often been contrasted with the 'melting-pot' metaphor of American society.[39] In theory at least, these two societies view ethnic diversity quite differently. Canadians claim to see an advantage in diversity. They criticize the demand for assimilation implied in the American motto, *e pluribus, unum* (out of the many, one). The United States has insisted on 'Americanizing' its immigrants. It has expected them to conform to the ideals and aspirations formally expressed in the sacred documents of America's founding. But to become a Canadian has never meant giving up another culture, nor adopting a code, credo, or way of life. Candidates need only state their 'loyalty to the crown'. Lacking a tradition of ideological purity, Canada has permitted, even supported, nonconformity of many types. For example, Canadians have been able to accept socialism as a legitimate political ideology; Americans have not.[40]

The conception of Canada as a bicultural partnership between the 'two founding races' of English and French was the implicit underpinning of the Royal Commission set up by the Pearson government in the early 1960s. Though this conception ignores the primacy of the aboriginal presence in Canada, its strongest critics at the time were the many ethnic groups that did not enjoy the British or French 'charter status'. So insistent were these groups in challenging biculturalism that the Royal Commission felt obliged to publish a separate volume of their report on *The Contribution of the Other Ethnic Groups*. More significantly, the Trudeau government declared in 1971 that although Canada had two official languages, it had no official culture. On the contrary, henceforth Canadian federal policy would work to preserve the country's multicultural heritage. Thus began the policy of official 'multiculturalism within a bilingual framework'. Its supporters hoped it would enshrine the concept of the mosaic and hence differentiate Canada from the U.S. melting pot. Funds would be spent to assist ethnic groups with cultural activities, heritage language training, and historical research. As the policy evolved, it came to include concern about racism and the need to promote 'cross-cultural understanding'. Even the Charter of Rights endorses multiculturalism through section 27: 'This Charter shall be interpreted in a manner consistent with the preservation and enhancement of the multi-cultural heritage of Canadians.' Six years later the Mulroney government passed what was hailed as 'the world's first multiculturalism act', and created for the first time a Department of Multiculturalism and Citizenship.

Critics of multiculturalism view all of this with cynicism verging on outrage. For them multiculturalism excuses the refusal to become Canadian. Indeed, according to best-selling author William Gairdner, multiculturalism is *The Trouble With Canada*.[41] Picking up on this undercurrent of negative feeling about multiculturalism, several of the newly formed political parties have adopted platforms critical of the program. The Reform Party committed itself to terminating the multiculturalism policy.

But the problems of multiculturalism are not simply the result of a federal policy. Ethnic identity is on the increase in most parts of the world. It is not surprising that the so-called 'other ethnic groups' in Canada have expressed strong feeling about their place in Canadian society, and have demanded a say in the process of constitutional reform. Ethnic groups (along with groups representing aboriginal people) were among the most vocal and articulate critics of the Meech Lake Accord.

Particularly galled by the clauses in the Accord that recognized Quebec as a 'distinct society', native and ethnic spokespersons alike attacked both the conception of Canada they believed the Accord embodies, and the process of constitutional reform which privileged as the major stakeholders only first ministers representing the provincial and federal governments. Alan Cairns has analysed this debate over Meech Lake as a contest between the 'official discourse' of federalism and the 'non-official' (or in this case 'anti-official') discourse of ethnicity and identity.[42] As our society changes demographically to become much more diverse ethnically and socially, our political culture is changing as well. Ethnic consciousness has increased, and demands for a redefinition of our political process have begun to transform political discourse.

The changes have taken a rather different course in Quebec than elsewhere in Canada, reflecting some of the unique and distinctive characteristics of the political culture of that province.

Though the 'mosaic' is an attractive enough ideal, we must examine the way Canadians behave if we are to understand Canadian society. To begin with, the mosaic concept has not always been put into practice, or even paid lip service. For example, Quebec francophones have until very recently thought that ethnic diversity threatened their rights. Francophones are part of the Canadian mosaic, but they do not accept the mosaic in either principle or practice.[43] They resent its implications of equal status for all minority cultures, especially since most of the other minorities have chosen to learn English, the dominant language. Francophone support for multiculturalism at the time of Confederation gave way to a belief in the principle of two cultures, or biculturalism; francophones insisted on special status as one of the two 'founding races'. They have not reversed their opinion in the years that have intervened.

And just as the mosaic is incompletely accepted as a symbol of Canadian society, so too the history of relations between groups sometimes makes the mosaic image seem inappropriate. Over the years, various ethnic minorities have chosen to fight out their long-standing hatreds in the New World. For example, fights between Orangemen and Catholics became standard fare in the social diet of Canada during its earliest years. Later arrivals have sometimes kept up this unfortunate custom.

The Problem of Racism

Nor have Canadians always wanted to make room for foreign customs. At times Canadians have defined very narrowly the range of ethnic groups the Canadian mosaic could accept. Two years after Confederation, for example, Robert Grant Haliburton lectured the Montreal Library Club on Canada's 'national spirit'. He stressed the influence of Canada's northern geography and climate on this spirit, asking, 'may not our snow and frost give us what is more value than gold or silver, a healthy, hardy, virtuous dominant race? [For Canada] must ever be . . . a Northern country inhabited by the descendant of Northern races.' Haliburton and many like him in the nineteenth century assumed that no country could hold on to its national character without keeping its racial purity. For, 'If climate has not had the effect of moulding races, how is it that the southern nations have almost invariably been inferior to and subjugated by the men of the north?'

From the happy marriage of northern races and a northern climate would be born a Canadian people worthy of the ideals of 'the true north, strong and free', Haliburton argued.[44] Several early nationalists even took the trouble to prove that the French Canadians had descended from the Normans, not from the peoples of southern France. They therefore shared with British, German, and Scandinavian Canadians the genetic advantages all northern people enjoyed. They were acceptable.

Not until near the end of the nineteenth century did non-Aryans immigrate to Canada in sizeable numbers. To central Canada and the Prairies came Southern and Eastern Europeans; to British Columbia, the Chinese and Japanese. Many Canadians hated the newcomers and wanted to push them out. Arguing against such intolerance, an editorial, 'Immigration and Race', in the Toronto *Globe* of 11 July 1901, called for moderation: 'Objection is taken to the character of immigration to Canada on racial grounds. . . . In Canada it is often argued that we get people from the British Isles or "Teutons", all others being branded by our ethnological experts as inferior. . . . The Slav is supposed to be the traditional enemy of the Saxon, against whom he will be arrayed in some earth-shaking conflict, and he is unfit for free institutions.'

Several months later, a *Globe* editorial observed: 'National character is now in the formation stage in Canada. There are many different [cultural] elements which are not yet assimilated and the process of assimilation may be slow' (28 October 1901). Nine years after that, the *Globe* notes with relief that 'Canadianization of the West' was indeed taking place: 'The vexed question of the variety of languages remains with us, but in the West it no longer appears so formidable an obstacle to unity as it once did. There are many languages spoken in the city of Winnipeg and there are a few taught in the schools, but the pupils all learn English as in Toronto.' One could not expect miracles, however; yellow and brown people remained beyond the pale of acceptability. A *Globe* article of 9 November 1906, titled 'Stop Hindoo Immigration', opined that 'This country is wholly unsuited to such people and they cannot be assimilated by our people.' A *Queen's Quarterly* article on current affairs appearing in October 1906 similarly commented that 'the Chinese are the product of a civilization so different from ours that probably many generations would pass before they assimilated with us.'[45]

Canada's philosophy of tolerating ethnic diversity was given its clearest voice by John Murray Gibbon, in his book *The Canadian Mosaic* (1938). Gibbon's imagery is noble and inspiring enough: 'The Canadian people today present itself as a decorated surface, bright with inlays of separate coloured pieces, not painted in colours blended with brush on palette. The original background in which the inlays are set is still visible, but these inlays cover more space than the background, and so the ensemble may truly be called a mosaic.' But even while celebrating the mosaic that immigration had brought into being, Gibbon argued that eventual assimilation was to be preferred. The mosaic was no more than a stage along the way to a 'new northern nation'. This notion is not far from the Americans' 'melting-pot'. In such a nation the 'European racial groups' that make up the Canadian people would eventually be 'blended into one type. Possibly, in another two hundred years, Canadians may be fused together and standardized so that you can recognize them anywhere in a crowd.'[46] Gibbon's book rarely refers to blacks (though they arrived in Canada with the white Loyalists), to Asians, or to Orientals. It focuses instead on the European groups that had come to Canada. The faces in Gibbon's mosaic are white—never red, yellow, brown, or black.

For Gibbon and his fellow Canadians ethnic cultural diversity was one thing, racial diversity quite another. Until the 1960s, Canadian immigration policy was designed, as Prime Minister Mackenzie King put it, to keep Canada 'as a white man's country'. The myth of Canadian racial tolerance does not stand up well under close scrutiny. The appalling treatment of Canada's native people (who today make up about one-quarter of Canada's prison population); the disgusting internment of Japanese people during the Second World War;

the present plight of those who descended from black Loyalists in the Maritimes; and countless other examples of racism give the lie to our society's pretence of encouraging diversity.

Surveys show abundant evidence of racism among many Canadians. Over one-quarter of all immigrants to Canada between 1967 and 1974 were blacks or Asians, and by 1976 most of Canada's roughly one-half million non-whites (two per cent of the country's population) lived in large cities like Toronto. That year, York University anthropologist Frances Henry conducted a survey of Toronto residents to study the extent and dynamics of racial prejudice. Over fifty per cent of the people she interviewed expressed racist attitudes, by her criteria.

Groups most prone to racism included housewives, older people, the poor and uneducated, members of certain religious groups (particularly Baptists, Lutherans, and Presbyterians), and immigrants from Southern and Eastern Europe. Those falling into the 'very racist' category tended to have had the least contact with non-whites; yet they believed firmly in racist stereotypes. 'Thus it is very clear that racists believe Whites are intelligent and willing to work hard whereas Blacks are thought to be sloppy, slow moving, and like to drive big cars.'[47]

Nonwhite immigration to Canada continued at a relatively high rate over the next fifteen years, and so too did the problem of racism. Virtually every province established a Human Rights Commission to investigate complaints of discriminatory practices. The official political culture was developing strong injunctions against discrimination, and broadening the conception of offensive practices beyond race, ethnicity, and language to include gender, sexual preference, physical or mental disability, and age. Canada was truly entering the epoch of human rights, and facing head-on the complex problem of balancing individual with collective rights.

Unequal Opportunity

Racism and discrimination are not the only challenges to concept of 'mosaic'. John Porter's classic, *The Vertical Mosaic*, revealed nearly thirty years ago another equally serious difficulty in accepting the mosaic as Canada's unifying symbol. Porter concluded from his data that social position in Canada was closely tied to ethnic background. In describing the development of 'a reciprocal relationship between ethnicity and social class', Porter pointed out that various ethnic groups assume a low level 'entrance status' on arriving in the country:

> A given ethnic group appropriates particular roles and designates other ethnic groups for the less desired ones. Often the low status group accepts its inferior position. Through time the relative status positions, reinforced by stereotypes and social images—the Irish policeman and the Irish maid, for example—harden and become perpetuated over a very long time. Over time the position of entrance

status may be improved or it may be a permanent caste-like status as it has been, for example, with the Chinese in Canada. Thus most of Canada's minority groups have at some time had this entrance status. Some, but not all, have moved out of it.[48]

Canadian ethnic groups have unequal standing and unequal chance to move between classes. Although few Canadians of minority origins appear to want to assimilate culturally, they all want full economic, social, and political rights. But the line that separates ethnic solidarity from discrimination is a fine one. Does the equal opportunity for jobs demand that all ethnic groups be found, in equal numbers, in all occupational settings? Would we require that Caucasians be allowed to wait on tables in Chinese restaurants? And should we enact quotas or 'affirmative action' policies to remove inequality?

TABLE 3.1   THE TEN MAJOR SOURCE COUNTRIES OF IMMIGRATION TO CANADA, 1961, 1978, AND 1984

1961	%	1978	%	1984	%
Italy	20.4	Britain	13.7	Vietnam	12.4
Britain	18.5	U.S.A.	11.5	Hong Kong	8.7
U.S.A.	16.1	India	5.9	U.S.A.	7.8
Germany	8.6	Hong Kong	5.5	India	6.2
Greece	5.4	Philippines	5.1	Britain	5.8
Portugal	4.2	Jamaica	4.5	Poland	5.1
Poland	3.8	Portugal	3.6	Philippines	4.2
Yugoslavia	3.2	Italy	3.4	El Salvador	2.9
Netherlands	2.7	Guyana	2.6	Jamaica	2.8
France	2.4	France	2.0	China	2.5
Total ten major countries	85.3	Total ten major countries	57.8	Total ten major countries	58.4
Other countries	14.7	Other countries	42.2	Other countries	41.6
Total	100.0	Total	100.0	Total	100.0

Source: Statistics Canada, *Canadian Social Trends* (Autumn 1986): Employment and Immigration Canada.

Putting the mosaic notion into practice raises many such questions. Indeed, the mosaic concept must be rehabilitated if it is to serve as a unifying symbol, even in anglophone Canada. Purged of class connotations and racial prejudice, the mosaic notion may prove a unique stage upon which to gather Canadians from varied backgrounds without first doing away with all the differences. Cross-cultural understanding and a celebration of diversity can become vital elements of Canadian identity, but only if Canadians reject as national heresies intolerance and discrimination and only if our official discourse is modified to capture the legitimate concerns for status and identity expressed by Canadians of all ethnic and racial backgrounds.[49] The federal government needs to do more than support ethnic cultural activities; it must make it possible for ethnic, native, and minority voices to be heard in debates about the future of our country; and it must also promote the democratic values that nourish multicultural harmony and justice.[50] But, conversely, it must also protect the society against cultural anarchy.

TABLE 3.2	NATIVE-BORN AND FOREIGN-BORN POPULATIONS, CANADA, 1871-1986				
	CANADIAN POPULATION (THOUSANDS OF PERSONS)			PER CENT FOREIGN-BORN	
YEAR	TOTAL	FOREIGN-BORN	NATIVE-BORN	CANADA	U.S.
1871	3,689	625	3,064	16.9	14.0
1882	4,325	603	3,722	13.9	13.3
1891	4,833	644	4,189	13.3	14.7
1901	5,371	699	4,672	13.0	13.6
1911	7,207	1,587	5,620	22.0	14.6
1921	8,788	1,956	6,832	22.3	13.2
1931	10,377	2,309	8,069	22.2	11.6
1941	11,507	2,019	9,488	17.5	8.8
1951	14,009	2,060	11,949	14.7	6.9
1961	18,238	2,844	15,394	15.6	4.0
1971	21,568	3,295	18,273	15.3	4.7
1981	24,083	3,867	20,216	16.1	6.2
1986[a]	25,022	3,908	21,114[b]	15.6	5.9
			21,078[c]		

[a] The years of American censuses, the source of our American data, are one year earlier: that is, 1870, 1880, and so on.

[b] Non Immigrant Population

[c] Native Born Population — *Table 5A.* — The Nation — 1987 Census.
CAN 1 CS8.7 1986 93-108, 93-209

Source: Canadian data: *Census Canada* 1981, 1986, and *Immigration Statistics*, Department of Manpower and Immigration, 1972, Table 1; U.S. data, *Historical Statistics of the United States, Colonial Times to 1957*, 1960; *Social Indicators 1976*, Table D; and *Statistical Abstract 1990*.

Teaching the Canadian Identity to Newcomers

A nation's ability to protect the integrity of its culture depends on, among other things, the original soundness and unity of its culture, its ability to teach this culture to newcomers, and the rate at which the population changes through the addition of newcomers. John Porter reminds us, in *The Vertical Mosaic*, that throughout history Canada has imported immigrants to do the jobs native Canadians had not been trained, or were unwilling, to do. Such immigration tended to keep institutions of higher education from developing, because they seemed unnecessary to national well-being. The immigrants who came to Canada fitted readily into the Canadian economy and made it prosper.

But they did not fit into the culture quite so easily. Compared to the number who immigrated there were too few Canadian-born people—particularly adults—to preserve and teach the culture both to immigrants and to new-born children. The small ratio of these 'tradition-carriers' to new arrivals strained Canada's capacity to absorb immigrants. This has hindered the development of an English-Canadian identity as much as anything we have discussed so far. Further, it suggests that cultural diversity may result as much from a failure to socialize immigrants as from a desire for multiculturalism.

Like other societies in the New World, Canada was colonized by immigrants from the Old World in gradually increasing numbers. In 1871, after more than two centuries of immigration and child-bearing, Canada's population exceeded three million persons (see Table 3.2). At the earliest stages of settlement each arrival of immigrants, however small, had meant a large proportional increase in Canada's population. For example, the town of York (Toronto) increased in size from 720 persons in 1816 to 9,252 in 1834 and to 44,821 in 1860 (of whom over half were foreign-born in the last tally). This was a 6,000 per cent increase in one and a half generations, obviously significant to social organization.

Canada's population renewed itself, or turned over, very rapidly for a number of reasons. As we have noted, immigration was considerable. But so was emigration. For a long time—indeed, until this present century—as many were leaving Canada each year as were entering it, making for a rapid change of faces. But also, rates of birth and death were very high, as in all pre-industrial or early-industrial societies. Every year two per cent or three per cent of the population died and slightly more children were born to replace them. This turnover also worked to keep the society in rapid flux. Because of high mortality rates and fertility rates, old people were in short supply. For example, the proportion of men sixty years or older in Upper Canada (Ontario) in 1848 was only four per cent. Today the percentage is twice as high. The rapid, yearly turnover of population, the high percentage of immigrants, and the absence of old people to teach and preserve the culture all worked together. The result was cultural confusion: the lack of a single, unifying culture and people who could teach it to newcomers.

Ever since Confederation, people born elsewhere have constituted ten to twenty per cent of the Canadian population. Except during the Depression, every decade in the twentieth century has seen a great deal of immigration. In many decades more than a million people migrated to Canada. Many decades have witnessed almost equally high rates of emigration. The inflow of immigrants has increased the numerator, and the outflow of native-born persons has reduced the denominator in the percentage of foreign-born Canadians. Such rapid turnover has kept the ratio of immigrants to total population high, and, stated otherwise, it has kept the ratio of 'tradition-carriers' to 'new arrivals' low.

From the data in Table 3.3 we can compute a 'ratio of tradition-carriers to new arrivals', which measures the extent of this turnover of population over a long period of time.[51] This ratio has several interesting characteristics. First, throughout the last hundred years the ratio has ranged between one and three tradition-carriers per new arrival. Of course some of these 'tradition-carriers' are no more than teenagers or immigrants of a mere ten years' standing who, therefore, carry tradition in name more than in substance. By continuing to live in Canada and learning its culture, they have carried some of the Canadian tradition; but most tradition-carriers are native-born adults. For Canada to become culturally homogeneous, tradition-carriers must train the many newcomers in the 'Canadian way'. Canada's ability to do this has varied greatly over time, but compared to the United States the ratio of tradition-carriers to new immigrants has been relatively low.

The ratio shows several peaks and dips since Confederation, notably between 1891 and 1911, and between 1931 and 1951. In both of these periods, a depressed economy reduced the numbers of newcomers: both new-born children and immigrants. This led to a higher ratio of tradition-carriers to new arrivals. In each instance a return to prosperity later allowed immigration (and child-bearing) to resume on a large scale. The resulting decline in the ratio of tradition-carriers to new arrivals made cultural stability precarious once again.

The Increase in Tradition-Carriers

Leaving these fluctuations aside, the overall trend in this ratio of tradition-carriers to newcomers is upward. The data in Table 3.3 indicate that this upward trend is not due to major declines in immigration or emigration. Indeed *net* migration (the excess of immigration over emigration) has been greater since 1900 than before. Rather a major change in the longevity and turnover of the Canadian-born population accounts for this trend. Canada's population is 'older' today than it was one hundred years ago; the median age today is probably ten years higher. And, as we have noted, old people are proportionately more numerous than ever before. That means a higher ratio of adults to children, and a smaller percentage of infants and children each decade than in the one before. A longer lifespan also means a slower disappearance of old faces through death.

For demographers the age structure—the proportion of men and women at

TABLE 3.3		COMPONENTS OF POPULATION GROWTH CANADA, 1861-1986					
DECADE	POPULATION START OF DECADE	BIRTHS	DEATHS	NATURAL INCREASE	IMMIGRATION	EMIGRATION[a]	NET MIGRATION
				(Thousands of Persons)			
1861-71	3,230	1,369	718	651	183	375	-195
1871-81	3,689	1,477	754	723	353	440	-87
1881-91	4,325	1,538	824	714	903	1,109	-206
1891-1901	4,833	1,546	828	718	326	506	-180
1901-11	5,371	1,931	811	1,120	1,759	1,043	716
1911-21	7,207	2,338	988[b]	1,350	1,612	1,381	-231
1921-31	8,788	2,415	1,055	1,360	1,203	974	229
1931-41	10,377	2,294	1,072	1,222	150	242	-92
1941-51	11,507	3,186	1,214[b]	1,972	548	379	169
1951-61[c]	14,009	4,468	1,320	3,148	1,543	462	1,081
1961-71	18,238	4,063	1,360	2,703	1,429	802	627
1971-81	21,568	3,537	1,660	1,877	1,263	625	638
1981-86[d]	24,083	1,871	876	993	499	235	264

[a] A residual, calculated by adding natural increase and immigration to the population count at the start of the decade and subtracting the population count at the end of the decade.

[b] Includes deaths resulting from the two world wars, numbering 120,000 and 36,000 respectively.

[c] Includes Newfoundland.

[d] These immigration statistics begin 31 June 1981 and end 31 May 1986.

Sources: Department of Manpower and Immigration, *Canadian Immigration and Population Study* (1974), Table 1.4; *Vital Statistics*, 1971-85, Vols. 1-3; *Immigration Statistics*, 1971-1981 and 1981-1986.

each age—is probably the most important characteristic of a population. The average age of a population clearly reflects a population's rate of turnover: a higher age means a slower turnover. In a society without immigration and emigration, the percentage of people at each age can be derived mathematically from stable rates of birth and death, which are the components of turnover. Migration aside, as rates of birth and death rise, the population turns over more quickly, the ratio of newcomers to tradition-carriers rises, and the average age falls.

Most significant in affecting the ratio of tradition-carriers to newcomers in this past century has been the decline in child-bearing as a result of the increased use of birth control. Today's fertility rate is about half the rate in the 1950s, just under two children per mother who has completed her child-bearing. This rate is the lowest ever recorded in Canadian history and since the early 1970s has remained below the 'replacement level' (i.e., the level required to prevent a natural decrease in Canada's population). Fertility, like mortality, has declined markedly throughout the whole Western world. Indeed the same processes that are gradually slowing down the turnover of the Canadian population are doing the same in the other modern countries.

As a result, the median age of the Canadian population increased from twenty years in 1881 to almost twenty-eight years in 1976. Demographers predict that it will rise to almost thirty-six years by the year 2001, if birth and death rates remain as low as they are now and present migration patterns persist. And as the proportion of young people (tradition-consumers) decreases, the proportion of older people (tradition-carriers) increases accordingly. In fifty years slightly more Canadians will be over age sixty-five than under age twenty.[52] This will reverse the classic 'dependency problem', the problem of providing for those who are too young to support themselves. In the future the many who are too old to support themselves will have to be provided for. This is not an easier problem to solve, but it is a different one. But whatever its economic consequences, this 'aging' of the Canadian people is likely to help promote cultural unity.

The ratio of tradition-carriers to new arrivals has varied over time in exactly the same way in the United States as in Canada. In both countries, it reaches a peak immediately after the Great Depression, when fewer newcomers (immigrants or babies) came to either country. However, the American ratio of tradition-carriers to new arrivals is always higher than Canada's. This difference is probably due to lower rates of immigration and emigration in the United States. Data in Table 3.2 show that throughout the present century, foreign-born persons have been proportionately fewer in the American than in the Canadian population. One must conclude that, among other factors favouring its stronger national culture, the United States has had a slower population turnover as well.

Some of Canada's cultural problems seem destined to disappear with a continuing low level of fertility and mortality, if immigration is kept down to a modest amount. But problems remain, largely because of the number, longevity, and geographic segregation of Canada's immigrants. Canada's cities pose the greatest challenge to cultural unity, as the ratios of tradition-carriers to new-comers are lowest there. Young immigrants have come mainly to Canada's cities, where they have lived in separate groups and set up institutions for keeping their own cultures alive. Now those institutions have taken on lives of their own, slowing the inevitable assimilation of Canadian-born ethnics.

Consider the ratio of immigrants to total population in the various parts of Canada. At least in this century, cities have always contained more immigrants per native Canadian than the rural areas of Canada. For example, in 1921, only 22% of the national population but almost 30% of the people in Canada's twelve largest cities had been born in other countries. In 1971 the proportion was still over 20% in these largest cities, only 15% in the national population. In 1921, over one-third of the populations of Toronto, Hamilton, Winnipeg, Calgary, Edmonton, and Vancouver were foreign-born (almost one-half in the last four cities named). In 1971, over 40% of Torontonians and over one-third of Vancouverites had been born in other countries. By 1981 these proportions had fallen slightly but were still very high. In Montreal almost one person in five has been counted as foreign-born in the censuses of 1921, 1931, 1961, and 1971, and about one in six in 1981.

To summarize, a great many immigrants have come to Canada throughout its history. However, even higher rates of emigration than immigration in the nine-teenth century kept the population small. Immigration and emigration com-bined with high levels of mortality and fertility in the nineteenth century to turn over, or renew, the population more quickly than in any other equally developed nation. This rapid turnover was most marked in the cities. But the cities are normally responsible for preserving a modern society's culture (in institutions such as universities, museums, and art galleries) and transmitting it outward (by the mass media). In Canada's cities, the population has turned over most. There the ratio of tradition-carriers to new arrivals is lowest and the institution-alization of rival, ethnic cultures is most developed.

Conclusion

John Porter has compared English Canada to a huge railroad station. 'As well as a society receiving immigrants, it has been one producing emigrants, either naturally or by harbouring the 'birds of passage' who have stopped over in Canada while making the move from Europe to the United States.' 'What,' he asks, 'is likely to be the effect on social institutions . . . of such a kinetic popu-lation?'[53] He might have added: and what are its likely effects on Canadian political culture and the national identity?

We must answer this question tentatively, as follows: When a nation whose

TABLE 3.4	TOTAL AND FOREIGN-BORN POPULATIONS IN SELECTED CITIES, 1921, 1971, AND 1981								
	1921			1971			1981		
POPULATION	TOTAL	FOREIGN-BORN	FOREIGN-BORN % OF TOTAL	TOTAL	FOREIGN-BORN	FOREIGN-BORN % OF TOTAL	TOTAL	FOREIGN-BORN	FOREIGN-BORN % OF TOTAL
St. John's, Nfld.	—	—	—	88,102	3,160	3.6	161,901	5,095	3.1
Saint John, N.B.	47,166	4,836	10.3	89,039	4,030	4.5	121,265	5,655	4.6
Halifax	58,372	8,996	15.4	122,035	9,850	8.1	295,990	20,425	6.9
Quebec City	95,193	2,879	3.0	186,088	3,730	2.0	603,265	13,660	2.2
Montreal	618,506	115,582	18.7	1,214,352	228,400	18.8	2,921,360	459,490	15.7
Ottawa	107,843	18,095	16.8	302,341	49,195	16.3	619,050[a]	110,125	17.8
Toronto	521,893	197,125	37.8	712,786	310,595	43.6	2,192,720[b]	782,935	35.7
Hamilton	114,151	44,346	38.8	309,173	93,375	30.2	557,025	134,480	24.0
Winnipeg	179,087	85,233	47.6	246,246	61,295	24.9	625,305	111,995	17.9
Calgary	63,305	30,208	47.7	403,319	82,595	20.5	671,325	138,290	20.5
Edmonton	58,821	26,129	44.4	438,152	82,800	19.1	785,465	143,010	18.2
Vancouver	117,217	59,957	51.2	426,256	146,715	34.4	1,380,730	391,845	28.4
TOTAL	1,981,554	593,386	29.9	4,537,889	1,076,740	23.7	10,935,201	2,317,005	21.2

[a]Ottawa considered as Ottawa Ontario only, not the entire National Capital Region.
[b]Toronto considered only within its metropolitan boundaries; not the Greater Toronto area.
Source: Censuses of Canada, 1921, 1971, and 1981. Note: data are drawn from central cities, not from metropolitan areas. However 1981 data are for Metropolitan Toronto.

identity is already weak and confused—its very existence regarded as ironic[54]—turns its population over rapidly, even greater confusion will result. But the potential for such confusion was present at the beginning. Loyalism never could provide English-speaking Canada with a Hartzian 'fragment identity'.[55] No fragment ideology existed to be 'nationalized', so no particular ideological outlook could be elevated to a Canadian way of life, because Loyalism was never ideologically 'pure' to begin with. Its main component, liberalism, had already been claimed by the United States, and was forcibly denied to the Loyalists. This complication aside, an ideological identity derived from the Loyalist heritage would have conflicted with the identity of the French fragment.

Inheriting the Loyalist tradition was the imperialist movement that grew up in the late nineteenth century. Although it served as a useful antidote to continentalist thinking,[56] imperialism ultimately hindered true nationalism. It kept alive symbols from the colonial past and delayed the adoption of symbols that might have stirred the loyalty of both major founding groups.[57] Canada's identity crisis, one full century after Confederation, was preordained.

The only element of Loyalism that can be said to have any value today—namely, multicultural tolerance—has been tested and found wanting. On the one hand, the mosaic proves to be vertical. On the other hand, the faces in the mosaic as originally conceived were white only. Accordingly non-whites have frequently encountered alarming racism in Canada. And yet a rehabilitated mosaic concept, drawn from the Loyalist tradition, might help Canadians to modify their identity to take account of the complex problems of multiculturalism. Loyalism offers very little help, however, in resolving the problems of Anglo-French relations, or the equally profound conflicts caused by regionalism. These topics are taken up in the next chapters.

Notes

[1] Donald Smiley, *The Canadian Political Nationality* (Toronto: Methuen, 1967): ix.

[2] Hugh MacLennan, 'Canadian National Identity', in *Canadian Identity: A Symposium held at Mount Allison University, 25 September 1969* (published by the university): 23.

[3] Margaret Atwood, *Survival* (Toronto: Anansi, 1972): 33.

[4] Linda Hutcheon, '*As Canadian As . . . Possible . . . Under the Circumstances*' (Toronto, York University and ECW Press, 1990): 9.

[5] Stuart Keate, as cited in *ibid*.: 23.

[6] *Ibid*.: 44.

[7] '[I]t is impossible to attempt to deal with problems unless our attempts are built on the strongest foundation of self-knowledge.' *The Symons Report*. An abridged version of volumes 1 and 2 of *To Know Ourselves*, the Report of the Commission on Canadian Studies. Published by The Book and Periodical Development Council, 1978: 19. Note also Keith Spicer's comment in his 'Foreword' to the report by the Citizens' Forum on Canada's Future: 'This country is dying of ignorance, and of our stubborn refusal to learn.'

[8] *Symons Report*: 20, 15.

[9] A proposal to abolish the monarchy met stiff, bitter opposition at the annual meeting of the Canadian Bar Association in Halifax (August 1978). The 1991 decision by Susan Eng, the newly appointed Chair of the Police Commission in Ontario, to change the oath sworn by Ontario's Provincial Police Officers from allegiance to the Queen to allegiance to Canada evoked such strong reaction that the Provincial Government was forced to review the matter.

[10] This is the classic interpretation propounded by Louis Hartz in many writings. Some critics have discounted the influence of John Locke and others have disputed the assumed ideological consensus Hartz implies. The criticisms are summarized by Kenneth McNaught in his article in J.H.M. Laslett and S.M. Lipset, eds, *Failure of a Dream? Essays in the History of American Socialism* (Garden City, NJ: Doubleday-Anchor Books, 1974). Sacvan Berkovitch provides a persuasive account of the American ideology in *The American Journal* (Madison: University of Wisconsin Press, 1978). For another excellent analysis see Samuel P. Huntington, *American Politics: The Promise of Disharmony* (Cambridge: Belknap Press, 1981).

[11] Cited in D. Bell, 'Nation and Non-Nation', ch. 4. For a thorough and sensitive assessment of Tory ideology see Janice Potter, *The Liberty We Seek: Loyalist Ideology in Colonial New York and Massachusetts* (Cambridge: Harvard University Press, 1983).

[12] Even Jonathan Boucher, widely touted as an 'arch-Tory' entirely unsympathetic to liberal ideas, later dedicated his *View of the Causes and Consequences of the American Revolution* to George Washington. He congratulated the 'late dignified President' for having framed the US constitution 'after a British model'. See Bell: 119-20.

[13] G.T. Borrett, 'The Levelling Principle in Canadian Life' in *Letters from Canada and the United States* (1865). Reprinted in G.M. Craig, ed., *Early Travellers in the Canadas* (Toronto: Macmillan, 1955): 279. This myth of Britishness grows best in isolation. The Loyalist builds an American Society in Canada and calls it by British names. So long as the Loyalist never goes to Britain, never sees the 'pure form' of which his image is such an imperfect copy, his myth can stay alive.

The Loyalists who left America for England were not permitted this luxury. In England the Loyalists saw themselves as they truly were, real Americans. The path followed by the Canadian Loyalists, through a world of imaginary Britishness and 'Loyalism for its own sake' was not available to them. No action could lessen their pain, and the Loyalists in England suffered terrible torment. They pined their life away longing for their homeland. They packed their bags, anticipating the return voyage they would never make. See Mary Beth Norton, *The British Americans* (Boston: Little, Brown, 1972).

[14] For an excellent overview of changing themes in Loyalist mythology, see Dennis Duffy, 'Upper Canadian Loyalism: What the Textbooks Tell', *Journal of Canadian Studies* 12,2 (Spring, 1977). Duffy writes that 'the structure of the Loyalist myth stresses a pattern of defeat, exile, hardship and struggle followed by future triumph in a righteous cause' (p. 17). Note as well Carl Berger's statement: 'It is startling to realize how many English Canadian historians in the late nineteenth century traced their roots back to the old loyalist families' (*The Sense of Power* [Toronto: University of Toronto Press, 1970]: 90).

[15] *The Centennial of the Settlement of Upper Canada by the United Empire Loyalists, 1784-1884* (Toronto: Rose, 1885): 13.

[16] Quoted in Carl Berger, 'The Vision of Grandeur' (unpublished PhD dissertation, University of Toronto, 1966): 167.

[17] For a sober critique of this account see Garth Stevenson, 'Foreign Policy', in Conrad Winn and John McNemeny, *Political Parties in Canada* (Toronto: McGraw-Hill Ryerson, 1976).

[18] *Centennial of the Settlement*: 14, 16.

[19] Some writers treat imperialist sentiment as a form of Canadian nationalism, following Stephen Leacock's declaration that 'I am an imperialist because I refuse to be a colonialist'. See for example Carl Berger, *The Sense of Power*. Berger's main thesis is that 'Canadian imperialism rested upon an intense awareness of Canadian nationality combined with an equally decided desire to unify and transform the British Empire so that this nationality could attain a position of equality within it' (p. 49).

[20] Quoted by Genevieve Jain, 'Nationalism and Educational Politics in Ontario and Quebec, 1867-1914', in Alf Chaiton and Neil McDonald (eds), *Canadian Schools and Canadian Identity* (Toronto: Gage, 1977): 42. Like Leacock, Ross saw 'no antagonism between Canadianism and Imperialism. The one is but the expansion of the other' (quoted in Robert M. Stampp, 'Empire Day in the Schools of Ontario: The Training of Young Imperialists', *ibid.*: 103).

[21] See Stampp, for a description of the celebration of 'Empire Day' in Ontario Schools. The cover of Berger's *The Sense of Power* bears an 1898 Canadian stamp that speaks volumes about the illusion of grandeur possessed by Canadian imperialists. The stamp pictures the Mercator projection of the map of the world with all the Empire shown in pink. Canada's bulk looms large at the centre of the map—Britain is virtually undetectable. The caption reads, modestly, 'We hold a vaster Empire than has been.'

[22] Duffy: 25.

[23] Quoted in Nelson: 169. The phrase became the title of Ann Condon's book on the Loyalists: *The Envy of the American States: The Loyalist Dream for New Brunswick* (Fredericton: New Ireland Press, 1984).

[24] Quoted in Mildred Schwartz, *Public Opinion and Canadian Identity* (Berkeley: The University of California Press, 1967): 5.

[25] The Loyalist experience in the Maritimes differed from that in Upper Canada in interesting ways. Although committed Loyalists all shared a certain antipathy toward the United States, anti-American feeling was much weaker in the Maritime colonies. There it was moderated by ties, formed before the Loyalist migration, that joined the neutral Yankees to their cousins in New England. The Maritime Loyalists also felt less threatened by the United States. They even continued to trade with Americans during part of the War of 1812. According to Murray Barkley, Maritime Loyalists assigned to nature, rather than to the Americans, the role of 'chief obstacle to the accomplishment of the Loyalist experiment'. Upper Canadian Loyalism was 'militaristic and anti-American', but Maritime Loyalism was not. Hostility to the Americans showed strength in the Maritimes only twice during the nineteenth century: in the 1840s and the 1890s. See Murray Barkley, 'The Loyalist Tradition in New Brunswick: the Growth and Evolution of an Historical Myth, 1825-1914', in *Acadiensis* (Spring, 1975): 3-45.

[26] Lord Durham wrote of the 'constant intercourse' between the 'identical population' of Canadians and Americans, separated in some places by an 'imaginary line', in others by 'rivers, which are crossed in ten minutes', or by lakes required a 'six hours' passage'. Gerald M. Craig (ed.), *Lord Durham's Report* (Toronto: McClelland & Stewart, 1963): 132-3.

[27] See Gerald Craig; Hazel Mathews, *The Mark of Honour* (Toronto: University of Toronto Press, 1965); S.D. Clark, *Church and Sect in Canada* (Toronto: University of Toronto Press, 1948): especially 85, 95; and D. Bell, ch. 7.

[28] Fred Landon, *Western Ontario and the American Frontier* (Toronto: McClelland & Stewart, 1967): 129.

[29] A.G. Bradley, *The Making of Canada* (London: Constable, 1968): 168.

[30] S.F. Wise, 'Colonial Attitudes from the Era of the War of 1812 to the Rebellions of 1837', in S.F. Wise and Robert Craig Brown, *Canada Views the United States* (Toronto: Macmillan, 1967): 21-2.

[31] Quoted in Berger, *Sense of Power*: 56. Note that Berger argues against the use of the term 'anti-Americanism' in describing the imperialists' sentiments because it is 'too loaded with unsavoury connotations and too ill-defined to faithfully encompass outlooks which ranged from Denison's conspiratorial fantasies to G.M. Grant's hopes for Anglo-American understanding' (p. 175).

[32] Wise (p. 96) has suggested that over-concern with the United States has 'had a paralytic effect upon the Canadian mind'. At the same time, the obsession with comparing means that Canadians have measured their worth by praise from the outside, a classic symptom of sensed inferiority.

[33] Under Canadian law, the crown has until recently been able to appeal a jury verdict of not guilty,

as it did in the case of Dr Henry Morgentaler's abortion trial. Such appeals were eliminated in Britain and the United States more than a century ago. For a more general discussion of Canadian civil liberties, see Lorne Tepperman, *Crime Control: The Urge Toward Authority* (Toronto: McGraw-Hill Ryerson, 1977); Walter S. Tarnopolsky, *The Canadian Bill of Rights* (Toronto: McClelland & Stewart, 1975); Edgar Friedenberg, *Deference to Authority: The Case of Canada* (White Plains, NY: Sharpe, 1980). On post-Charter Canadian attitudes, see the many interesting articles and papers that have been based on the ambitious survey conducted by Paul Sniderman, Peter Russell, Joseph Fletcher *et al.*

[34] For a sensible critique of the October crisis policies of the federal government, see Denis Smith, *Bleeding Hearts . . . Bleeding Country: Canada and the Quebec Crisis* (Edmonton: Hurtig, 1971). Note that an RCMP officer testified in an investigation concerning questionable RCMP tactics that after 1970 police officers felt they had an implicit 'licence' to use extreme measures against suspected political subversives.

[35] Of course, one thing not lost through Canada's unheroic beginning was human lives. Indeed a strongly articulated national identity is far from an unmitigated blessing. It can lead to excessive nationalism, a disease which has produced considerable suffering in the world. For this and other reasons, some highly intelligent Canadians have expressed anti-nationalist sentiments, arguing either that nationalism is dangerous (witness the response to Walter Gordon's nationalistic economic measures in the 1960s, or Diefenbaker's ambiguous demise, much 'lamented' by George Grant); or, more positively, that nationalism is old-fashioned, in Trudeau's words a 'rustic, clumsy tool'. In this view Canada's non-nationalism and non-identity put it about a century ahead of other states.

While attracted by these arguments, I find them ultimately unconvincing. Canada's legendary identity crisis has with few exceptions failed to promote a wider identification with global issues that lie beyond the nation state. Instead it has increased or prolonged subnational identities while facilitating the spread of culture from the imperial centre. In short, it has exacerbated the colonial mentality.

In my view, Canada will probably not be able to 'skip' the nationalist stage in its political evolution. The increased concern in the late 1960s and the 1970s with nationalism and national identity represented a welcome transition, and by and large avoided xenophobic excesses. Cf. Northrop Frye: 'The nationalism that has evolved in Canada is on the whole a positive development, in which self awareness has been far more important than aggressiveness. Perhaps identity only is identity when it becomes, not militant, but a way of defining oneself against something else' ('Conclusion' to Carl F. Klinck, ed., *Literary History of Canada: Canadian Literature in English* 2nd ed. Vol. III, [Toronto: University of Toronto Press, 1977]: 321). The challenge for the 1990s will be to avoid the disintegration of Canada because of the rise of francophone nationalism or other equivalent forces.

[36] William Nelson, *The American Tory* (Boston: Beacon, 1961): 89.

[37] See G. Elmore Reaman, *The Trail of the Black Walnut* (Toronto: McClelland & Stewart, 1957). This aspect of the Loyalist tradition received a revival in recent years. Writing to the *Globe and Mail*, James P. Lovelaine, president of the Toronto Branch of the United Empire Loyalist Association, took great pains to point out that 'large numbers' of Loyalists were 'neither English speaking nor Anglo-Saxon', but instead included 'a caravan of nationalities' (reprinted in *The Loyalist Gazette* [April 1964]: 2).

[38] The UEL Association of Canada recognizes the Indian Loyalist in its coat-of-arms, which shows a red arm joined with a white, a tomahawk as well as a sword. See Duffy: 18.

[39] Allan Smith, 'Metaphor and Nationality in North America', in *Canadian Historical Review* 51,3 (September 1970): 245-75.

[40] This point is more fully discussed below in Chapter 7. Note that applicants for US citizenship are asked whether they have ever experienced 'socialist thoughts or leanings'.

[41] William Gairdner, *The Trouble with Canada: a Citizen Speaks Out* (Toronto: Stoddard, 1990). The book sold over 20,000 copies by summer 1991. See the two-part feature on multiculturalism in the *Toronto Star* 23 and 24 June 1991.

[42] Alan Cairns, 'Political Science, Ethnicity, and the Canadian Constitution', in David Shugarman

and Reg Whitaker (eds) *Federalism and Political Community, Essays in Honour of Donald Smiley* (Peterborough: Broadview Press, 1989).

[43] At the time of Confederation, G.E. Cartier supported the notion of multiculturalism and protection of minority group rights because it provided an umbrella to shelter francophones without their demanding special consideration. As this policy was abandoned under the strain of non-anglophone immigration in the late nineteenth century, francophones found that they had 'to distinguish themselves from, not identify themselves with, the other minorities' in order to avoid the assimilationist fate ultimately suffered by Ukrainians, Germans, Scandinavians and others. Smith: 267-8.

At that point, French Canadians asserted the principle of duality in place of the obsolete pluralistic conceptions of multiculturalism. For more recent, quantitative evidence that francophones are less tolerant than anglophones of ethnic, racial, and religious minorities, see James E. Curtis and Ronald D. Lambert, 'Educational Status and Reactions to Social and Political Heterogeneity', *Canadian Review of Sociology and Anthropology* 13,2 (1976): 189-203.

[44] Quoted by Carl Berger, 'The True North Strong and Free', in Peter Russell, ed., *Nationalism in Canada* (Toronto: McGraw-Hill, 1966): 6. See also Berger's account of Canadian imperialists' conception of 'Canadian Character' in *The Sense of Power* (ch. 5). Even more militant views about the need to protect Canada's racial purity are expressed today by right-wing extremists like Western Guard.

[45] All quotations are from a compilation of public opinion prepared by Paul Marshall when he was a graduate student in political science, York University, and are included as an Appendix to an unpublished seminar paper he wrote in 1976. Note that J.S. Woodsworth's book *Strangers Within Our Gates*, published in 1909, in the course of assessing the merits and future prospects of immigrant groups in Canada, similarly concluded that Orientals were unassimilable. See the discussion in John Porter, *The Vertical Mosaic* (Toronto: University of Toronto Press, 1965), ch. 3.

[46] John Murray Gibbon, *Canadian Mosaic* (Toronto: McClelland & Stewart, 1938): vii, viii.

[47] Frances Henry, 'The Dynamics of Racism in Toronto', Research Report, York University, February 1978: 45.

[48] Porter: 63-4.

[49] 'Speculatively, it might be said that the idea of an ethnic mosaic, as opposed to the idea of a melting pot, impedes the process of social mobility' (*ibid.*: 70).

[50.] [T]he essence of authentic nationalism in Canada lies, ideally, in the experience of celebrating and deriving joy from the encounter with the diversification of Canadian existence. Ideally, what we share in common is the experience of converting our differences into a mosaic of creative fidelity to each other' (Lionel Rubinoff, 'Nationalism and Celebration: Reflections on the Sources of Canadian Identity', *Queen's Quarterly* 82,1 [Spring, 1975]: 1-13).

[51] To calculate the proportion of persons surviving one decade, demographers take the population at the start of the decade and subtract the numbers who die or emigrate during the decade. They then divide this number by the population at the start of the next decade. The resulting percentage is subtracted from 100 per cent to show the proportion of 'newcomers'.

[52] Lewis Auerbach and Andrea Gerber, *Implications of the Changing Age Structure of the Canadian Population*: Study on Population and Technology. Perceptions 2 (Ottawa: Science Council of Canada, 1976). See also Warren Kalbach and Wayne McVey, *The Demographic Basis of Canadian Society*, rev. ed. (Toronto: McGraw-Hill Ryerson, 1979), especially Table 6.3 on median age.

[53] Porter: 33.

[54] Cf. William Kilbourn: 'The Canadian Identity—the phrase is both a chimera and an oxymoron—is full of odd conjunctions, split visions, and unresolved tensions.' 'The Peaceable Kingdom Still', *Daedalus* 117,4 (Fall, 1988): 1.

[55] Many would agree with W.L. Morton that the absence of an ideologically based national identity has its advantages: 'One of the blessings of Canadian life is that there is no Canadian way of life,

much less two', but a culture that admits 'of a thousand diversities'; W.L. Morton, *The Canadian Identity* (Toronto: University of Toronto Press, 1972): 111. Echoing this theme, Donald Smiley decried the excess of 'racial nationalism—of French-Canadian delusions of a providential mission, of notions of British imperial destiny, of latter-day Anglo-Saxon assimilationism'. Instead he calls for 'a Canadian political nationality divorced from cultural considerations' (*The Canadian Political Nationality*: 130-1).

[56] 'Those of Denison's generation had fought to preserve the British connection in a period of pessimism and to an incredible extent their thought was dominated by fear of annexation to the United States and by the chief advocate of continentalism in Canada, Goldwin Smith. . . . The new generation of imperialists became preoccupied with the consequence of prosperity and industrialization, with the emergence in English and French Canada of a nationalism which hoped for the breakup of the imperial system, and with the problems of imperial defence' (Carl Berger, *Sense of Power*: 42-3).

[57] Writing in 1965, Donald Smiley observed that 'Recent English-Canadian nationalism has been notoriously devoid of distinctive myths and symbols capable of evoking strong emotional responses. Since the British traditions have lost their power to inspire, almost all English Canadians have at some time felt embarrassed by these deficiencies in the ritualistic manifestations of nationhood' ('Federalism, Nationalism, and the Scope of Public Activity in Canada', in Peter Russell, ed.: 100).

Attempts since 1965 to remedy these 'deficiencies' are assessed by Philip Resnick, *The Land of Cain: Class and Nationalism in English Canada, 1945-1975* (Vancouver: Star Books, 1977, ch. 5); and from a different perspective by Abraham Rotstein, 'Is There an English Canadian Nationalism?' *Journal of Canadian Studies* 13,2 (Summer, 1976). Rotstein answers his own question with a tentative 'yes', although he points with caution to the danger that a unidimensional 'territorial nationalism' stressing the integrity of Canada 'from sea unto sea' at any cost, will displace a more balanced, creative 'democratic nationalism' embodying concepts of social justice and political equality.

See also the contributions of John Conway and others to the Fall 1988 issue of *Daedalus*, and the discussion that appears in Lipset, *Continental Divide*.

4 | La Survivance in Quebec and Anglo-French Relations

Ideological diversity and a high rate of population turnover have weakened and confused the English-Canadian identity. In francophone Quebec, the opposite has occurred. The conquest served to purify an already distinctive society by pushing out merchants and other bourgeois elements and breaking the link to France. Isolation largely put a stop to the importation of new ideologies and kept population turnover due to immigration at a very low level. Given its different fragment origins, formative events, and destination language, Quebec's distinctive cultural evolution is not surprising.

Although many francophones left Quebec (particularly in the latter half of the nineteenth century) very few francophone immigrants arrived after the advent of British rule.[1] From the time of the conquest to the Second World War, with the exception of the period leading up to the Rebellion of 1837-38,[2] traditional conservatism prevailed. These and other differences in development ensured that Québécois and English Canadians would view Canada and each other differently.

A study carried out in the 1960s on behalf of the Royal Commission on Bilingualism and Biculturalism compared 'young people's images of Canadian Society' and found important differences between anglophones and francophones. The former thought of Canada the way Americans perceive their country, emphasizing the country's resources, industries, economic prospects, and opportunities for advancement. By contrast, francophones spoke of Canada in political terms; they mentioned federalism and provincial autonomy. English-Canadian youth saw Canada as full of opportunity for success through hard work. French Canadians instead believed that succeeding in Canada depends on good social connections and the ability to speak English as well as French. Most anglophones, not surprisingly, felt more like Americans than like francophones in their culture and social relationships.[3] (The 1968 Election Survey found anglophones expressing similar attitudes of social and cultural distance from francophones.)

Another study compared English-Canadian and French-Canadian textbooks. It found, to no one's surprise, two distinct versions of Canadian history: one for French, another for the anglophones. Anglophone authors approached their subject in varied ways and emphasized different events. But they shared a 'common view of the past, . . . one which differed markedly' from that of francophone authors. Anglophone histories tended to see 'the establishment and survival of Canada as a political entity in North America', against attacks from the United States, as central to our national history. By contrast, the francophones emphasized *la survivance*: survival not of Canada *vis-à-vis* its powerful neighbour but of *les Français vis-à-vis les Anglais*.

| Table 4.1 | CANADIAN CHILDREN'S IDENTIFICATION WITH HISTORICAL SYMBOLS AND ERAS (IN PERCENTAGES) |

	FRANCOPHONE	ANGLOPHONE
A. *Nationality of the heroes*		
Canadians	60.6	63.3
Foreigners	11.9	11.0
Columbus	14.9	11.6
Other	8.9	9.6
Not sure	3.7	4.5
Total percentage	100.0	100.0
Total N	473	335
B. *Cultural membership of the Canadian heroes*		
French-Canadian heroes	98.1	49.5
English-Canadian heroes	1.9	50.5
Total percentage	100.0	100.0
Total N	267	190
C. *Historical eras*		
Before 1760	80.5	49.5
After 1760	19.5	50.5
Total percentage	100.0	100.0
Total N	267	190

Source: Jean Pierre Richert, 'The Impact of Ethnicity on the Perception of Heroes and Historical Symbols.'

Typically, half of the space in French texts studied took up the period before the 1763 'catastrophe' (their term for the conquest). English texts paid this early period much less attention and treated the events of 1763 as a triumph, not a catastrophe. Francophone historians honoured leaders that anglophones ignore, and presented English-Canadian heroes in a way that, if not entirely negative, suggested contradictory feelings. Likewise, 'Facts which seem significant to Francophone authors are often omitted by Anglophone authors. When all agree to include the same event, they often give divergent interpretations of the historical implication of the incident or of the contribution and motives of the men involved.'[4]

Table 4.2   TEN MOST FREQUENTLY CITED HISTORICAL FIGURES

| | FRENCH CANADIANS | | ENGLISH CANADIANS | |
	PERCENTAGE	N	PERCENTAGE	N
Bourassa (R)	2.3	11	—	—
Cabot	—	—	5.7	19
Cartier*	31.9	151	6.0	20
Champlain*	7.6	36	10.4	35
Columbus*	14.8	70	11.6	39
De Gaulle	1.3	6	—	—
Hudson	—	—	3.3	11
Iberville	1.5	7	—	—
Laporte	3.2	15	—	—
Maisonneuve	1.7	8	—	—
Macdonald	—	—	6.0	20
Mackenzie (W.L.)	—	—	3.3	11
Napoleon	4.2	20	—	—
Radisson	—	—	4.8	16
Trudeau*	2.1	10	3.9	13
Wolfe	—	—	5.1	17
Total	70.6	334	60.1	201

*Reconciliation symbols.

Source: Jean Pierre Richert, 'The Impact of Ethnicity on the Perception of Heroes and Historical Symbols.'

Jean Pierre Richert carried out a subsequent study of English-Canadian and French-Canadian school children to determine the effect of these different historical portraits. He gathered data from 'nearly 1,000 questionnaires, 330 essays, and over fifty in-depth, personal interviews of elementary school children' in three Quebec locations. His findings, summarized in Tables 4.1 and 4.2 above, showed

> first of all that children overwhelmingly identified with the historical symbols of their own culture, and that their ethnocentric perception of historical figures

increased with age. Second, the data showed that Francophone and Anglophone children identified with different eras of Canadian history. The former identified primarily with the pre-1760 era, while the latter identified most with the post-1760 era. . . . There are few *reconciliation* symbols in Canadian history which was, therefore, viewed as a divisive rather than a binding force.[5]

Clearly, therefore, differences in outlook between anglophones and francophones are not confined to textbooks. Thinking their own history is the more important, many anglophones look upon themselves as the only true Canadians. French Canadians, in their view, are a throwback to earlier times and should have been assimilated long ago. By contrast, many francophones note with pride that French has been spoken in Quebec since 1608. For this and other reasons, they regard their own people as the true, natural *Canadiens*. In their eyes, *les Anglais* are 'recent arrivals linked still to another land'.[6]

The shock of the conquest further unified the French-Canadian fragment. A strong sense of national identity began to develop then, and it was based on traditional French Catholic values. Francophone Quebec differed from the rest of Canada not only linguistically but also ideologically. There, as in other true fragment cultures, ideologists took hold of the popular mind and imbued it with a sense of mission and destiny. In the words of one nineteenth-century nationalist, 'Every nation must fulfil its own destiny, as set by Providence. It must understand its mission fully and strive constantly towards the goal Divine Providence has assigned it. . . . The mission with which Providence entrusted French Canadians is basically religious in nature: it is, namely, to convert the unfortunate infidel local population to Catholicism, and to expand the Kingdom of God by developing a predominantly Catholic nationality.'[7]

The Fight for Ideological Conformity

Although it took decades to do so, the Catholic Church eventually expanded to fill the vacuum created in French Canadian society after the conquest. The image of Quebec as a 'priest-ridden society' had little validity even by the middle of the nineteenth century. The remarkable growth in the clergy occurred in the latter part of the nineteenth century and reached its apogee in approximately 1951, by which time Quebec had more clerics per capita than any other society in the Western world. (See Table 4.3.) By controlling the agencies of cultural production and political socialization (including even labour unions), the Catholic hierarchy set about zealously to promote and safeguard this national consciousness. It turned aside any attempts to import the changes that occurred in French culture after Quebec's founding—notably, the Enlightenment, the Revolution, and the all-too-worldly Empire. The church threatened to excommunicate as heretics any whose belief in traditional Catholicism was shaken by exposure to alien ideas. It forbade the reading of books that advanced ideas contrary to the accepted doctrine. It carefully monitored school curricula (which remained under its control in Quebec until 1963) to keep alien points of view from being taught. In the twentieth century, church censors banned films that might undermine Catholic teachings, and stood fast against competing viewpoints, like Marxism. Catholic labour unions were even set up to organize workers within the traditional system. Uppermost in the minds of Catholic leaders was the need to remain 'free from fatal contact with foreign influence, from the mortal pressures of a selfish, mercantile civilization', i.e., anglophone North American civilization.[8] This was the key to *la survivance*.

Table 4.3   NUMBER OF CATHOLICS PER CLERIC IN QUEBEC, 1810-1961

| | | CATHOLICS PER MEMBER OF RELIGIOUS ORDER | | |
	CATHOLICS PER PRIEST	PER MALE	PER FEMALE	PER TOTAL
1810	1,375	9,418	1,009	912
1851	1,080	2,068	1,100	722
1911	652	457	120	96
1931	567	355	90	71
1951	504	309	88	68
1961	509	367	98	78

Sources:From Fernand Ouellet, 'The Quiet Revolution: A Turning Point' in Thomas S. Axworthy and Pierre Elliott Trudeau, eds, *Towards A Just Society* (Markham: Viking 1990): L.E. Hamelin 'Evolution numérique séculaire du clergé catholique dans le Québec,' *Recherches sociographiques*, 2 (1961): 189-241; B. Denaut and B. Lévesque, *Eléments pour une sociologie des communautès religieuses au Québec* (Montreal/Sherbrooke, 1975).

Ideological conformity was never complete, however. The Patriotes of the 1837 uprising were inspired by 'alien' liberal ideas. A group of more articulate radicals formed in the mid-nineteenth century to promote left-wing liberalism. Called the *Institut Canadien*, these 'rouges' maintained an anti-clerical, anti-traditional outpost surrounded by hostile Catholic conformity. They were always under attack, and never widely accepted in Quebec. Only after he turned his back on important elements of the rougist doctrine did the Liberal leader Wilfrid Laurier receive grudging acceptance from the Catholic hierarchy. It was only then that his party succeeded electorally in Quebec and, ultimately, formed the government of Canada.

   In the twentieth century, ideological conformity finally dissolved. The Quiet Revolution offered Québécois a rapid succession of alternatives to the defensive, conservative nationalism of Catholic *survivance*. The ideological spectrum of Quebec politics widened dramatically to include liberalism, socialism, and radicalism of various shades.[9] At no point did Quebec's thinking successfully capture the imagination of English Canada, binding all of Canada to a single, united

identity. At the turn of the present century, however, a few anglophone imperialists attempted to find such a common ideology. They believed that organic conservatism might serve to link the two cultures: 'There were some
imperialists . . . who were attracted to Quebec exactly because of its "back-
wardness". They discovered in the province conservative principles, traditional
values, and a hostility to capitalism which they themselves admired and
shared.'[10] A short-lived and unsuccessful attempt was made in 1896 to set up
a 'Loyal Aryan and Seigneurial Order'. The project failed miserably through a
lack of interest in English Canada and outright hostility in Quebec. Even if
francophones were conservatives, they put nationalism first and conservatism
a distant second.

Moreover, they found the imperialist trappings of anglophone conservatism
very distasteful. 'In their attempt to harmonize the French Canadian with their
conception of the national character the imperialists showed some sincerity,
ingenuity, and not a little blindness. By thinking in such terms they often con-
cealed from themselves the degree to which imperialism was repugnant to
French Canadians.'[11] Similarly, A. Perrault wrote in 1924, 'We must not dream
of tighter imperial solidarity. This would hasten the breaking apart of everything
else . . . .'[12]

To most francophones, the anglophone imperialists did not seem true conservatives to begin with. French-Canadian nationalists like J.M.R. Villeneuve
thought English Canada was hopelessly Americanized in its tastes and customs,
as he deduced from the 'licentiousness in their moral life: religious indifference,
divorce, birth control, women's rights . . . (etc.)'. Such similarities to American
behaviour proved beyond doubt that the English-Canadian mind was 'tarred
with the same brush, and a civilization as limited in its horizons' as that of the
godless Americans. For this reason, among others, Villeneuve insisted: 'There
is not the slightest meeting-point between our [Canadian anglophones' and
francophones'] languages, social traditions, religious aims, habits of mind, spir-
itual formation, public institutions, or civil laws. The only way in which these
could be closely united would be through the complete abdication of our Catholic and French personality.'[13]

Francophone nationalists cherished the mission God had given to French
Canada. Of this Villeneuve declared: 'Our main ambition is that our Catholic
faith be maintained and strengthened in every soul born of our race.' Although
many francophones had already left Quebec for other parts of North America,
he remained confident that: 'a strong French State, practically homogeneous
and completely free in its activities, would be the surest guarantee of the survival
and integrity of our people of the Diaspora, since they would, in a sense, be
protected by the zeal of a powerful French and Catholic civilization, which
would command the respect of, and finally triumph over, the always ephemeral
forces of those civilizations rising to surround us, which are ambitious, but
divergent and materialistic, in their aims.'[14]

Villeneuve's remarks illustrate two permanent features of the French-Canadian identity: the will to survive (*la survivance*), and the fear that Confederation may not be the best means of ensuring this survival.

Anglophones and francophones have lived together in what is now Canada for over 200 years. Observers have characterized the Anglo-French relationship in every conceivable metaphor of conflict and co-operation. Images have varied from Lord Durham's famous phrase, 'two nations warring in the bosom of a single state' to the more benign 'true partnership' typified in the words of Janet Morchain: 'Canada, by her existence, demonstrates that two peoples . . . can live in peace under a single Federal government. In fact we have aspired to more than simple coexistence; we have attempted positive tasks together. And we have learned . . . that we can act only when there is a true partnership on the basis of voluntary agreement.' If, however, equal partnership was idealized, even Morchain admits that 'a measure of co-operation was the reality.'[15] In a classic volume that attempted for Canada what Alexis de Tocqueville's *Democracy in America* accomplished for the United States, André Siegfried termed Anglo-French relations in Canada 'a *modus vivendi* without cordiality'. Writing in 1906, Siegfried described Canadian politics as 'a tilting-ground for empassioned rivalries'. In his view, 'an immemorial struggle persists between French and English, Catholics and Protestants . . . .'[16]

A particularly well-known metaphor of the Canadian 'experiment in race relations' is Hugh MacLennan's 'two solitudes'. This image conjures up the almost total indifference in one group toward the other. A different metaphor used by Quebec premier Pierre Chaveau in 1876 is more graphic still: 'English and French, we climb by a double flight of stairs toward the destinies reserved for us on this continent, without knowing each other, without meeting each other, and without ever seeing each other except on the landing of politics. In social and literary terms, we are far more foreign to each other than the English and French of Europe.'[17]

Chaveau's assessment still applies to a remarkable extent. In 1977, then CBC president Al Johnson candidly admitted that 'the CBC has failed generally to adequately reflect English Canada to French Canada and vice versa.'[18] The electronic media have not yet bridged the cultural isolation of these two groups. The gap, the distance, the solitude remain. But despite literary and artistic ignorance of one another, French and English Canadians have always had to meet, as Chaveau reminds us, on 'the landing of politics'.

The Political Culture of Anglo-French Relations

The political culture of Anglo-French relations comprises the wide variety of basic values, beliefs, and attitudes that French and English Canadians hold about each other and their relationship. Contradictory images and diverse out-looks are rooted in the distant past; they can be traced back to the beginning of sustained contact between the two groups. The Treaty of Paris (1763) was assimilationist in its tone. Though promising to prevent religious persecution, it limited francophone rights, and kept Catholics from taking part in politics. The Quebec Act of 1774 embodied a different view, which favoured accommodation over assimilation. Faced with growing unrest in the Thirteen Colonies, the Act largely restored the place of the Church and guaranteed linguistic and religious integrity—that is, survival—in return for loyalty. For the rest of Canadian history, public policy and private sentiment have ranged endlessly between the two poles of tolerance and hostility. Francophones' attitudes have fluctuated over a similarly broad spectrum, from hating their conquerors to appreciating the advantages of living under British institutions.

The ingredients of mutual hostility were natural, obvious, and immediate: differences in religion, language, culture, and power. The harmonizing elements were artificial, obscure, and distant: mainly, an awareness that toleration and restraint were needed to keep the nation together. At critical points in Canadian history, Anglo-French relations have degenerated into bitter accusation, even violence. These incidents often resulted from ignorance and were always viewed through the distorting lens of stereotype and prejudice.

To many French, the English (their conquerors) have seemed the perpetrators of historic injustices. They had, after all, deported the Acadians and beaten down the 1837 Patriotes. Such memories were kept alive well into the twentieth century. The francophone intellectual Jean C. Falardeau recalled that in his boyhood he had learned that 'The English Canadians were the descendants of those who had crushed the Papineau rebellion, had hanged Riel, had approved the Canadian participation in the Boer War, and had imposed conscription in 1917.'[19] Aggressive, godless, and obsessed with commercialism, *les maudits Anglais* were to be feared and hated. To many English, on the other hand, the French have appeared backward, ignorant ('a nation lacking entirely literature and the arts,' as Lord Durham had put it), the docile mass in a priest-ridden society. They spent their time raising large families they couldn't feed, *n'est-ce pas?* Anglophone bigots showed their contempt for the French language with the curt phrase 'speak white', uttered until the 1970s even in Montreal. (FLQ ideologist Pierre Vallières reflected the response of French Canadians by naming his polemic on behalf of Quebec independence, *White Niggers of America*.)

Negative views and stereotypes have not always dominated Anglo-French relations. But in times of conflict between the two groups, extremism has crowded out moderation. Typically, these conflicts have grown out of opposing images of Canadian development, or differing views about Canada's role in foreign wars, or more recently contending attitudes toward language rights. Particularly when Canadian soldiers were risking their lives across the sea, English Canadians would express feelings of resentment against the French: 'Almost always, in the heat of their passion, their insults came to a climax in the word "treason". In this very popular term their inveterate mistrust of the other race finds expression.'[20]

Anglo-French Relations Before Confederation

English and French clashed repeatedly in the early nineteenth century. Francophones, controlling a majority of the seats in the Lower Canada Assembly, opposed the Château Clique (most of whom were English-speaking). This latter group dominated the executive and legislative councils and was pressing to expand the economy in its own interests. The controversy erupted into warfare in 1837, with Louis Joseph Papineau leading the *Patriotes*. Commissioned to investigate these disturbances in Lower (as well as Upper) Canada, Lord Durham traced the root cause to the francophone presence. He advised eliminating the French by assimilation. By uniting Upper and Lower Canada into a single political unit and giving equal representation in the Assembly to the numerically smaller anglophone population, Durham hoped that eventually the stubborn francophone minority would be dissolved in an ocean of anglophones.[21]

But during the next few decades the English and French learned to co-operate with and accommodate one another; and this meant the defeat of Durham's plan for cultural assimilation. Historians divide the years from 1841 to 1867 into periods characterized by the rule of one or another dual administrations: Baldwin/Lafontaine, MacNab/Taché, Brown/Dorion, and so on. Every ministry was split in two, and thus was led by both an anglophone *and* a francophone. In 1848, the French language was granted a status in the legislature equal to English. So that both anglophone and francophone citizens of this new united Canada could see their government in action, the capital moved back and forth, periodically, between Kingston and Quebec City. Legislation that interested only one-half of the united Canadas was placed under the exclusive jurisdiction of members from that half. These and other similar measures allowed the English and French to live together on 'the landing of politics' without either pushing the other over.[22]

But having to work out endless compromises between the two groups was politically exhausting. Deadlock was inevitable. For one thing, the demographic balance had shifted. Originally benefited by equal French and English representation in the legislature, the rapidly growing anglophone population in Canada West now found itself increasingly victimized by under-representation. The demand for more equitable political arrangements was one of the factors that moved the colonies toward federation in the 1860s. Finally the British North America Act, which provided for two levels of government, emerged as the most practical replacement for the union enacted in 1841.

The Confederation debates of this period refer frequently to these difficulties. The Hon. David Reesor stated on 13 February 1865: 'We have had so many political crises, and the changes have been so varied, that it becomes necessary for some great constitutional change to be made . . .'. Premier Taché observed on 3 February 1865, that 'Legislation in Canada for the last two years had come almost to a standstill. . . . From the 21st May 1862, to the end of June 1864, there had been no less than five different Governments in charge of the business of the country . . . .' Although many factors stalemated the situation, Anglo-French conflict featured prominently among them. The Hon. John Ross, on 8 February 1865, recalled that 'when difficulties between Upper and Lower Canada began to thicken', colonial federation was suggested as a possible solution.[23]

Sir John A. Macdonald put the idea of federation into a broader perspective by laying out the alternative 'modes' of solution then available: 'One was the dissolution of the union between Upper and Lower Canada, leaving them as they were before the union of 1841 . . . '. But this proposition 'had no supporters . . .' because it 'was felt that a dissolution would have . . . left us two weak and ineffective governments, instead of one powerful and united people . . . '. The next mode suggested was 'the granting of representation by population . . . '. Despite strong support for this option in Upper Canada, 'it would have left the Lower Province with a sullen feeling of injury and injustice' (6 February 1865).

In throwing his support behind the remaining option of federal union, Sir John A. Macdonald illustrated some important maxims of healthy Anglo-French relations. First, avoid policies or solutions that will permanently alienate one of the two linguistic groups. Second, be prepared to compromise, and do what is practical even if it is not preferred. Macdonald himself followed these maxims:

> I have again and again stated in the House, that, if practicable, I thought a Legislative Union would be preferable. . . . But, . . . with a desire to arrive at a satisfactory conclusion, we found that such a system was impracticable. In the first place it would not meet the assent of the people of Lower Canada, because they felt that . . . in case of a junction [union] with the other provinces, their institutions and their laws might be assailed, and their ancestral association . . . attacked and prejudiced. (6 February 1865)

The theme of compromise arose repeatedly during the debates. The Hon. Alexander Campbell chided his fellow members to keep the need for flexibility always in mind. 'Where, honourable gentlemen, is the union effected between our two countries, or any two individuals even, which has lasted for any length of time without mutual forbearance and mutual concessions? . . . You must give up all thoughts of union unless you are willing to give and take, and cease persisting for everything you think best' (17 February 1865).

George Brown was well known for his bitter criticisms of the francophones. But even he realized the importance of give and take, and stated flatly that 'the French Canadians must have their views consulted as well as us. This scheme can be carried, and no scheme can be that has not the support of both sections of the province' (8 February 1865).[24]

Why the French Accepted Confederation

For the francophones, a federal union offered the best choice among several imperfect alternatives. Chiefly, it allowed Lower Canada to 'preserve its autonomy together with all the institutions it held so dear' (Premier Taché, 3 February 1865). Also it gave 'to Lower Canada the local government of its affairs, and the control of all matters relating to its institutions, to its laws, to its religion, its manufactures and its autonomy' (Hon. Sir Narcisse F. Belleau, 14 February 1865). George Etienne Cartier told members of the legislature of Canada that the reason French Canadians still 'had their institutions, their language, and their religion intact today . . . was precisely because of their adherence to the British Crown'. Monarchical institutions counterbalanced the democratic, homogenizing influences of the republic to the south: 'In our Federation,' Cartier insisted, 'the monarchical principle would form the leading feature, while on the other side of the line [i.e., in the United States], judging by past history and the present condition of the country, the ruling power was the will of the mob.'[25]

By assigning educational and related matters to the provincial legislatures, Confederation returned legislative self-rule to Quebec and enshrined the 'tacit bargain' between English and French élites. In this way the former could dominate the economic and the latter the cultural portion of Quebec life.[26] The large number of seats (sixty-five) given Quebec in the proposed federal House of Commons further safeguarded French rights. In a statement that has proved uncannily prophetic, Belleau insisted that 'The influence of Lower Canada will enable her to make and unmake governments at pleasure, when her interests shall be at stake or threatened . . .' (14 February 1865).[27]

Despite these guarantees, many francophones opposed Confederation. They argued, for example, that Confederation would actually deprive francophones of their rights 'by substituting for them a political organization which is eminently hostile to us' (Hon. Joseph X. Perrault, 3 March 1865). Others insisted that, assurances to the contrary, Confederation was simply 'the first necessary step' toward the legislative union that most anglophones preferred (Hon. Antoine A. Dorion, 16 February 1865).[28] In the end Lower Canadian members of the legislature voted by a margin of 27 to 21 in favour of Confederation, a frail foundation on which to build a new, bicultural society. Indeed, more than a century later Claude Morin opined that even so fragile an acceptance as this rested on a 'deep misunderstanding . . . Quebeckers thought [Confederation] would forever guarantee them . . . self-determination, while at the same time other Canadians . . . look[ed] forward to the establishment of a very strong central government in Ottawa.'[29]

The BNA Act and Anglo-French Relations

Historians and constitutional experts have disagreed, sometimes colourfully, over Confederation's meaning for Anglo-French relations. To what extent was the BNA Act a 'compact' or 'treaty' between the 'two founding races'? George Stanley declared in 1956 that Confederation should indeed be viewed as a 'pact' or 'entente between the two racial groups of Old Canada, between the two provinces which were each the focus of a distinctive culture'.[30]

After carefully reviewing the evidence for the period 1867 to 1921, on behalf of the Royal Commission on Bilingualism and Biculturalism, historian Ramsay Cook qualified this view. The compact notion enjoyed some legitimacy as it applied to the provinces, but very little as it applied to cultural groups, that is, to the English and French fragments. Confederation clearly assumed a spirit of Anglo-French amity; this spirit was supposed to well up as soon as the 'ethnic' issues which divided Canadians—cultural, religious, and linguistic issues—were removed from the federal forum to the provinces.[31] The survival of French-Canadian culture under Quebec's protection was thought by nearly everyone to be 'une chose donnée'.

But the BNA Act itself gives little hint of such an implied agreement. According to Professor Cook, 'the most that can be said about Confederation is that, while it was clearly intended to meet the needs of both French and English Canadians, there was no detailed contract stating the conditions of the agreement.' Indeed, Cook believes that most supporters of Confederation were 'far more concerned about the survival of British North America against outside pressures than about internal threats to the survival of either French or English Canadians'. It was those who opposed Confederation, according to Ramsay Cook,[32] who raised the French-English issue to prominence. The 'compact theory of Confederation' emerged after the fact, in the heat of French-English political battles un-anticipated by the Fathers of Confederation, over issues that the BNA Act had failed to address.

Surprisingly few provisions of the Act deal explicitly with French-English relations. The major direct references serve to protect the rights of the English minority in Quebec. (These constitutional guarantees were later put in jeopardy by the Parti Québécois' controversial Bill 101 and the Liberals' Bill 178.) Section 93 of the Act places a magic circle of constitutional protection around 'any Right or Privilege with respect to Denominational Schools which any Class of Persons have by Law in the Province at the Union'. It guarantees the Protestant minority in Quebec the same rights to separate schools as the Roman Catholic minority received in Ontario. But because this provision is framed in terms of religion rather than language, and because control of education was vested in the pro-vincial government, francophones outside Quebec had to fight for the right to education in the French language from the outset. Two other provisions of Section 93 allow for appeals to the federal cabinet in the event that educational rights are infringed. They permit the federal Parliament to legislate remedies 'for the due Execution of the Provisions of this Section and of any Decision of the Governor General in Council [i.e., the Cabinet] under this Section'.

Other aspects of the BNA Act were indirectly addressed to the question of Anglo-French relations, and formed a part of the federal bargain that both élites finally approved. The old province of Canada was split into Quebec and Ontario, the one province mainly French-speaking, the other English-speaking. Although Ontario was more heavily populated, it was given the same representation in the Senate (twenty-four members) as Quebec. Quebec was also guaranteed sixty-five seats in the House of Commons (this was later amended to seventy-five when the size of the House increased). Legislative proceedings of Parliament and court actions at the federal level and in Quebec were to be conducted in both English and French. Yet not until legislation was passed in 1969 did more widespread bilingualism receive a written warranty in the Official Languages Act.

The final two sections of the BNA Act enabled Canada to grow by adding new provinces. But no attempt was made at this time to define the character these new provinces would assume. Would the model of bilingual Quebec extend to the West? Would denominational schools in the mother tongue be guaranteed? The BNA Act remained silent on these issues, which were to become matters of hot controversy in the years that followed.

Anglo-French Relations, 1867-1917

Manitoba, the first Western province to enter Confederation, initially seemed to be evolving toward bilingualism or even francophone hegemony. But after two decades of controversy over the linguistic character of the new province, the experiment in bilingualism ended forever. French was abolished in provincial institutions in 1890, and French school rights originally granted to francophone Manitobans were revoked shortly afterward. Some francophone leaders continued to plead for the federal government to intervene on behalf of the minority, under Section 93 of the BNA Act, which obligated the federal government to protect language rights. Faced with two irrepressible opposing forces, Prime Minister Sir Wilfrid Laurier acted in classic federal style: he worked out a compromise.

Separate schools would not be revived, but a limited amount of religion could be taught at the end of each school day. In city schools with forty Catholic pupils and rural ones with more than twenty-five, Catholic teachers could be hired. Finally, the compromise permitted instruction in a language other than English, on a bilingual basis, where the numbers justified it. But this other language need not be French![33]

Similar incidents in other provinces set off equally intense conflict between English and French. New Brunswick had taken away francophones' school rights in the 1870s. The issue arose anew as Saskatchewan and Alberta were added to Confederation. A version of the same conflict broke out in Ontario, where it continued to simmer throughout the present century.[34]

Generally speaking, the federal politicians showed considerable restraint in dealing with these issues. Dalton McCarthy proposed in 1890 to remove the provision in the 'Northwest Territories Act' that permitted the use of French; this extreme idea met defeat in the House of Commons. In 1915, the Senate passed a motion expressing 'regret' over the bitterness surrounding the bilingual schools debate in Ontario. The following year, the House passed an even sterner motion taking the Ontario government to task for its stand on the issue.[35] But no federal government was ever willing to disallow offensive provincial legislation or enact remedial laws, although Section 93 clearly authorized such actions. Francophone nationalists have never forgiven these sins of omission by the federal government.

In addition to disputes over school rights and the status of French in political institutions in Western Canada, anglophones and francophones have clashed repeatedly over Canada's foreign involvements. Formally, Britain controlled Canada's foreign policy into the present century. Informally, Canadians enjoyed some freedom in deciding how much to assist the 'mother country' militarily. Many anglophones, spurred on by the Orange Lodge and other organizations, urged Canada to take full part in British imperial adventures. An articulate group of francophones, led by the nationalist Henri Bourassa, opposed this view. During his tenure as Prime Minister, Sir Wilfrid Laurier was caught in the middle. Again his strategy was to seek a compromise, appealing to moderates on both sides in the hopes of preventing a national split. On the questions of Canadian participation in the Boer War in 1896, and Canadian support for the British navy a decade later, compromise worked. But as the First World War dragged on, extremists on both sides gradually gained the upper hand over moderates.

In 1917, Prime Minister Borden gave in to pressures from English Canada to conscript men into the army. Laurier, then leader for the opposition, refused to support conscription and enter a coalition 'Union Government'. The election of 1917 split apart both the Liberal Party and the country as a whole. A number of anglophone Liberals joined Borden but francophone party members, along with a handful from English Canada, did not. Conscription was legislated against the backdrop of violent demonstrations in Quebec and in the face of bitter opposition from Laurier's Liberals.[36]

Conflicts between the French and English dominated Canadian politics during the half-century following Confederation. They have remained part of the political culture of Anglo-French relations, leaving a legacy of mistrust. Some anglophones felt that because they opposed conscription, the French had acted like traitors and troublemakers, and should lose all of their rights and privileges in Confederation. Other anglophones drew quite a different conclusion. William

Lyon Mackenzie King, for example, was deeply worried by the threat these conflicts posed to Canadian unity. Moderation and compromise were for him the *sine qua non* of Canadian survival. King believed that such confrontations between the two groups must be avoided at all cost.

These conflicts and their resolution convinced many francophones that, despite the presence of a bloc of francophone MPs from Quebec, the federal government could not be counted on to protect francophone rights. They therefore turned their attention from Ottawa to Quebec City, where francophones controlled decision-making. They also transferred federal allegiances from the Conservative to the Liberal Party. In francophones' eyes the Liberals had lined up on the 'correct' side of most important issues and had shown themselves willing to be led by a francophone.[37] Thus, in the period 1867-1917, the ethnic and religious bases of electoral support for the two major parties underwent realignment.[38] Whereas Conservatives had won most federal Quebec seats previously, the Liberals dominated federal elections there until 1958. Moreover, for many francophones Confederation lost whatever emotional appeal it had ever previously enjoyed. From now on they would assess the benefits of staying in Confederation pragmatically, without the influence of sentimental attachment.

Indeed some leaders openly counselled Quebec to withdraw. In 1922, francophone nationalist J.M.R. Villeneuve added up the costs and benefits of Confederation and found the costs were, by far, the greater.

[W]as it not Confederation that prevented confessional schools in New Brunswick? And that also deprived us of them in Manitoba in 1896, in Alberta and Saskatchewan in 1905, in Keewatin in 1912? And was it not Confederation that refused to intervene on a federal level, and Confederation whose timid remedial bills were disdained when we tried to have recourse to them? . . . Is it not Confederation that imposes upon us divorce, and women's suffrage, and imperial conscription, all principles of social dissolution fatal to a race? Is it not Confederation that gives us State schools, unilingual and neutral, and uniform laws in which perish the last traces of the French spirit that enlivened our civil and judicial institutions? Is it not Confederation that refuses to recognize the rights of our national, liberating unions, incapable as it is of judging the true meaning or order and the advantage of safeguarding sensible freedoms? And is it not Confederation that doles out our French language in the most parsimonious amounts in the public services; that keeps it from our youth in many provinces, and ostracizes it with insult and injury?

And finally, is it not Confederation that has anglicized the entire policies of our public representatives, subordinating them to the most risky naval, military, or imperialistic forces? It is impossible to calculate to what extent our morale and our political sense have been depressed by the role we have been fulfilling since 1867.

Taking his assessment to its obvious conclusion, Villeneuve insisted that only by withdrawing 'from the political association of provinces' can the francophone nation be assured of surviving. Confederation had at first conferred the 'advantage of protecting us from our former bugbear, annexation [by the U.S.]'. But it had now outlived its usefulness for francophones. It promised no 'religious or national protection for French minorities outside Quebec'.[39]

Conservative Nationalism in Quebec

Leaders like Villeneuve expressed separatist sentiments in the 1920s, but nearly half a century would pass before Canadian unity was seriously threatened. In the interim, although some francophone nationalists favoured separation, the majority did not. Instead their nationalism remained conservative and traditional.[40] It continued to enshrine the practices and ideals of rural, agricultural, Catholic Quebec. At the same time, these nationalists acquiesced, even collaborated, in the domination of commerce and industry by anglophone Canadians and Americans. The anglophone industrialists, in turn, were wedded to liberal concepts of economic progress and development and felt unfettered by francophone nationalism; so they ignored it.

Hugh MacLennan's important novel *Two Solitudes*, written in 1942, casts into relief the contrast between English and French cultural outlooks. In MacLennan's book, M. Athanase Tallard, the vaguely aristocratic seigneur, embodies the values of the *ancien régime*. His own life is rural, Catholic, and built around the life of the community, his village. The community accepts him as its natural leader; his father, grandfather, and other ancestors for generations before him had played a similar role. Through his farm runs a stream that Tallard has simply regarded as a permanent, unchanging feature of the natural setting. But then Mr McQueen, a 'city man' who is therefore by definition 'English', visits the farm and instantly imagines a factory built there, drawing power from the waterfall in this stream.

Tallard's reflections make crystal clear the contrast in outlooks: 'Suddenly the full force of the idea exploded in his mind. All his life he had lived here without so much as dreaming of the possibilities that lay under his nose, while McQueen had taken a single look at the falls and had seen everything at once. Why could people like himself never see such things unless they were pointed out first by someone else?'[41] Tallard agrees to let McQueen build the factory, but this decision ends up destroying his health, position, and life-style. Anglophone industrialists prosper while the local francophones fall into decline. This tale is clearly an allegory of the industrialization of traditional Quebec and the suffering and dislocation it brought to many thousands of Tallards and lesser francophones. At the same time, it embodies the stereotypical portraits of English and French that have themselves been transformed over the past 50 years.

The election of Maurice Duplessis as premier in 1936 promised change for Quebec, but actually entrenched tradition even more firmly. Duplessis' Union

Nationale Party campaigned to clean up corruption and strengthen provincial autonomy. Duplessis later promised to protect Quebec from the incursions of the federal government: to make French Canadians *maîtres chez nous*, 'masters in our own house'. However, under his regime anglophones continued to control Quebec business and industry. Meanwhile the Catholic church kept its control in the remaining vital areas of labour, health, and education.

Conservative nationalists like Duplessis urged francophones to turn their backs on the ways of commerce and industry, and to avoid the 'contaminating' influence of the city. That traditional conservatism was still the dominant ideology in Quebec is abundantly clear from the following statement, broadcast on Radio-Canada in 1956 on election day:

> Sovereign authority, by whatever goverment it is exercised, is derived solely from God, the supreme and eternal principle of all power . . . . It is therefore an absolute error to believe that authority comes from the multitudes, from the masses, from the people, to pretend that authority does not properly belong to those who exercise it, but that they have only a simple mandate revocable at any time by the people. This error, which dates from the Reformation, rests on the false principle that man has no other master than his own reason . . . . All this explanation about the origin, the basis, and the composition of this alleged [!] sovereignty of the people is purely arbitrary. Moreover, if it is admitted, it will have as a consequence the weakening of authority, making it a myth, giving it an unstable and changeable basis, stimulating popular passions and encouraging sedition.[42]

As late as the mid-1950s Duplessis' government was urging people to move back to the land, encouraging agricultural resettlement in Quebec. His party ruled Quebec with an iron hand. Except for the period between 1939 and 1944, Maurice Duplessis controlled Quebec until his death in 1959, using a powerful political machine, well greased with patronage and corruption.[43]

Although Quebec City and Ottawa sometimes came into direct conflict during this period, federal politics, hence the fortune of the country, remained under the control of the Liberal Party from 1935 to 1957. It was largely within the confines of that party that the federal bargain between English and French had to be worked out. The federal success of the Liberals 'was founded on the solid electoral support of Quebec'. But despite this, the Liberal Party remained weak in Quebec provincial politics.[44]

To ensure patronage was available to federal Liberal politicians,[45] francophone leaders were given the most lucrative patronage portfolios in Ottawa: public works, the post office, and other similar ministries. Duplessis called an election in 1939 on the issue of conscription and promised to keep francophones out of the Canadian army. In a manner without precedent in Canadian history, federal Liberal leaders took over the provincial party's electoral campaign. So powerful were the federal Liberals in Quebec that they managed to defeat Duplessis almost by themselves.

Despite their immediate success, in the long run, intervening this way hurt the provincial Liberal Party quite badly. Viewed by voters as a client government totally dependent on Ottawa, Godbout's provincial Liberals easily went down to defeat in 1944. Mackenzie King's eventual and reluctant adoption of conscription, however, offended francophone Québécois far less than did the Tories' 'fanatical devotion to conscription as an end in itself, and to the greater glory of the British Empire'.[46] Consequently, the Liberal Party continued to dominate federal elections in Quebec until the astounding (but temporary) success of John Diefenbaker in 1958.

Bitterness soured the long debate over conscription during the Second World War. Yet, surprisingly, French-English relations remained relatively good. Many leaders spoke enthusiastically about biculturalism as an essential feature of the Canadian identity. For example, Vincent Massey, later to become the first Canadian-born governor general, said in 1948: 'In English-speaking Canada we have abundant reason to value the contributions made by our fellow-citizens who speak French as their native tongue. It is no mere cliché to say that we would be a far poorer and weaker country without it. Canadians of French origin do not think less of us in English-speaking Canada because we too cherish our traditions—from England and Scotland and Ireland.'[47] Similarly, Mason Wade would write over a decade later: 'The English Canadian now accepts the fact that Canada must be both French and English if it is not to become American. The Massey Report and the action taken upon it by both the St Laurent and Diefenbaker governments reflect this new acceptance of Canada's bi-culturalism as a national asset rather than a liability.'[48]

But at best this biculturalism was very unbalanced. In trying to assess 'the national political scene', Norman Ward observed the following: 'In the past, biculturalism in national politics has meant that the French Canadians in Quebec remained French (on "some sort of reservation," as one of their representatives remarked sardonically in Parliament) and the English Canadians spoke English; and whenever the two groups made contact, the French spoke English too.'[49] The pattern of English domination was particularly striking in the federal civil service, where francophones were badly under-represented, particularly at the senior levels. Francophone citizens were often unable to carry out their business with the federal government in French; francophone civil servants often were forced to speak English, especially when dealing with their superiors in the bureaucracy.[50]

Moreover, this political inequity underlined an even more disturbing pattern of social and economic inequality 'discovered' by sociologists such as John Porter. Porter found that French Canadians, even the Québécois in their own province of Quebec, were treated like second-class citizens. Their classical educations had failed to prepare them for urban industrial and commercial life. But also, the discriminatory practices of anglophone business and industrial élites put francophones at a great disadvantage. Even immigrants recently arrived from Europe, who adopted the English language, were better off. Findings of such widespread and persistent inequality added fuel to the new French nationalism, itself responding to more fundamental changes in Quebec society.[51]

Modernization and the Quiet Revolution

Between 1939 and 1950, the number of manual labourers in Quebec doubled. The population working in agriculture dropped by 25%. Industrialization increased dramatically and the number of jobs in manufacturing went up accordingly.[52] These trends accelerated over the next two decades. The number of farms in operation fell by more than half between 1951 and 1971; the number of Québécois living on farms declined even more astonishingly, from one in five to one in twenty. Similarly, the percentage of the francophone male labour force involved in primary industry (farming, logging, mining, fishing and the like) fell to about a quarter of its earlier level. Accordingly, the numbers working in services, or tertiary industry, rose from 34% to 51% during these two decades.[53] Quebec was becoming a modern society, and as it did so, it rapidly outgrew its traditional ideology and the supporting political institutions.

In 1960, a rejuvenated provincial Liberal Party, led by former federal cabinet minister Jean Lesage, defeated the Union Nationale, now bereft of Duplessis to guide it. Lesage introduced extensive policy changes that amounted to a 'quiet revolution'; the changes brought social modernization and political modernization a little closer together in Quebec. In place of the defensive commitment to survivance, Lesage's liberals spoke confidently of *épanouissement* (roughly, 'expanding outward'). Thus, the Quebec ship of state steamed out of the backwaters of traditionalism, but it was headed on a collision course with the federal government.

Quebec's new policy of expansion would lead inexorably to jurisdictional disputes with Ottawa. Policy matters the Quebec government had previously ignored—immigration, external affairs, communications, and even official language policy—would become matters of concern. The new nationalism replaced fatalism and resignation with optimism and commitment. It aimed not to avoid modernization, but to take control of the process and shape it to the needs and wishes of Quebec society. It saw Quebec's machinery of state as the prime instrument for attaining these new goals.

Quebec society was changing in other ways as well. New life infused the arts and letters. New plays, novels, and vital works of social criticism and political theory began to appear in quantity. Artists, dancers, and popular singers gave voice and form to the new wave of national consciousness and purpose that was sweeping over francophones in Quebec.[54] But the forces of change had a darker side too. Impatient with the slow pace of political change, a small group of political extremists came together, forming the *Front de Libération du Québec* (FLQ).

Leading ideologist for the FLQ, Pierre Vallières, drew upon Marxist notions of socialist revolution, black American radicalism, and the anti-colonial writings of Africans and other third-world people. He wrote his book, *Nègres blancs d'Amérique* (*White Niggers of America*), while he was in prison for committing an act of terrorism; it opens with this powerful statement:

> In writing this book I claim to do no more than bear witness to the determination of the workers of Quebec to put an end to three centuries of exploitation, of injustices borne in silence, of sacrifices accepted in vain, of insecurity endured with resignation; to bear witness to their new and increasingly energetic determination to take control of their economic, political, and social affairs and to transform into a more just and fraternal society this country.

Throughout the sixties, the FLQ carried out dozens of bombings. These and other terrorist activities were intended to build up the strength and visibility of their cause: the complete separation of Quebec from Canada, and the transformation of Quebec society into a socialist republic. Again in Vallières' words, 'the relations between men must be radically transformed and . . . imperialism must be definitively overthrown' in order to create a 'new classless society' in which 'solidarity' replaces 'money . . . [and] the exploitation of man by man' as the 'cement' holding the social order together.[55]

Growing alongside these FLQ activities was a sense of dissatisfaction with the limited policies of the Liberal Party. One of the dissatisfied Québécois was a former journalist who had played a major part in nationalizing Hydro in Quebec, René Lévesque. Lévesque had increasing difficulty accepting the moderation of his Liberal Party colleagues. He wanted the Quebec state to intervene more forcefully in the provincial economy and to secure the place of the French language in Quebec.

The Liberal Party went down to defeat in 1966 in a last thrust by the Union Nationale, led by Daniel Johnson. Johnson's book, *Egalité ou indépendance*, reflected the new aggressiveness of nationalists in Quebec, even those whose nationalism was, like Johnson's, rooted in conservative ideology. But the Union Nationale lost its progressive momentum in 1968 when Johnson died and a more traditional leader, Jean-Jacques Bertrand, succeeded him.

Meanwhile the provincial Liberal Party, now out of power, was coming apart faster and faster. Seeing that the moderates, committed to federalism, would not endorse the policies he supported, Lévesque withdrew and formed a new party committed to 'sovereignty-association'—political independence for Quebec in the context of strong economic links with the rest of Canada. In the following year (1968) when the Parti Québécois (PQ) formed out of his *Mouvement Souveraineté-Association* and several other small parties, Lévesque assumed its leadership.

The Parti Québécois

At the next provincial election, held in 1970, the PQ received over twenty per cent of the popular vote. But this secured for the Péquistes only 6% of the seats in the National Assembly. Under its new leader Robert Bourassa, the Liberal Party had won a stunning victory. Unable to believe that a separatist party might ever gain power by election, the radical FLQ embarked on its boldest and costliest venture: it kidnapped James Cross and Pierre Laporte. The violent murder of Laporte alienated most FLQ supporters, leading to that organization's rapid demise. But the brutal tactics of the provincial and federal governments, operating under the authority of the War Measures Act in October 1970, also disgusted many moderate francophone nationalists. These tactics probably contributed in some degree to the later electoral success of the PQ.

Public opinion polls of the 1960s and early 1970s indicated a growing feeling among francophones and anglophones that French-English relations were getting worse, particularly after the October Crisis. Yet separatism continued to attract little attention from most Canadians. Even in 1973, three-quarters of anglophones and more than three-fifths of francophones still thought separation was unlikely. In that year, the Liberals won another election and virtually eliminated all opposing parties except the PQ, which won six seats with 30% of the popular vote. Between 1970 and 1976, popular support for the idea of independence-with-economic-association apparently grew, particularly among PQ supporters. More important, in 1974 the Parti Québécois moderated its policies. By emphasizing good government and progressive policies, the PQ was able to offer voters a credible alternative to the increasingly unpopular Liberal Party. PQ strategists agreed to postpone the debate over independence until after the Parti came into power and a referendum was held. This apparent watering down of the PQ's separatist policy, and the declining popularity of the Liberals, enabled the PQ to win the 1976 provincial election.[56] Canada had come to the brink of an English-French divorce.

The growth of Quebec nationalism in the previous decade had already transformed the situation irrevocably; the PQ victory simply turned up the volume, so everyone could hear what had changed. Some scholars believe the program of the PQ simply extended the changes introduced during the Quiet Revolution, changes which had led many Québécois to expect a major realignment of economic power in the province. No longer would francophones stand being denied entry to the best jobs. No longer would they willingly learn English to move up the occupational ladder. Quebec would become a French state, controlling its own destiny, not an appendage to the powerful anglophone society surrounding it. These ideas were well advanced and widely supported even before the PQ came into power.

Indeed the language issue has always been a central one to francophones. Studies conducted in the 1960s showed that if current patterns of immigration continued, anglophones would outnumber francophones in Montreal by the year 2000. Arresting this trend meant revoking the privileges anglophones enjoyed in Quebec. In particular, immigrants could not be allowed to send their children to anglophone schools. Furthermore, businesses operated in Quebec would have to be forced to use French rather than English, so that francophones could compete effectively for the top jobs.

Strong public pressure made the reluctant provincial Liberals propose (in 1975) a bill which would, in effect, make French the official language of Quebec and relegate English to a minor role. After entering office the next year, the Parti Québécois went even further, however. They presented to the National Assembly a Bill explicitly declaring French the official language of Quebec. The Bill took away most of the special privileges accorded to anglophones in Quebec under the BNA Act. Its presenter, Minister of State for Cultural and Development Dr Camille Laurin, claimed this Bill was designed to make up for previous injustices perpetrated against French Canadians: 'The charter of a French language in Quebec is the supreme affirmation of the French fact in America, the victory of the Québécois nation over the anglophone occupier, the annulment of the defeat upon the Plains of Abraham and the cultural Magna Carta of the Québécois.'[57]

The Federal Government Responds

Throughout the turbulent decades of the sixties and seventies, the new nationalism in Quebec forced a puzzled federal government to respond, however hesitantly. Upon assuming office in 1963, the minority Liberals led by Lester Pearson attempted to loosen up Confederation. Quebec, and any other province, would be permitted to 'opt out' of federal schemes and receive additional tax dollars as compensation. Similarly, efforts were made to give the provinces additional powers. Federal-provincial conferences at all levels of government, from the prime ministerial down to the middle-range bureaucratic, would become ever more common. Here the sharing of jurisdictions would be carefully negotiated. Such attempts as these to adjust the mechanics of federalism to ever-growing provincial desires for autonomy will be discussed more fully in the following chapter.

Also in 1963, the Pearson government appointed a Royal Commission on Bilingualism and Biculturalism to study English-French relations in Canada and to recommend policies that would unify the nation. The Commission engaged the talents of a large part of the Canadian academic community. Its staff travelled throughout the country, sounding out public opinion on a variety of important issues. In the end, the Commission was disbanded before it had made its recommendations for basic constitutional change. But it did recommend changes in language policy—no mean achievement.

The Royal Commission's advice proved of questionable value, however. After reviewing the experiences of other bilingual societies, the commissioners identified two different ways of approaching bilingualism. One, the 'territorial principle', suggested designating certain large areas of a country as unilingual unless the minority exceeded a certain percentage of the local population. In that event, the area would become officially bilingual. The competing 'personality principle' attempts to provide bilingual services to all citizens, regardless of the local majority language. The commissioners rejected any consistent application of either principle, opting for a combination of the two. They urged the federal government to serve citizens everywhere in Canada in both languages *and* also to designate certain areas with a concentration of francophones as bilingual regions. They believed that this dual principle would protect French Canadian culture and language throughout the country in two distinct ways.

By making French Canadians feel linguistically at home everywhere in Canada, the commissioners hoped to undermine narrow Québécois nationalism. Francophones could once again feel a part of the federal state and take pride in the country's new bilingual achievement. Rather than looking to Quebec City as the focal point of a francophone state, they would turn instead to Ottawa, the centre of a truly bilingual Canada.

The commissioners' views were close to those of a certain intellectual who, as editor of *Cité Libre*, had been one of Duplessis' most articulate critics in the 1950s. This man, Pierre Elliott Trudeau, had written in 1965 that 'to prevent the country from breaking up', the federal government must move quickly to grant 'French minorities in other provinces, as well as in Ottawa, the same rights and privileges as the English minority in Quebec'. If these rights were truly guaranteed, Trudeau believed francophones could be persuaded 'to abandon their role of oppressed nation and decide to participate boldly and intelligently in the Canadian experience'.[58]

That same year Trudeau and two colleagues, Gerard Pelletier and Jean Marchand, were enticed to join the Pearson government. By adding these 'three wise men' to his cabinet, Pearson attempted to divert French-Canadian sentiment in Quebec from the separatist cause. Trudeau's political fortunes rose quickly from that time on. By 1968, when the Commission issued its recommendations, Pierre Trudeau had already succeeded Pearson as leader of the Liberal Party, and he had won the party a decisive victory: the first clear majority government elected in a decade. During the election, Trudeau campaigned vigorously against any notion of a 'special status' for Quebec. Indeed he dismissed as a dangerous fallacy the Conservative Party's endorsement of the '*deux nations*' concept. Trudeau thus demonstrated his strong anti-nationalistic bias, as he had in condemning Maurice Duplessis during the 1950s. The landslide win temporarily ended all discussion by federal politicians of a change in Quebec's constitutional position within Confederation. The Conservative Party abandoned its *deux nations* concept, and Trudeau made it clear that he intended to avoid 'weakening' the federal government's position vis-à-vis the provinces any further.

Committing his government to federal bilingualism, Trudeau personally piloted through Parliament new legislation designed to establish both the 'English and French languages as . . . the official languages of Canada for all purposes as the Parliament and Government of Canada.' The Official Languages Act was supported by all political parties and passed in 1969 with few dissenting voices.

Through this and earlier legislation, the federal bureaucracy for the first time became bilingual at all levels, and a number of French-language units came into existence. By 1977, 21% of senior executives in the federal public service were francophones. Federal institutions and installations such as airports were given a bilingual façade. The CBC set up 92 French-language television stations and 137 radio stations across Canada. The government increased its support of French-language training in public schools and of the use of bilingual phrases and words as titles for major governmental departments such as Environment Canada, Transport Canada, Information Canada, and so on. The national airline was renamed Air Canada. Some even spoke of changing the name of the national police force from Royal Canadian Mounted Police to something less British in tone. Thus, at the symbolic level, Canada became more obviously a bicultural nation; francophones received a better chance to rise in the federal civil service; and French-language radio and television stations were established throughout the country.

Some segments of Canadian society opposed these measures bitterly. Such opposition was epitomized in the popular book entitled *Bilingual Today, French Tomorrow: Trudeau's Master Plan and How It Can Be Stopped*, by J.V. Andrew. Yet most English Canadians accepted most of these policies. A survey conducted in 1977 revealed that over eighty per cent of Canadians agreed with their main thrust.

But the bilingualism policies failed to address the aspirations of the new Québécois nationalism. Québécois francophones continued to think of the Quebec state as the fulcrum of change. They wanted a truly francophone society in Quebec, not a bilingual society in Canada as a whole. Thus while Ottawa moved toward bilingualism, Quebec City continued to pursue unilingual policies that culminated in Bill 101, which declared French the official language of Quebec. The contradiction between these two policies symbolizes the growing tendency of francophone Québécois and English Canadians to talk past one another.[59]

Francophone Canadians, especially those who live in Quebec, place a great premium upon being able to speak French outside Quebec. English-speaking Canadians sympathize with this position; but they are more likely than the francophones to lack concern about this issue or even oppose the French position. Indeed, all the responses to a recent survey suggest a lesser concern with the issue outside Quebec than in it, and a general lack of sympathy with the needs and fears of the other linguistic group, with the fears of French Canadians who journey outside Quebec and of anglophones and 'others' who venture into it. These data show little sign of mutual understanding, but rather of something more reminiscent of 'two solitudes'.[60]

The language policies of Quebec and Ottawa rest on contradictory conceptualizations of the 'language problem' and how it can best be solved. Federal policy sees language use as an individual right, and attempts to make it possible for every individual to use either of the official languages when dealing with the federal government or its agencies and in federal institutions such as airports anywhere in Canada. It also offers support for the maintenance of both official languages by supporting radio and television outlets in both languages in all parts of the country; and mandating educational facilities in either language 'where numbers warrant'. Using its regulatory authority, the federal government is able to require bilingual messages and advertising on commercial products, labels, instructions, etc. Competence in both languages is required for a number of positions in the public service. In short, federal language policy stresses bilingualism, individual language rights reflecting the 'personality principle'.

By contrast, Quebec's language policy is based on the 'territorial principle' that connects language use not to individuals but to groups living in a particular geographical location, namely, the province of Quebec. Convinced that French can only survive if it has a secure territorial base, successive Quebec governments, both Liberal and Parti Québécois, have strengthened the legal preeminence of French even to the point of requiring that all commercial outdoor signs feature French. When this provision of Quebec language law was declared unconstitutional by the Supreme Court, Prime Minister Robert Bourassa moved immediately using the 'nothwithstanding clause' to override this decision and enact Bill 178.

In effect, the competing policies of individual bilingualism and territorially based unilingualism offer two different visions of Canada, two alternative views of Canadian identity, two contrasting prescriptions for national unity (In important respects Quebec language policy is a prescription for survival of the francophone *nation* rather than an attempt to preserve national unity for Canada as a whole. And it has generated strong resentment among some anglophones who regard it as a betrayal of the principle of bilingualism.)

Nearly twenty years after the passage of the Official Languages Bill, according to a 1986 Decima survey a large number of Canadians had no clear understanding of the objectives of federal bilingualism. Four years later a majority of Canadians surveyed by Gallup regarded bilingualism as a 'failure.' Little wonder, 'Linguistic duality is a vision of Canada at variance with the social reality most English-speaking Canadians experience. Most anglophones have little or no contact with francophones.'[61]

Conclusion

Writing one year after the centenary of Canadian Confederation, René Lévesque and his associates warned that the 'Canadian constitutional crisis' was 'growing more and more acute; it is nearing the boiling point.' For Lévesque the crisis was of Quebec's own making, and 'it is therefore Quebec's responsibility to find within itself the clear thinking and the courage to bring it to its conclusion.'[62]

Quebec's politics in the next decade absorbed the talents and energies of that province's best minds. Among both the élite and the mass, opinion crystallized around the issue of constitutional change. Few francophones in Quebec supported the status quo. Over eighty per cent of Québécois surveyed in June 1978 wanted either fundamental change in Confederation or outright independence. The scene was set for a monumental political struggle between federalism and sovereignty-association, featuring two protagonists who had sparred many times before. Leading the federalist forces was their most brilliant champion— Pierre Trudeau —who had miraculously returned to power after Joe Clark's minority Conservative government, elected in spring of 1979, was forced to resign in December following a defeat on a key vote in Parliament. Trudeau's chief opponent was of course René Lévesque, founder and leader of the Parti Québécois, darling of the Quebec nationalists. At stake was a referendum to authorize the Quebec government to begin negotiating with Ottawa to achieve sovereignty association.

The federalists urged Québécois to vote no—an act which would simultaneously affirm their loyalty to Canada. Hence their slogan 'mon non est Canadien'. At the same time Trudeau appeared to promise fundamental constitutional change that would address a number of key Quebec grievances and aspirations. He even used the language of 'renewed federalism' that had appeared in the Provincial Liberal Party's 'Beige Paper', which had argued for special recognition of Quebec's unique position in Canada. A majority of Quebec referendum voters, including a very high proportion of anglophones and a large number of francophones, voted against sovereignty-association. Francophones who opposed it appear to have been motivated by economic concerns about the financial costs of leaving Canada, and political assurances from Trudeau that the constitution would indeed be 'renewed'.

Following the successful defeat of his old adversary René Lévesque, Trudeau turned nearly all his energy to the task of constitutional change. His objectives were to patriate the Constitution and add to it a Charter of Rights. Trudeau had no intention of offering any sort of special status to Quebec, though he was ultimately forced to make compromises in his proposed constitution package in order to win the support of provincial premiers, all of whom (except René Lévesque) eventually backed the initiatives. And so in 1982, the Canada Constitution Act was passed with the support of the nine other provinces, despite the opposition of Quebec.

Among the compromises was the addition of a clause which allowed governments to pass laws which override certain provisions of the Charter, so long as the offending legislation is prefaced with a clause explicitly stating that the law applies 'notwithstanding' the Charter.

The federal government proposed to include in the Charter language that would strengthen aboriginal land claims. When several premiers objected vociferously, that clause was removed and replaced by a less radical formation that merely 'recognized and affirmed' '*existing* aboriginal and treaty rights of the aboriginal peoples of Canada' (emphasis added). In the closed process of executive constitution making by the 'first ministers', the aboriginal people of Canada's 'first nation' once again lost.

On the other hand, representatives of dozens of women's groups scored an unprecedented victory. They formed an amazingly effective national coalition to force the first ministers to add to the Charter a provision (Section 28) *guaranteeing* the 'rights and freedoms of the Charter' equally to male and female persons.

Five years after the patriation of the Constitution, Trudeau's successor, a Quebec anglophone, persuaded all ten provinces to accept proposed amendments to the Constitution that satisfied Quebec's demands, and would have brought Quebec into the constitutional fold. When in June 1990 these agreements lapsed because they failed to achieve ratification in Manitoba and Newfoundland, relations with Quebec went into a dangerous tailspin. Anxious efforts to find a new basis for consensus have opened new divisions and irritated old wounds. Steadfastly refusing to participate in joint intergovernmental constitutional negotiations, Quebec set a timetable of fall 1992 for a referendum on new constitutional arrangements and/or the option of independence

Like all true crises, the English-French conflict presents opportunity as well as danger. In light of the prospect of a Canada without Quebec, many anglophones have begun to look at their country anew. English-Canadian nationalism and a viable, identifiable English-Canadian culture are probably more necessary now than ever. Yet even the prospects of unifying the 'rest of Canada' are poor, for this presupposes a unified purpose that transcends regional differences. And, as we shall see, the disparity between regions in English Canada is another source of conflict and disunity.

Notes

[1] Intermarriage did take place between French and Irish and French and Indians particularly. But not until 1977, following the transfer from Ottawa to Quebec of certain powers to select immigrants, did francophone immigrants to Quebec outnumber anglophones.

[2] See Denis Monière, *Ideologies in Quebec: The Historical Development* (Toronto: University of Toronto Press, 1981).

[3] John Johnstone, *Young People's Images of Canadian Society* (Ottawa: Queen's Printer, 1969). A study of how high school students label their own national identity reached similarly interesting results. Over 90% of anglophone students described themselves as 'Canadian' whereas only 65% of francophone students did so. The percentage of francophones choosing the labels French Canadian or Québécois was 78 and 79 respectively. (Multiple choices were permitted.) When forced to choose only one label, over 80% of anglophones chose Canadian, whereas 70% of francophones chose French Canadian. See H.D. Forbes, 'Conflicting National Identities among Canadian Youth' in J. Pammett and M. Whittington, *Foundations of Political Culture*: 293, 295.

[4] *Report of the Royal Commission on Bilingualism and Biculturalism*, vol. II: Education (Ottawa: Queen's Printer, 1968): 276.

Note however Lipset's more recent assessment: 'Both Canadian linguistic cultures continue to differ systematically from the American . . . . [O]n most issues, Francophones are at one end of the spectrum, Anglophones in the middle, and Americans at the other. Quebec, once the most conservative part of Canada, has become the most liberal on social and welfare issues. English Canada is also consistently more progressive than the United States.' *Continental Divide, op.cit.*: 216.

Note also that in his Foreword to the *Report of the Citizens' Forum on Canada's Future*, Keith Spicer spoke of 'a deep similarity of values and ideals among Canadians' that 'includes British-origin Canadians, Quebeckers and other French-speakers'. (p. 7).

[5] Jean Pierre Richert, 'The Impact of Ethnicity on the Perception of Heroes and Historical Symbols', *The Canadian Review of Sociology and Anthropology* 11, 2 (1974): 156, 157.

[6] *Preliminary Report of the Royal Commission on Bilingualism and Biculturalism* (Ottawa: Queen's Printer, 1965): 55. From the perspective of native peoples, of course, both groups are recent immigrants. Insofar as the Amerindians themselves migrated to this continent from Asia, some have argued that only the Métis are a truly indigenous people. See Duke Redbird, 'We are Métis: A Métis Perspective of the Evolution of an Indigenous Canadian People' (unpublished MA thesis, York University, 1978).

[7] L.F.R. Laflèche, 'The Provincial Mission of the French Canadians', in Ramsay Cook (ed.), *French-Canadian Nationalism* (Toronto: Macmillan of Canada, 1969): 92, 98.

[8] Nelson Wiseman argues that this progression reproduced the dialectical development of socialism in Europe. See 'A Note on "Hartz-Horowitz at Twenty": The Case of French Canada', *Canadian Journal of Political Science* 21,4, (1 December 1988): 803.

[9] J.M.R. Villeneuve, 'And Our Dispersed Brethren . . .?' in Cook (ed.), *French Canadian Nationalism*: 203.

[10] Carl Berger, *The Sense of Power*: 140. The idea of a common conservative link between imperialists and Francophones found no favour with many leading figures in the imperialist movement. To Charles Mair and Colonel George Denison, the French were an unfortunate relic of 'medieval inertia', impediments to the progress of enterprise in Canada. See *ibid.*: 58 ff., 134 ff., *et passim*.

[11] *Ibid.*: 145. Some francophones, however, supported the Empire because they believed it offered sounder protection for their culture than would, for example, the United States. See pp. 138-9.

[12] Antonio Perrault, 'Inquiry into Nationalism', in Cook (ed.): 220.

[13] Villeneuve, *ibid.*: 206-7.

[14] *Ibid.*: 209, 205, 210.

[15] Janet Kerr Morchain, *Search for a Nation*, general editor: Mason Wade (Toronto: J.M. Dent and Sons [Canada] Limited, 1967): 1-2.

[16] André Siegfried, *The Race Question in Canada*: 11, 14.

[17] Quoted in Mason Wade, *Canadian Dualism* (Toronto: University of Toronto Press, 1960): xviii.

[18] Al Johnson, 'Touchstone for the CBC' (mimeo., 1977): 39.

[19] Jean C. Falardeau, *Roots and Values in Canadian Lives* (Toronto: University of Toronto Press, 1961): 21.

[20] Siegfried: 97. Note as well retired military officer J.V. Andrew's incredible book about the 'conspiracy' to turn Canada into a unilingual francophone country. The book is a distillation of stereotypes and historical grievances. Andrew reminds readers, for example, that 'Many Canadians can easily recall that French-Canadians were a scarce commodity for the Armed Forces when they were needed during the two world wars' (*Bilingual Today, French Tomorrow* [Richmond Hill: BMG Publishing Ltd, 1977]: 19).

The amazing popularity of the book appears to indicate deep currents of anti-francophone sentiment in Canada.

[21] Of Durham's recommendations, Denis Monière writes: 'Thus, over the ignorant, uncultural, jealous, inert and conservative French, the civilized and progressive English were to be given control of the state apparatus, so that trade and industry could grow in Britain's own interest. Moreover, this apparatus was to be more powerful, and not less . . . . Durham suggested that Britain . . . concede the system of responsible government [to Canada] (op.cit.: 116.) To a Quebec nationalist like Monière, Durham's Report represents the epitome of racist-like neo-colonialist thinking. A rather different perspective appears in Janet Azenstadt's interpretation of Durham as an enlightened liberal with very progressive ideas about government and freedom.

[22] For an account of the accommodative practices worked out in Canada during the period 1841-67 see William Ormsby, *The Emergence of the Federal Concept of Canada, 1839-1845* (Toronto: University of Toronto Press, 1969). Although on a much more informal basis, some similar practices have been continued ever since. The Liberal Party of Canada has alternated between a francophone and an anglophone as leader since Laurier. When an anglophone has been in charge, he has invariably appointed a strong francophone lieutenant to oversee political matters related to Quebec. Cabinet appointments usually include a significant number of francophone Québécois. Two of the nine Supreme Court justices are francophones familiar with Quebec law. Recently the Speakership of the House of Commons has alternated between a francophone and an anglophone. Prime Minister Trudeau set about to increase francophone representation in the Civil Service, particularly at middle and upper levels.

[23] Quoted speeches are reprinted in Peter B. Waite (ed.), *The Confederation Debates in the Province of Canada, 1865* (Toronto: McClelland & Stewart, 1963): 21, 22, 25.

[24] *Ibid.*: 38, 39-40, 40-1, 65.

[25] Quoted in Frederick Vaughan, 'The Political Philosophy of the Canadian Founding' (paper presented to the Conference on Political Thought in English Canada, York University, March 1978): 6, 7.

[26] Reginald Whitaker, *The Government Party* (Toronto: University of Toronto Press, 1977): 41.

[27] Waite (ed.) *The Confederation Debates*: 35. Other quotes appear *passim*.

[28] Reprinted in Morchain: 127, 128.

[29] Claude Morin, 'Address', reprinted in S.D. Berkowitz and Robert K. Logan (eds), *Canada's Third Option* (Toronto: Macmillan, 1978): 35-6. Morin clearly exaggerates the extent to which non-Quebeckers favoured centralization, as Chapter 5 will show.

[30] George F.G. Stanley, 'The Federal Bargain: The Contractarian Basis of Confederation', in Kenneth D. McRae (ed.), *Consociational Democracy: Political Accommodation in Segmented Societies* (Toronto: McClelland & Stewart, 1974).

[31] Ramsay Cook, *Provincial Autonomy, Minority Rights and the Compact Theory 1867-1921* (Ottawa: Queen's Printer, 1969). Cf. Donald Smiley, *The Canadian Political Nationality* (Toronto: Methuen, 1967): 118: 'Responsible politicians have for nearly a century tried to realize the confident expectations of the Fathers of Confederation that the conflicts of federal politics should not range English-and French-speaking Canadians against each other as such.'

[32]Cook, *Provincial Autonomy*: 53. Cook's assessment rests on an impressionistic opinion. The only quantitative study of the Confederation Debates yields less conclusive results. Although about one-quarter of the representatives from Lower Canada who opposed Confederation devoted considerable attention to preservation of French culture, no significant differences showed up among other participants in the debate. See Walter Soderund, Ralph Nelson, and Ronald Wagenberg, 'Canadian Confederation: An Empirical Test of the Hartz Theory' (paper presented to the Canadian Political Science Association, Annual, 1976), Table 6 *et passim*.

[33] Laurier came into office supporting provincial autonomy in school rights and urging 'sunny ways' in dealing with this kind of issue, i.e., encouraging moderation and compromise. He won electoral support in French Canada through appeals to ethnic solidarity—the chance to have a francophone as prime minister. Some francophones also agreed with the policy of provincial autonomy, fearing

that a more interventionist federal government might some day tamper with Quebec's autonomy. For an account of the controversy, see *inter alia*, Robert Brown and Ramsay Cook, *Canada: 1896-1920* (Toronto: McClelland & Stewart, 1974): 12 ff; W.L. Morton, *Manitoba: A History* (Toronto: University of Toronto Press, 1967): 240 ff.

[34] See the articles on francophones 'Outside Quebec' in Mason Wade (ed.), *Canadian Dualism*, Part IV.

[35] Cook, *Provincial Autonomy*: 60-3.

[36] A concise study of the issue appears in *Conscription 1917* (Toronto: University of Toronto Press, n.d.). Note particularly Ramsay Cook's essay 'Dafoe, Laurier and the Foundation of Union Government' where Cook notes that 'The ugly sore of racial friction had been irritated by the years of debate over imperial policy and the racial question; the language controversy and the Lapointe resolution requesting the Province of Ontario to recognize French Language rights brought it to a head only to have it burst explosively by the conscription crisis' (p. 35).

[37] Of the Liberal Party's seven leaders since Confederation, three have been francophones. In the same period the Conservatives have had fourteen leaders, all anglophones. In times when both major parties have had anglophone leaders, the party with a strong francophone lieutenant has tended to do better in Quebec. See Conrad Winn and François-Pierre Gingras, 'The Bicultural Cleavage' in Winn and McNemeny: 63 ff.

[38] The realignment took place more gradually and less completely than some writers suggest. Gingras and Winn assess the evidence more carefully, taking into consideration actual voting figures in Quebec rather than merely counting seats (*Ibid.*: 57 ff).

[39] Villeneuve in Cook, *French-Canadian Nationalism*: 211, 210. Even present-day supporters of federalism express bitterness at the inadequacies of the BNA Act. Solange Chaput-Rolland noted that 'The Constitution of Canada is the very document that permitted our fellow Francophones in Alberta and Manitoba and Saskatchewan to become second-class citizens. The present constitution made this possible, so we must be very sure that the next one will be more just.' Solange Chaput-Rolland and Gertrude Laing, *Face to Face* (Toronto: New Press, 1972): 87.

[40] Henri Bourassa expressed a more progressive form of French-Canadian nationalism but even he in the end subscribed to Abbé Groulx's traditional version. See Laxer and Laxer: 162 ff.

[41] Hugh MacLennan, *Two Solitudes* (Toronto: Macmillan of Canada, 1942): 99.

[42] See Herbert Quinn, *The Union Nationale*; and McRoberts and Posgate, *op. cit.*, ch. 5, which contains a careful assessment of the social and cultural forces sustaining Duplessis.

[43] Reginald Whitaker, *The Government Party* (Toronto: University of Toronto Press, 1977): 270.

[44] For a thorough and stimulating analysis of the role of patronage in Quebec political culture, see Ralph Heintzmann, 'The Political Culture of Quebec, 1840-1960', *Canadian Journal of Political Science*, 16,1 (March, 1988): 3-60. Proof that patronage still lives in Quebec is the career of M.P. Maurice Gravel—'The Godfather of Hull'—who served a jail sentence for his activities. See *The Globe and Mail*, 27 June 1991.

[45] Whitaker: 289. King exercised what some anglophones regarded as maddening caution in introducing conscription, and was able to secure the support of Louis St Laurent, later his successor as prime minister. The effects of conscription were consequently less severe than in the First World War.

[46] Vincent Massey, *On Being Canadian* (Toronto: J.M. Dent, 1948): 18.

[47] Wade, *Canadian Dualism*: 416. Note, however, that Wade was unjustifiably optimistic in concluding in 1958 that 'it would appear that there is much co-operation and adjustment between English and French in Canada today, although some ancient and deep-rooted misunderstandings remain. There is little evidence of serious friction and conflict' (p. 417).

[48] Norman Ward, 'The National Political Scene', in *ibid.*: 274.

[49] See V. Seymour Wilson, 'Language Policy', in G. Bruce Doern and V. Seymour Wilson, eds, *Issues in Canadian Public Policy* (Toronto: Macmillan, 1974).

[50] J. Porter, *The Vertical Mosaic*. Note that Nathan Keyfitz questions whether the classical education of francophones accounts in any way for their relatively low socio-economic status. The Quebec curriculum, he points out, strongly resembles the Oxford education, highly prized by the British imperial élite. See Wilson: 257-8.

[51] Marcel Rioux, *Quebec in Question* (Toronto: James, Lewis & Samuel, 1971): 65-7.

[52] McRoberts and Posgate: 34.

[53] Cf. James de Wilde's contrast between the 'old' and 'new' nationalism in Quebec, in Richard Simeon, ed., *Must Canada Fail?* (Montreal: McGill-Queen's University Press, 1977): 20-2.

[54] Note Nick Auf der Maur's comment that 'wherever one looks, be it in the arts, education, politics, the unions, the best and the brightest of the French element is apt to be péquiste' (quoted by Simeon: 7).

[55] Pierre Vallières, *White Niggers of America*, translated by Joan Pinkham (Toronto: McClelland & Stewart, 1971): 17, 14.

[56] See Maurice Pinard and Richard Hamilton, 'The Parti Québécois Comes to Power: An Analysis of the 1976 Quebec Election', in *Canadian Journal of Political Science* 11,4 (December 1978): 739-76; and François-Pierre Gingras and Neil Nevitte, 'Nationalism in Quebec: the Transition of Ideology and Political Support' in Allen Kornberg and Harold Clarke (eds), *Political Support in Canada: The Crisis Years* (Durham, Duke University Press, 1983).

[57] Camille Laurin, quoted in *The Globe and Mail*, 8 July 1977.

[58] Pierre Elliott Trudeau, *Federalism and the French Canadians* (Toronto: Macmillan, 1968): 31, 32.

[59] Similar contrasts in outlook appeared within the francophone community, particularly between federalists and independentists. Jean Chrétien, first francophone to hold the federal post of minister of finance, sarcastically rejected the preoccupation with 'injustices of the past' that led PQ leaders to propose the 'intolerable' remedy of imposing injustices on present-day Quebec anglophones. To Chrétien, René Lévesque was lamentably inward-looking. Chrétien prefers bilingualism as a guarantee of access to the 'big leagues'. Unilingualism in Quebec is a backward step taken in disregard of the 'irreversible progress' made in extending bilingualism federally and in the provinces of New Brunswick, Ontario, and Manitoba. See his 'Address' reprinted in Berkowitz and Logan.

[60] Michael Ornstein *et al.*, 'The State of Mind: Public Perceptions of the Future of Canada', in R.B. Byers and R.W. Reford (eds), *Canada Challenged: The Viability of Confederation* (Toronto: Centre for International Affairs, 1979).

[61] Michael O'Keefe, 'An Analysis of Attitudes towards Official Language Policy among Anglophones'. Office of the Commission of Official Languages, Policy Analysis Branch, October 1990: 8.

[62] René Lévesque *et al.*, *An Option for Quebec* (Toronto: McClelland & Stewart, 1968): 7.

5 | Regionalism: Co-operation and Conflict

Canada is a land of vast size and startling contrasts. Its millions of square miles touch three oceans and take in radically different climatic areas, zones of vegetation, and physical formations. The forms of political life vary across Canada in equally startling ways. Issues, attitudes, life styles, leadership types, and political parties differ from one region to another. As of 1978, for example, the NDP (and its predecessor the CCF) had held power for twenty-eight of the previous thirty-five years in Saskatchewan and for eight of the previous ten years in Manitoba. Yet this same party had never won a single parliamentary seat in four of the five provinces east of Ontario.[1] The vast regional differences in political life cannot be ascribed to geography or vegetation, at least not directly. The political character of any region is moulded by the historical drama that has been played out on its stage.

We must start our analysis by noting what has been pointed out many times before: Canada began as an outpost of the competing empires of France and Britain. Finally winding up in British hands, it found itself threatened almost immediately as the new nation to the south began to grow and expand. Each of the original provinces developed economically as a separate colony and incorporated different traditions into its political culture. In each, development was shaped by imperial needs at the time and the presence of hinterland resources or 'staples' available for export to the European metropolis and to the United States.[2] Different environments combined with different technologies and opportunities to produce distinct regional economies. The fishing economy of Newfoundland had little connection with the timber economy of nearby New Brunswick. Agriculture in southern Ontario and Quebec sustained the fur trade farther west but it was quite distinct and self-sufficient as well. In the twentieth century wheat and to a lesser extent pulp, mineral, and energy resources came to dominate Canadian development. The east-west linkage forged by the staple trade in fur, timber, and wheat weakened. New north-south patterns appeared, linking Canadian regions to the United States and encouraging balkanization within Canada.

At this stage, large parts of the economy came under direct foreign ownership. As particular exporting regions rose or fell in economic importance, their prominence in the nation's politics did likewise. Some regions became very rich and powerful while others declined. Always the international demand for particular staples, not the wishes of Canadians, had the most important impact on which regions would develop, and when, and how. Thus in the 1970s Alberta grew prosperous and politically important as the price of oil increased. Efforts of the federal government to improve the economy in other, poorer regions suffered as a result. Higher prices for oil and gas came to enrich Alberta while the economy of the vulnerable Atlantic provinces languished. Just as the Liberal government moved to curb Alberta's profits through the National Energy Program, oil prices fell and Alberta's fortunes turned from boom to bust. In the following decade, central Canada (particularly Ontario) was running at full capacity economically while the other regions were still recovering from recession. Federal economic policies geared to the overheated Ontario economy were widely resented as inappropriate for the West and the Atlantic.

TABLE 5.1   SOME CHARACTERISTICS OF THE REGIONS OF CANADA, 1986

	POPULATION		AREA		DENSITY
	No.	%	Km^2	%	Per Km^2
CANADA	25,309,331*	100%	9,203,210	100%	2.8
Newfoundland	568,349	2.2	371,635	4.0	1.5
New Brunswick	709,442	2.8	71,569	.7	9.9
Nova Scotia	873,176	3.4	52,841	.5	16.5
Prince Edward Island	126,646	.5	5,660	.05	22.4
Quebec	6,532,461	25.8	1,357,812	15.4	4.8
Ontario	9,101,694	35.9	916,734	10.7	9.9
Manitoba	1,063,016	4.2	547,704	5.9	1.9
Saskatchewan	1,009,613	3.9	570,113	6.2	1.8
Alberta	2,365,825	9.3	638,233	6.9	3.7
British Columbia	2,833,367	11.4	892,677	9.5	3.2
Territories	52,238	.2	3,246,389	.35	
Yukon	23,504	.1	531,844	5.7	

Sources: 1986 Census, Profiles Census Divisions and Subdivisions for Each Province, Table 1 in each.

Throughout Canadian history, politicians have repeatedly tried to correct the economic disparity that underlies regional discontent. The extent of popular or élite support for such efforts toward equalization is 'impossible to gauge with any accuracy'.[3] Yet subsidies and transfer payments have often been used to equalize the regions. Indeed, the British North America Act itself spelled out the amounts the federal treasury was to pay individual provinces for entering

Confederation. Arranging for such fiscal transfers was of central importance in hammering out the original 'federal bargain'. Later, such payments helped to get Prince Edward Island and Newfoundland to enter Confederation as well. Regional disparities have been discussed at countless dominion-provincial conferences, and have occasioned numerous commissions of inquiry, the most influential of which was the Royal Commission on Dominion-Provincial Relations, appointed by Prime Minister Mackenzie King in August 1937. The Depression had burdened the provinces with expenses that far exceeded the revenues to which they were entitled under the BNA Act. This 'gulf' between assigned responsibilities and available revenues created a fiscal crisis for Canadian federalism, made worse by the vast discrepancy between provinces in overall wealth and level of economic development.

The Commission's 'Rowell-Sirois Report',[4] which diagnosed and prescribed treatment for Canada's ailing body politic, has become a landmark document. The commissioners found that the fiscal crisis was a product of public policy, economic change, and constitutional rigidity. To resolve it would require transferring large doses of federal funds to various provinces to enable them to discharge adequately their constitutionally defined duties. Tax equalization, unconditional federal grants, and regional development programs became increasingly important aspects of federal policy.

After the Second World War the federal government set up many agencies—among others the Atlantic Development Board, the Agricultural Rehabilitation and Development Agency (ARDA), and the Cape Breton Development Corporation—to reduce regional disparities in income, employment, and living conditions. Yet a government study in 1968 found that these agencies had only managed to prevent inter-regional gaps from widening even further. Much greater effort would be needed, the report continued, to reduce them.

In 1969, the federal government established a Department of Regional Economic Expansion (DREE) to foster co-operation in regional economic development. Aimed especially at helping the poorest regions of the country, DREE would oversee federal economic policies for all of the Atlantic provinces and certain areas of central Canada and the West. One year after accepting this newly created portfolio, the Hon. Jean Marchand summed up the government's philosophy of 'co-operative regionalism': 'A nation is nothing, it will not survive unless its parts can see their problems, and their solutions, in a national context; unless the federal government can and does act to assist in the solution of regional problems.'[5]

As frequently happens in politics, however, DREE's main achievements were symbolic—appearing to address a significant problem, symbolizing in words and names a commitment to equality. DREE failed to bring about any significant change in regional inequality. Tables 5.1 and 5.2 show that the regions are still very unequal, in spite of DREE's best efforts. As in 1927 so in 1976, per capita income in the richest province was almost twice that of the poorest.

The proportion had shrunk slightly by 1989, but it was still well over half as great. Unemployment rates varied among regions by a factor of almost three in 1976, just as in 1950. By the late 1980s, the rate in Newfoundland was more than three times higher than in Ontario.

TABLE 5.2   LEVEL OF PERSONAL INCOME PER CAPITA, BY PROVINCE*(IN CURRENT DOLLARS)

	YEAR			
PROVINCE	1927	1947	1976	1984
Ontario	509	981	5,559	16,433
Alberta	509	923	5,066	15,739
Quebec	378	709	4,505	14,168
British Columbia	535	980	5,374	13,723
Manitoba	455	875	4,733	13,339
Saskatchewan	499	818	4,702	12,534
Nova Scotia	299	676	3,990	11,960
New Brunswick	277	609	3,702	11,244
Prince Edward Island	248	477	3,274	10,796
Newfoundland	—	—	3,319	10,288
Average for Provinces	407	783	4,966	14,924

*Provinces are ranked in order of level of personal income per capita in 1984, and the data are for three-year averages centred on the year shown. Data for British Columbia include the Yukon and Northwest Territories in 1927 and 1947.

Sources: Based on data from Dominion Bureau of Statistics. Table published in Economic Council of Canada, *Second Annual Review*: Ottawa, December 1965: 101; 1976 statistics in Paul Fox, *Politics: Canada*, Toronto: McGraw-Hill Ryerson, 1977: 103; 1984 statistics, *Annual Estimates* 1977-1988: 40, Table 37.

In 1982 the Trudeau Liberals restructured DREE and gave it a new mandate. It was combined with the Department of Industry Trade and Commerce and re-named the Department of Regional Industrial Expansion (DRIE). Five years later, the Mulroney Conservatives transformed it again, this time folding in the Ministry of State for Science and Technology and calling it the Department of Industry Science and Technology (DIST). Under this reorganization, the responsibility for regional economic development was hived off and given to various new agencies including the Atlantic Canada Opportunities Agency (ACOA), The Western Diversification Office (WDO) and FEDNOR, which focused on development in Northern Ontario.[6] The many efforts to correct Canadian regional disparities reflect the existence of what Herschel Hardin calls the 'redistribution culture'. Its central 'ethic of redistribution' expresses the Canadian belief that justice requires the rich provinces to help out the poorer ones. So fundamental is this ethic to Canadian political culture that Hardin describes it as part of our national identity. It stands in contrast to American-style egalitarianism, which redistributes people to new sources of wealth. (Go west, young man!) The Canadian approach instead redistributes wealth to people, under the guise of 'bizarre locutions like "equalization payments" and "regional disparities"', terms as rich in meaning and tradition for Canadians as 'Remember the Alamo' is for Americans.

TABLE 5.3   UNEMPLOYMENT RATES, CANADA AND REGIONS, 1950-89 (SELECTED YEARS)

			PROVINCE OR REGION			
YEAR	ATLANTIC	QUEBEC	ONTARIO	PRAIRIES	BRITISH COLUMBIA	CANADA
1950	7.8	4.4	2.4	2.1	4.4	3.6
1954	6.6	5.9	3.8	2.5	5.2	4.5
1958	12.5	8.8	5.4	4.1	8.6	7.0
1962	10.7	7.5	4.3	3.9	6.6	5.9
1966	6.4	4.7	2.5	2.1	4.5	3.6
1968	7.3	6.5	3.5	2.9	5.9	4.8
1976	11.0	7.9	6.4	4.4	9.8	7.1
1987	16.1	10.3	6.1	8.1	11.9	8.8
1989	13.1	9.3	5.1	7.7	9.1	7.5

Sources: Dominion Bureau of Statistics, *Labour Force Survey* (Annual); 1976 Statistics in Fox, 1977: 102; Statistics Canada, *Canadian Economic Observer* Historical Statistical Supplement: 106, Table 12.5.

When the redistribution culture is 'healthy', regional equality is supported with little hesitation and few complaints, because 'to question redistribution is to question the existence of Canada itself'. Yet the ethic of redistribution is endangered because it lacks 'popular ideological expression by which Canadians can become aware of the importance of their own existence'. As Canadian mass media become more and more dominated by American popular culture, Canadians increasingly come to see redistribution through American cultural lenses, and view it as a humiliating or totally unnecessary form of 'charity', instead of regarding it as expressing 'solidarity and generosity'.[7]

Regionalism and Political Culture

Hardin's observations raise a much broader issue. As its suffix suggests, regionalism, like other 'isms', involves values, sentiments, and beliefs. The term *regionalism* implies a sense of regional identity, an attachment to one's own region, and usually a belief that it is somehow victimized by other regions or by the larger whole. Thus, Mildred Schwartz states that

> we associate 'regionalism' with situations of politically relevant divisiveness and territorial cleavages, often accompanied by some consciousness on the part of the residents that they have distinctive, regionally based interests.[8]

It is this subjective element of awareness that leads to the overt political problems implied by the term regionalism. To describe regionalism as an ideology would be an exaggeration, but it is an important aspect of political culture: the politically relevant values, attitudes, beliefs, and symbols that exert an unseen but crucial influence on the political life of a society. Political culture helps shape the outlook and discourse of both ordinary citizens and political leaders. It affects the way they react and talk to one another, the problems they consider politically significant, the kinds of solutions and government policies deemed legitimate. When regional identities, allegiances, and grievances are embedded in a society's political culture—especially among the political élite—residents and political leaders of different regions will perceive political problems and priorities differently. Thus, when oil prices became an issue in the federal elections of 1979 and 1980, Westerners (particularly Albertans) saw higher prices as both economically necessary and a matter of simple fairness. Ontarians, by contrast, viewed this attitude as sheer greed and selfishness on the part of the 'blue-eyed Arabs'. These contradictory outlooks demonstrate the strength of regionalism in Canadian political culture. So deeply rooted are these concerns that the Pepin-Robarts Task Force on Canadian Unity observed:

> To many foreign observers, the fact that Confederation is widely evaluated from the particular point of view of how given provinces have fared over the years is a remarkable feature of Canadian life. In other countries, cleavages such as social class, religion, race, or creed have been of decisive importance to the collective lives of citizens. In Canada, how much the people of any given province have participated in the benefits of the federation, or shared its losses, has been at the forefront of our politics.[9]

What is a region? If regionalism connotes the subjective elements, the concept of a region at first appears much more objective. Ralph Matthews is explicit on this point: 'Region and regionalism refer to the *objective* and *subjective* aspects of the same phenomenon.'[10] Although geographers use the term region to refer to an area with distinctive natural characteristics—usually physical—that differentiate it from surrounding areas, political boundaries have a way of overwhelming natural boundaries, so that geographic regions have little relevance to the political phenomenon of regionalism.

Nevertheless, regionalism is affected by a number of objective factors, and we must therefore examine its structural underpinnings: aspects of the economy, settlement patterns, and other demographic patterns that reinforce territorially based cleavages in Canadian society. These latent divisions become political forces through a process of political socialization and as a result of the activities of political élites and institutions.

Precisely how all these factors are linked together has never been unequivocably established, although several detailed models have been proposed and several competing paradigms of analysis continue to vie for supremacy.[11] For our purposes, it is sufficient to use a rather crude distinction between the environment within which political institutions operate and the institutions themselves. On this basis we can examine the structural aspects of the environment that contribute to or sustain regionalism and then go on to consider the role of political institutions and political culture.

The Structural Underpinnings of Regionalism

Economic Factors
As mentioned at the beginning of this chapter, the various regions of Canada have historically had different economic bases. Efforts to integrate the regions into the national economy have had some limited success, but regional differences persist. Manufacturing has become the economic mainstay of Central Canada; agriculture and, more recently the petroleum industry and potash of the Prairies; forestry and mining of British Columbia; fishing of the Atlantic region; precious metals in the North. Thus, each region has a unique set of economic interests and has experienced markedly different economic fortunes: Unemployment rates, income per capita, and the structure of the economy vary enormously as one moves across the country. Furthermore, these varying economic bases have generated conflicting political interests that have inhibited the development of an overall economic policy for the country. By the 1970s, the various provincial governments had begun to adopt policies more appropriate to independent countries than to the parts of a supposedly unified national economy. In some instances, provincial governments actively discouraged trade with out-of-province suppliers or manufacturers, attempted to prevent nonresidents of the province from owning land or taking certain kinds of jobs, and manipulated sales taxes to favour local products. These practices continued throughout the next decade. Indeed, as a recent report on economic co-operation in the Maritimes pointed out, 'In an era of U.S.-Canada free trade, Canadian provinces have been remarkably adept at turning a blind eye to the obvious and pervasive system of interprovincial barriers restricting interprovincial trade. Few Canadians realize the sheer pervasiveness of these interprovincial barriers . . .'.[12]

The balkanization of Canada's political economy has been worsened by economic pressure and penetration from the United States. The boundary between the two countries artificially severs geographic regions that have as much potential for economic coherence as the national economy. As long as the railway dominated transportation, the east-west linkages were the most powerful.

However, beginning in the 1930s, trucking and airlines strengthened north-south linkages and therefore helped tie each province or region of Canada to its American neighbour. These tendencies were reinforced by the Auto Pact in the 1960s and the Free Trade Agreement of 1988. Continental integration of this kind occurs at the expense of national integration. The more provinces look south for markets, finances, products, and services, the less opportunity exists for strong national economic policies or for political arrangements that could complement them. Finally, recent modernization and industrialization, far from helping nationalize the Canadian economic élite, have given birth to a new middle class strongly committed to the interests of the provincial governments, particularly in Quebec and Alberta. This new middle class was a major force behind the Quiet Revolution and the emergence of the Parti Québécois, and provided the backbone of the Alberta Conservative Party in the past two decades. These groups have used provincial state enterprise as an effective instrument for the expansion of provincial wealth and power. Although the political energy generated by these groups has not yet resulted in a successful separatist movement in either province (though separation is looming ever larger in Quebec), it is a crucial underpinning of provincial power and assertiveness and has put a razor-sharp economic edge on provincial-federal conflicts.

Fragment Origins
The first chapter of this book discussed Louis Hartz's theory that the culture and institutions of societies founded by immigration are significantly and permanently affected by the early settlers. Because these groups represented but fragments of the larger European whole, they introduced to the new society a particular cultural and ideological slice of Europe. Isolation from their home culture allowed these fragment groups to experience a different pattern of development.

Applying the fragment hypothesis to settlement within Canada, one immediately detects a source of regional variation. Each region of Canada has had a different fragment origin. Thus, the Maritimes were settled partly by migration from Europe but mainly by a wave of American colonists and Loyalists who moved north in the late eighteenth century. Newfoundland was founded by English and French settlers associated with the fishing trade, who settled as early as the seventeenth century, followed by a wave of nineteenth-century Irish immigration. Quebec was founded by francophone immigrants who came here in the seventeenth and eighteenth centuries from a parent culture that was largely feudal. Ontario was settled by an influx of Loyalists immediately following the American Revolution and then by British immigrants during the early nineteenth century. Manitoba was initially a bicultural society settled both by anglophones from Ontario and by francophones from Quebec; it received Central-European immigrants in the latter part of the nineteenth century and the early part of the twentieth century. Of the many different ethnic groups that settled in Saskatchewan and Alberta, a number retained their own languages until very recently. Alberta was also strongly influenced by nineteenth- and twentieth-century American immigrants. British Columbia has absorbed several immigrant groups, including the Chinese and Japanese, but was most influenced by British settlers, again in the late nineteenth and early twentieth centuries. The North—the only region where the aboriginal population remains high in proportion to the non-aboriginal 'settlers'—grew most dramatically during the gold rush at the turn of the century.

TABLE 5.4   ETHNIC ORIGINS/PROVINCIAL DISTRIBUTION, 1986

	BRITISH	FRENCH	B & F COMBINED	B OR F & O	OTHER
Canada	33.6	24.4	4.6	12.6	24.6
Newfoundland	88.9	2.0	4.3	3.0	1.5
Prince Edward Island	69.1	8.9	12.1	6.7	3.2
Nova Scotia	62.7	6.2	9.3	13.1	8.7
New Brunswick	46.9	33.3	10.0	6.6	3.2
Quebec	5.9	78.6	2.7	2.7	10.1
Ontario	43.9	5.9	5.7	14.3	30.2
Manitoba	29.6	5.3	3.4	17.7	44.0
Saskatchewan	29.9	3.4	2.8	22.5	42.4
Alberta	34.4	3.3	3.9	22.3	36.1
British Columbia	41.8	2.4	3.7	19.6	32.5

Source:1986 Census—*Tours on Canada*, Pamela White 'Ethnic Diversity in Canada': Ch. 1 Table 1.

Note the large category of British or French combined with other ethnic groups. This would explain why in some circumstances the 'Other' category has grown some in size as ethnic groups have intermarried and offspring claim combined backgrounds.

Given the diversity of the cultural backgrounds of these founding groups, it is not surprising that each region appears to have unique and distinctive cultural traits. This diversity is a source of richness. Socially, it has resulted in wide variations in culture and lifestyle, reflected in such things as divorce rates and crime rates. Politically it has created a series of settings in which the various political cultures have played out different policy scenarios. The diversity of Canadians' backgrounds has made it difficult for an overarching national political culture to emerge. The Western provinces have spawned third parties with distinctive ideological perspectives. As the next chapter will show, Western voters have tended to vote much more along class lines than voters in the rest of the country. Consequently, the traditional parties have had much more difficulty attracting voters in the Prairies than, for example, in Ontario. In most federal elections, the (combined) percentage of the popular vote won by the Liberal and Conservative parties has been lower in the West than in Ontario. Often these two parties have received less than two-thirds of the Western popular vote.

Demographic Patterns
One force that tends to erode regional difference is interregional migration. Whatever their historical origins, people tend to change their perspective and acculturate to the outlook of their friends and neighbours when they move to another province. But throughout Canadian history, the amount of interregional migration has been relatively small, particularly when compared with that of the United States. Most American college students prefer to attend college away from home, often in a different region of the country entirely. Their first job may take them to yet another region, and they have little compunction about changing residence if the opportunity for a better job arises. Canadians, by contrast, tend to go to university in their home town or at an out-of-town university in their own province. They rarely venture to a different region for post-secondary education, or for employment purposes afterwards. In 1981, for example, only about 8% of Canadian university students and 3% of community college students moved to another province for their education. After graduation there was slightly more inter-provincial movement, with about 12% of university and 5% of community college students changing provinces. (Some of these, however, moved back to their home province.)[13]

This lack of demographic mobility in Canada has reinforced historical regional differences. Canadians tend to live and die in the province or region in which they were born. The 1971 Census showed that approximately 90% of native-born Canadians living in provinces east of Alberta had been born in the province in which they lived. Though somewhat lower, the comparable figures for Alberta (75%) and British Columbia (63%) still constituted a majority. A study of Canadian migrants between 1966 and 1971 showed that only about 5% of all Canadians moved to another province. Ontario and Quebec seemed to serve as a buffer zone between western and eastern migrants. Only a small minority of migrants from the Atlantic provinces moved west of Ontario and very few migrants from the west moved east of Ontario. Thus, the most geographically remote regions of the country have had very little exchange of population.

During the 1970s, these interprovincial migration patterns changed considerably as a result of several factors, especially the economic boom in the West. For example, the percentage of out-migrants from the Atlantic provinces who headed to the West nearly doubled between 1970 and 1979. In that year more Atlantic residents moved to the West than to other Atlantic provinces. However, the reverse pattern of migration (from the West to the Atlantic provinces) changed very little over the course of the decade.

TABLE 5.5 NET MIGRATION FLOWS 1961-1986

	ANNUAL NET FLOWS[a]				
	1961-66	1966-71	1971-76	1976-81	1981-86
Between Atlantic and					
Quebec	-1,105	672	2,236	8,052	3,633
Ontario	-11,239	-9,514	5,393	-1,298	-13,288
Prairies[b]	-362	-220	139	-3,940	-223
Alberta	-526	-966	-727	-30,088	1,928
British Columbia	-1,001	-1,548	-911	-9,225	-13
Total[c]	-14,197	-11,620	6,001	-37,345	-8,155
Between Quebec and					
Atlantic	1,105	-672	-2,236	-8,052	-3,633
Ontario	-4,497	-19,309	-9,388	-101,519	-67,772
Prairies[b]	176	-74	-314	-3,700	-1,338
Alberta	-53	-1,351	-1,511	-27,208	-3,384
British Columbia	-704	-2,953	-2,063	-15,732	-3,198
Total[c]	-3,9272	-24,547	-15,522	-156,498	-79,320
Between Ontario and					
Atlantic	11,239	9,514	-5,393	1,298	13,228
Quebec	4,497	19,309	9,388	101,519	67,772
Prairies[b]	1,980	4,163	114	-9,847	5,122
Alberta	869	-289	-4,895	-99,581	26,206
British Columbia	-1,864	-2,671	-6,729	-49,493	9,801
Total[c]	17,074	30,142	-7,712	-57,826	122,061
Between Prairies[b] and					
Atlantic	362	220	-139	3,946	223
Quebec	-176	74	314	3,700	1,338
Ontario	-1,980	-4,163	-114	9,847	5,122
Alberta	-5,441	-10,227	-8,229	-42,902	+73
British Columbia	-5,976	-9,965	-4,989	-26,423	-3,200
Total[c]	-13,113	-24,418	-13,516	-51,930	-6,391
Between Alberta and					
Atlantic	526	966	727	30,088	-1,928
Quebec	53	1,351	1,511	27,208	3,384
Ontario	-869	289	4,895	99,581	-26,206
Prairies[b]	5,441	10,227	8,229	42,902	-73
British Columbia	-5,668	-6,243	-3,635	-18,193	-6,216
Total[c]	-397	6,401	11,714	186,314	-29,319
Between British Columbia and					
Atlantic	1,001	1,548	911	9,225	13
Quebec	704	2,953	2,063	15,732	3,198
Ontario	1,864	2,671	6,729	49,493	-9,801
Prairies[b]	5,976	9,965	4,989	26,423	3,200
Alberta	5,668	6,243	3,635	18,193	6,216
Total[c]	15,549	22,993	18,457	121,595	4,226

[a] This table outlines differences in interregional migration. A postive figure indicates that more people came to the indicated region from the sub-region than went from that region to the sub-region. A negative figure, of course, indicates the opposite. For example, in 1961-66 an average of 1,105 more people moved from the Atlantic region to Quebec than moved eastward from Quebec to the Atlantic region than in the opposite direction.
[b] Includes Manitoba and Saskatchewan.
[c] Total migration figures include persons moving to and from the Northwest and Yukon Territories.
Source: Statistics Canada , Catalogue 91-208, *International and Interprovincial Migration in Canada*, 1977 and 1978, and Demography Division, unpublished estimates; table from *Social Trends* Autumn 1987, p. 25.

The West was a popular destination for migrants from Ontario as well. In 1970-71, more than 21,000 Ontarians moved to Quebec, fewer than 17,000 to British Columbia, and fewer than 9,000 to Alberta. By the end of the decade, Ontario migration to Quebec had fallen less than 16,000, while migration to British Columbia rose above 22,000 and migration to Alberta more than quadrupled to over 36,000. In percentage terms, Quebec's share of Ontario out-migration fell from 26.1 to 14.4, while Alberta's share rose from 10.8 to 32.7. British Columbia's share stayed about the same at 20.5. Ontario remained the most popular destination for migrant Quebeckers, attracting at least 60% of them throughout the decade. It was widely believed that anglophone Que-beckers left the province in droves during the late 1970s and early 1980s, disillusioned by the restrictive, pro-francophone language policies of the Quebec nationalist Parti Québécois, which held power until 1985. However, although some large companies moved their head offices—with much publicity—from Montreal, Quebec out-migration figures for the years after 1976 are very similar to those for the first half of the decade. What did change was the number of Canadians moving to Quebec from other provinces; this figure fell about 20%.

TABLE 5.6	PER CENT OF LANGUAGE DISTRIBUTION BY PROVINCE, 1986		
	ENGLISH	FRENCH	OTHER
Canada	62.1	25.1	12.8
Newfoundland	98.8	.5	.8
Prince Edward Island	94.1	4.7	1.2
Nova Scotia	93.8	4.1	2.1
New Brunswick	65.3	33.5	1.3
Quebec	10.4	82.8	6.8
Ontario	78.0	5.3	16.7
Manitoba	73.4	4.9	21.8
Saskatchewan	81.9	2.3	15.7
Alberta	82.3	2.4	15.3
British Columbia	82.1	1.6	16.3

Source: 1986 *Census Focus on Canada, a Statistical Profile*: Chapter 1, Table 1.

National migration figures for the 1980s show a few significant changes but the overall pattern has remained constant. Only about 6% of Canadians moved from one region to another. Ontario gained most from this movement, while all other provinces except British Columbia lost residents. The biggest absolute decline was in Quebec, which lost nearly 80,000 residents. Proportionally, however, the biggest shifts occurred in Alberta, which lost more than 20% of its population while attracting almost as many new residents from other parts of the country.

Another important source of demographic change in Canada is immigration. Approximately one Canadian in seven was born outside the country, a ratio that has stayed relatively constant for the past forty years. Very few of these immigrants have settled in the Atlantic provinces or Quebec. Indeed, for the period 1951 to 1971, fewer than 5% of the residents of the Atlantic provinces were foreign-born. Between 5% and 10% of Quebec residents were foreign-born. The comparable figure of the Prairies was close to 20%; for both Ontario and British Columbia it was above 20%. Hence, the ethnic composition of the five provinces east of Ontario is quite different from the rest. (Concern over the number of immigrants to Quebec and the percentage of those who speak French was at the forefront of Quebec demands for a greater role in immigration policy. An agreement on these matters was reached immediately after the failure of the Meech Lake Accord, which would have strengthened the power of all provinces in this area.)

The Political Dimensions of Regionalism

Although regionalism has its roots in the social and economic environment, it is an intensely *political* phenomenon and it must be understood in relation to the political institutions of Canadian federalism. So powerful have these institutions become that some leading political scientists have emphasized what they call a 'state-centred' view of the relationship between the state and Canadian society. Rather than viewing regionalism as the product of social and economic forces, therefore, Alan Cairns argues that 'the support for powerful, independent provincial governments is a product of the political system itself, [and] . . . is fostered and created by provincial government élite employing the policy-making apparatus of their jurisdictions . . . '.[14] Taking maximum advantage of their control of education, for example, provincial political élites have at times actively encouraged the development of provincial political symbols and identity, even at the expense of the national identity. Similarly, provincial economic and social policies have frequently encouraged regional patterns of development. Accordingly, we now shift our attention to Canada's political institutions.

Canadian political institutions are the product of a unique constitutional hybrid; the BNA Act in effect grafted federalism onto a British parliamentary structure.[15] Paradoxically, the Act states that Canada will have a government similar in form and functioning to that of Britain. Yet the British political system is unitary. Britain has no political structures equivalent to Canadian provincial governments. The parliamentary system is not designed to represent territorially based political interests. The power of the British parliament is not circumscribed by a constitution that divides legislative authority between different levels of government. Federalism, however, requires both some form of territorial representation within the national political institutions (intrastate federalism) and a division of power between national and state or provincial government (intrastate federalism) and a division of power between national and state or provincial government (interstate federalism). Furthermore, there appears to be an inverse relationship between these two mechanisms of federalism; the more successfully regional interests are represented within national political institutions, the less regionally based conflict one finds between levels of government.

Although how the Founding Fathers of Confederation viewed federalism varied considerably, the key architect of the BNA Act, Sir John A. Macdonald, was a centralist at heart. With the dramatic and bloody example of the American Civil War before him, he told the Canadian Assembly in 1861:

> The fatal error which [the framers of the United States Constitution] have committed—it was perhaps unavoidable from the state of the colonies at the time of the revolution—was in making each State a distinct sovereignty, in giving to each a distinct sovereign power except in those instances where they were specially reserved by the constitution and conferred upon the general Government. The true principle of a confederation lies in giving to the general Government all the principles and powers of sovereignty, and in the provision that the subordinate or individual States should have no powers but those expressly bestowed upon them.[16]

Centrifugal tendencies could be overcome by putting into practice the 'true principle of confederation'. Giving the provincial governments some power could not be avoided, although doing so compromised the ideal of a unitary government. But by a variety of measures Macdonald hoped to ensure that the provinces would have little more autonomy than municipal councils. As his 1861 statement had insisted, the 'residual power' was supposedly lodged with the federal government. The power to disallow provincial legislation rested with the federal government too. But even this was not enough.

An arrangement known as the 'double mandate' permitted members to sit in both the federal Parliament and in their respective provincial legislatures at the same time. Macdonald felt this would enable politicians committed to a federal point of view to dominate provincial politics. Furthermore, the lieutenant governor appointed to each province was expected to represent the federal government. In order to keep the provinces from trespassing on federal power and prerogative, the lieutenant governor was given the power to withhold approval of provincial bills pending review by the federal cabinet.

Judging by what they intended and what they accomplished, 'the constitution-makers of 1867 took as their pattern not the American federal system, but rather the British Empire in which Ottawa replaced London and the provinces assumed the role of colonies.'[17] These arrangements gave the federal government the weightiest role. In theory the BNA Act created, at best, a 'quasi-federal state'.

However, theory and practice rarely go hand in hand. What the Fathers of Confederation had so sincerely intended counted for very little in the political and constitutional free-for-all of the next decades.

Efforts were made to govern strongly from the centre. Some predicted that the provincial governments would soon atrophy. However, a number of factors ensured that provincial institutions would survive, and would continue to focus local identities and aspirations. Indeed, the two most powerful agencies of political socialization—schools and political parties—continued to be controlled and directed by the province. 'Party politics tended to make the local governments a weapon against the central government. . . . Party politics established the nucleus about which would soon cluster the old provincial loyalties.'[18]

The movement toward Confederation had been rather quiet, negotiated by the élite over a period of several years and lacking in strong local support. Unable to attract Prince Edward Island or Newfoundland, Confederation even occasioned a display of black crepe by some residents of the other two Maritime provinces, and prolonged efforts in Nova Scotia to have the marriage annulled. In the words of one historian, 'New Brunswick was pushed into Union, Nova Scotia was dragooned into it, and Newfoundland and Prince Edward Island were subjected to all the pressure that could be brought to bear—short of force—and still refused.' The events leading up to Confederation, and its aftermath, attracted public interest, some of it favourable. But by and large, 'Confederation was not, except in Canada West, what is usually referred to as a popular movement. It was imposed on British North America by ingenuity, luck, courage and sheer force.'[19] Confederation had failed to inspire patriotic enthusiasm for the new nation brought into existence by a legal-sounding document that began unmusically, 'Whereas the Provinces of Canada, Nova Scotia and New Brunswick . . .'.

Even before Confederation, the way the BNA Act proposed to divide up powers roused ire in all of the provinces. J.E.B. Dorion bluntly stated the objections of many:

> I am opposed to the scheme of Confederation because the first resolution is nonsense and repugnant to truth; it is not a Federal union which is offered to us, but a Legislative union in disguise. Federalism is completely eliminated from this scheme, which centres everything in the General Government. Federalism means the union of certain states, which retain their full sovereignty in everything that immediately concerns them, but submitting to the General Government questions of peace, of war, of foreign relations, foreign trade, customs and postal service. Is that what is proposed to us? Not at all. In the scheme we are now examining, all is strength and power in the Federal Government; all is weakness, insignificance, annihilation in the Local Government.[20]

Critics who objected to the way the constitution centralized power were not about to give up struggling for greater provincial rights after the British North

America Act was passed. The leading figure in what historians later called the 'provincial rights movement' was the Liberal premier of Ontario, Oliver Mowat. As it turned out, Mowat and his colleagues helped convince the Judicial Committee of the Privy Council, which up until 1949 was the court of final appeal on constitutional matters, to weaken the clause by which Macdonald's associates believed they had irrevocably lodged residual power with the federal government. Likewise the federal government's power to disallow provincial legislation fell gradually into disuse.[21] The role of the lieutenant governor was redefined in law to prevent his acting on behalf of the federal government. Even the dual mandate arrangement was soon abolished.

Powers held by the provincial governments proved anything but the 'weakness, insignificance, annihilation' advocates of provincial rights had feared. For unwittingly, the Fathers of Confederation had given up to the provinces control over precisely those areas of policy that would later, in the era of the 'positive state', become the most significant. These areas include health, resources, education, and welfare.

Macdonald's critics took advantage of these changes from the beginning. They used the provincial capitals as bases from which to oppose his policies and the fortunes of the Conservative Party. 'In the first decade after 1867 political lines became clearly drawn, and much of the debate centred on questions of federal supremacy and provincial rights.' In Nova Scotia, all but two of the thirty-eight members elected in the 1867 provincial election were anti-Confederates. The following year the Provincial Legislature went so far as to declare the BNA Act 'unconstitutional and in no way binding' on the people of the province because they had not been adequately consulted in its preparation.[22]

Ever since Confederation, the federal Government has wavered between leading the nation and bargaining piecemeal with the provinces. The fluctuation has reflected changes in the health of the economy and changes in Canada's involvements abroad. Domestic political considerations, such as a minority government in Ottawa, weakness within the governing party, and the fiscal well-being of various governments, have also had an effect.

The Depression and Canada's heavy involvement in the Second World War seriously challenged government and increased the centralization of power in Canada. Writing afterward, in the late 1940s, James Corry and J.E. Hodgetts confidently predicted that the federal government would continue to grow in strength and prosperity to meet the national demands of advanced capitalism. Yet by the mid-1960s, events had already proved them wrong. Edwin Black and Alan Cairns then proposed a 'different perspective', which foresaw the exercise of much greater power by the provincial governments.[23] Their perspective soon became the new orthodoxy; nevertheless, provincial governments still faced problems that called for national co-ordination. Depending heavily on one another, the federal and provincial governments began to develop a dense network of agencies and relationships that Donald Smiley has called 'executive federalism'.[24] New ministries of intergovernmental affairs were set up in Ottawa and in nearly every province to sort out these new relationships.

The means of co-ordinating federal-provincial relations range widely in their splendour, from workaday committees discussing specific policies to lofty, highly publicized meetings of first ministers. Recognizing the increased clout of the provinces, political scientists began to describe intergovernmental activities in the language of international policies. They refer to 'summit conferences' and to the process of federal-provincial 'diplomacy'.[25] And, as with international diplomacy, interprovincial relations are often volatile and deeply troubled.

Regionalism and Federalism

For several reasons, federalism tends to stimulate regional distinctness despite the efforts of federal governments to unify the nation. First, federalism reminds the citizen of their dual political status and identity. Indeed, citizens of the United States are referred to in law as citizens of the state wherein they reside. Canadian practice does not make this dual citizenship explicit and refers instead to 'citizens' of Canada and 'residents' of the provinces. Yet Quebec is quickly and obviously becoming an exception to this rule. Just as they refer to Quebec and Canada as distinct entities, many Quebec nationalists distinguish Québécois (citizens of Quebec) from 'Canadians' (citizens of the other provinces and territories).

The competitive relationship between national and subnational political units encourages politicians to adopt a 'blame it on the other level' approach, tracing all evils and unpleasantness back to policies adopted by the national (or provincial) government.[26] Instead of attempting to defend their record while in office, provincial premiers often wage election campaigns that focus on the wrongs done their provinces by Ottawa and 'the feds' (a term that bespeaks the anger of regionalism).

Though they must work within the parameters established by federal policies, provincial politicians can stimulate a strong provincial economy by regulating transportation, communications, investment, and other processes.[27] In this way federalism allows the provinces autonomy that may weaken national integration. Provinces compete fiercely with one another to attract investors and stimulate expansion. Ironically, as a result of the Free Trade Agreement goods and services can flow more easily across the international border than between the provinces.

When a province emphasizes its own rather than national concerns in educational policy, the provincial point of view—its political culture—gets taught in the schools.[28] And when provinces manipulate the educational process, a provincial rather than a national identity may be bred into young people. This point was graphically illustrated during the 1991 St Jean Baptiste celebration in Montreal, where thousands of Québécois marched with the blue *fleur de lis* flags of

Quebec waving everywhere and countless placards proclaimed 'Notre vrai pays est Québec'.

In Canada, even geography aids regionalism. Few American states are large enough to make up complete ecopolitical systems in themselves. ('The south', for example, comprises at least thirteen separate states.) By contrast, each of the Canadian provinces alone, or combined with two or three others, can contain a whole system. The thinness of population between provincial centres—between Toronto and Winnipeg, or Calgary and Vancouver, for example—also isolates one region from another.

Conflicts between regions help to strengthen regional loyalties at the expense of other loyalties. The chief loss is that of class-consciousness, although other nation-wide loyalties are denied as well. Hence such subordinated people as women, the young, the old, native people, and racial minorities are kept from protesting their unfair treatment as strongly as they might if the nation were more united. By using regional conflict to promote regional loyalties, the élites can sometimes 'divide and conquer' the opposition pushing up from below.[29] The conditions under which such a strategy can succeed in Canada are clearly specified by S.J.R. Noel: 'the lack of a pan-Canadian identity combined with strong regional sub-cultures is not necessarily a dysfunctional feature . . . as long as *within each sub-culture demands are effectively articulated through its political élite* [and provided that there does not emerge] within any one of the provinces an élite who . . . are unwilling to provide "overarching co-operation at the élite level".'[30]

In Quebec a political élite officially and enthusiastically committed to 'sovereignty-association' emerged in the 1970s and expanded its influence after the defeat of Meech Lake, proving the fragility of élite accommodation and consociational democracy in Canada. But Quebec's nationalism is certainly not all that strains Canadian unity. In recent decades the term 'regionalism' has been reserved for strong local loyalties in other regions, particularly the West or the Maritimes.

At this point we need to distinguish between regional integration, or *co-operative* regionalism, and the dynamic of national disintegration, or *conflictual* regionalism. Regionalism as conflict began in Canada even before Confederation. In 1784 the aspirations of the newly arrived Loyalist settlers for regional independence led New Brunswick to break away from Nova Scotia. Upper Canada was carved out of the enormous territory of Quebec in 1791, when its predominantly anglophone residents demanded greater autonomy. Prince Edward Island's reluctance to enter Confederation in 1867, and the western rebellions led by Louis Riel, both challenged Canada's national solidarity. Ontario's Premier Oliver Mowat was a leading advocate of 'provincial rights' in the late nineteenth century. Indeed, at one time or another in Canadian history, just about every part of Canada has considered independence from the whole, though never with lasting results.

Because conflictual regionalism is simply political cleavage based on territory, it can be understood in relation to a general theory of political cleavages. Cleavages may be distinguished as either 'cross-cutting' or 'reinforcing': 'Roughly, cross-cutting cleavages assure that those persons who are divided by one cleavage (say, race) will be brought together by another (say, religion) and vice versa. Reinforcing cleavages, by way of contrast, assure that those who are divided by one cleavage (race) will also be divided by another (religion).'[31]

A conflict's intensity generally increases with the number and importance of reinforcing cleavages. When economic, racial, and religious-linguistic cleavages reinforce the territorial one, extreme conflict should be expected.[32] Imagine, for example, two geographically segregated racial groups, each practising a different religion; one whose members belong to the dominant social class, the other to the subordinate class. The potential for conflict, even internal war, is very great here.

Conflictual Regionalism in Canada

The course of conflict in Canada is hard to predict, for the regional differences are not clear-cut. No one can doubt that economic, linguistic, and ethnic differences do overlap regional cleavages to some extent. Although there are some homogenizing tendencies (notably the spread of American mass culture) that are eroding regional difference, on examination various social indicators such as drug offence rates, suicide rates, and divorce rates reveal considerable variation by province.[33] Economic statistics permit us to separate the 'have' provinces (Ontario, British Columbia, Alberta, and at times the other Prairie provinces) from the 'have nots' (all of the Atlantic provinces and Quebec). The line of separation coincides exactly with the eastern boundary of Ontario. Linguistically, of course, the first fact of Canadian politics is the regional concentration of the French minority, although a significant portion of this minority is found outside Quebec. Paradoxically, recent patterns of interprovincial migration, and the linguistic assimilation of francophones outside Quebec, have combined to increase the territorial segregation of anglophones and francophones in Canada.

Forty years ago, A.R.M. Lower assessed and perhaps even overstated the problem: 'The French-English cleavage is the greatest factor in Canadian life, not only because it is a racial and linguistic cleavage, but because it coincides with an economic cleavage, a legal cleavage, a cultural cleavage, a religious cleavage, and a philosophical cleavage.'[34] Kenneth McRae showed by means of a diagram the extent to which Quebec differs from the other provinces in both its language and religion. So different is it that Quebec seems to stand alone on the page. But other portions of Canada are ethnically distinct as well.

Historical census statistics show that until the last thirty years an ethnic 'mosaic' was most visible in the Prairies; by contrast, the French and British 'charter groups' chiefly populate the other regions of Canada. In 1971, the percentage of persons who were neither British nor French in descent ranged from less than 5% in Newfoundland and Prince Edward Island to over 50% in Saskatchewan. In 1986, over 90% of the population of each of the provinces east of Ontario had French or British ethnic roots. Comparable figures for the other provinces or territories ranged from a high of 70% for Ontario to a low of 36% for the Northwest Territories. Like geography, ethnicity may place a large obstacle in the way of the eastern and western provinces ever really getting acquainted.[35]

Multiple reinforcing cleavages do not invariably produce conflict. Cleavages are necessary for conflict to occur, but conflict also requires an awareness of the cleavages and a sense that regional inequalities are unjust. Like other 'isms', regionalism is cultural, based on a sense of deprivation relative to others. One cannot discuss the political side of regionalism without attending to the beliefs, values, and attitudes prevailing in a region. Only when this cultural factor, this regional awareness, is present—at least among the élite—does a region take on political, and not merely economic or geographical, significance.

Indeed, what people believe is true probably plays a greater part than what really is true in determining the nature and extent of conflict. Do the inhabitants of a certain place identify themselves with their region? Do they believe their region is victimized by other regions? If so, regionalism is likely to burst into conflicts pitting one region against another, or against the nation. Hence, the political culture of regionalism affects politics more directly than even the economics or sociology of regions.

Regional Awareness and Perceived Injustice

Although there is relatively little precise data on people's awareness of region, the 1974 federal election survey contained several useful questions. Responses show that about 60% of Canadians think of the country in regional terms, but not everyone defined region the same way. Some people thought regions exist within their own province. Others saw the region and province as coinciding. Regional awareness was greatest in the West, least in the Maritimes.[36] In general, young, fairly well off, geographically mobile Canadians are somewhat more aware of region than their rural, poorer, less mobile compatriots.

About half of the people in the 1974 survey who 'thought regionally' felt that some provinces carry 'more than their share' of the burdens of Confederation.[37] Such perceptions of regional injustice have long been part of the Canadian political culture. Examples could be taken from almost any region in the country, but for the sake of illustration the experience of the Maritimes and Prairies will suffice. These regions have at times suffered great economic hardship. Politics in these areas are infected by a profound sense of victimization and regional exploitation, much of it justified.

A belief in 'Prairie injustice' has roots that some trace back to the fact that 'the Prairie Provinces were conceived as a sort of colony of Central Canada'.[38] While not all westerners would state their views in such strong language, many think of the West as an exploited colony, victimized by eastern-dominated tariffs and transportation policies. Donald Smiley offered a more moderate, but nonetheless damning, assessment. He noted that 'the relations between the central heartland of Canada and its western hinterland have continued to be regulated by the classic devices and principles of mercantilism.'[39]

Survey data gathered in Alberta during 1968 showed people widely alienated from the federal government. Sixty-one per cent of David Elton's respondents agreed that 'the government in Ottawa is more concerned about the problems of Eastern Canada than they are about the problems of Western Canadians'. Nearly as many agreed that 'the Eastern Canadians receive more benefits than do Western Canadians from being part of the Dominion of Canada'. Yet despite these strong feelings of injustice, Elton found that less than 10% of Albertans supported annexation (to the United States) or secession. (Since 1968, however, several organizations have been set up to promote the independence of one or more western provinces.)[40]

Later surveys conducted by the Canada West Foundation, an organization established by Elton and others, found even higher levels of frustration in the 1980s. For example, in 1983, over 80% of Westerners sampled agreed that 'the West usually gets ignored in national politics because the political parties depend upon Quebec and Ontario for most of their votes'. More than half agreed that 'the West has sufficient resources and industry to survive without the rest of Canada'. And about 30% agreed that 'Western Canadians get so few benefits from being part of Canada that they might as well go it on their own'.[41]

A lack of strong representation in the federal cabinet may have helped to alienate Albertans. Just before the outbreak of the French Revolution, Abbé Sièyes summed up the predicament of the politically powerless French bourgeoisie in these words: 'What is the Third Estate? Everything. What has it been in the government of France? Nothing. What does it want? To become something.' Similar sentiments might help to explain why Crowfoot (Alberta) MP Jack Horner decided to abandon the Conservative Party and take a cabinet position in the Liberal government of Pierre Trudeau. Appointed in 1977 as minister of trade and commerce, Horner was the first Albertan in forty years to hold a major federal portfolio.[42] Partly because the West was for so long inadequately represented in the federal cabinet, provincial politicians (particularly premiers) have taken on the job of defending Western interests. In 1973 an unprecedented conference in Calgary discussed western economic opportunities. Pictured in the Western press as a *High Noon* style 'showdown' between Prime Minister Trudeau and the four western premiers, the conference symbolized the failure of federal politics to reflect western concerns.[43]

The election of the federal Conservatives, with their strong voter support in the West, was expected to end the West's frustrating sense of exclusion from central power. But the rigours of party discipline in a parliamentary system severely restrict the ability of MPs to represent regional interests. Alienation and anger with Ottawa flared up repeatedly once the Conservatives' honeymoon was over. Despite Mulroney's efforts to placate the West in the area of energy (through the Western Energy Accord of 1985), agriculture (through the Western Grain Stabilization Fund), and economic development (through the creation in 1987 of the Department of Western Economic Diversification), Western discontent with the feds was a major factor underlying the formation of the Reform Party in 1987. In the 1988 election, the Mulroney Conservatives won only 56% of the seats in the West, a considerable drop from the 75% they secured four years earlier. In nine of Alberta's 26 constituencies, Reform Party candidates finished second to Conservatives. The following year the Reform Party won the March by-election in Beaver River, and Stan Waters, campaigning under the Reform banner, won a province-wide election to determine who Alberta would nominate for an available Senate seat.[44] Meanwhile Alberta premier Don Getty continued to press hard for constitutional reform that would lead to a 'Triple-E Senate': Elected, Equal, and Effective.

Westerners are not the only ones to feel alienated from the powerful centre. 'Upper Canadians' have long been distrusted in the Maritimes as well. George Rawlyk asserts convincingly that 'Since 1867, two important ingredients in Nova Scotian regionalism have been an often profound dislike of Upper Canada and "Upper Canadians" and also a basic distrust of Confederation itself.'[45] These negative attitudes, Rawlyk continues, almost amount to a 'paranoid style'. Maritimers have tended to blame Ottawa and Toronto exclusively for Nova Scotia's economic and social decline, for example. A century after Confederation, Maritime alienation still remained remarkably strong. An opinion survey of all three provinces, conducted in connection with the Deutsch Commission investigators in 1970, showed that 40% of Maritimers felt they had 'most in common' with Maine, and only 33% 'most in common' with Ontario. Fully one-quarter declared that they 'would be in favour of political union with the United States'. Almost two-thirds favoured closer economic ties with their neighbours to the south.[46]

Negative feelings about Canada appear to have declined in Atlantic Canada. A survey conducted in 1978 under the auspices of the Pepin-Robarts Task Force on Canadian Unity found that 84% of Atlantic respondents felt that overall, Confederation had been 'a good thing' for their province, even though 38% favoured some sort of decentralization of power from Ottawa to the provincial government, and 62% felt that on average, people in Ontario were 'better off' than Atlantic residents 'in terms of their incomes and standard of living'.[47]

Regional alienation is not founded on economic disparity alone, but on disparity seen through a cultural lens that lines up the facts in a particular way. More recent research have clarified the extent of regionalism in Canada's mass political culture. Two considerations are key: the extent of regional identification, the perception of regional injustice. Not surprisingly, the question of identification revolves around provincial rather than regional loyalties, and is typically phrased with explicit reference to *government*. When Canadians are asked to which level of government they feel 'closest', they frequently respond in favour of the province. But when asked how they *identify themselves* in terms of their sense of community, they overwhelmingly respond in favour of Canada.

In part this paradox can be explained by distinguishing, as David Easton suggests, between orientations toward the political incumbents, the political regime, and the system as a whole. For most people questions about federal and provincial governments involve reaction to the incumbents, or at most the regime. Broader questions of identity tap into feelings about the wider community that is Canada.

Those who are reassured that most Canadians think of themselves as Canadians first, and therefore place national ahead of provincial identity, must temper their optimism with the knowledge that regional alienation is still very high. People in the West and the Atlantic feel hard done by Ottawa. Many believe that Quebec gets more than its full share, their province less. Many resent what they see as Ontario's stranglehold on economic policy-making in Ottawa. Decisions to allocate lucrative contracts to one region invariably create bitter resentment elsewhere.

This does not necessarily mean that Westerners or Maritimers want to leave Canada. On the contrary, many Westerners are demanding to be brought *in* more effectively, particularly in terms of the federal government: 'if Ontarians would listen carefully and respectfully to the voice of the West being articulated by the Reform Party, they would discover that many Westerners are being asked to be let in, not out.'[48] The finger of negative regionalism points clearly to the need for reform of our political institutions. But what of regionalism's happier side?

Co-operative Regionalism in Canada: The Extension of Community

Regionalism, like drama, has two faces. Conflictual regionalism, to be sure, wears the frown of tragic anger and sorrow. Co-operative regionalism, however, smiles out at us from the happy union of distinct people who, yet, can share common aspirations, needs, and cultures. Then, already-existing communities come together into a larger whole through 'political decisions made by those who have the authority to commit their communities to collective action.'[49]

A major study of 'the integration of political communities' listed ten factors that foster integration: proximity, homogeneity, transactions, mutual knowledge, functional interest, communal character, political structure, sovereignty, governmental effectiveness, and integrative experiences. Limited space rules out a detailed and systematic application of the complete model to the case at hand. However, the remainder of this chapter will consider the effects upon co-operative regionalism in Canada of political structure, governmental effectiveness, integrative experiences, and to a lesser extent functional interest.

The élitist bias of this approach poses problems on occasion. However, focusing on political decision-makers makes good sense when analysing co-operative regionalism in this country. For regional integration in Canada, at least as we have defined it, is like joining two or more semi-sovereign provinces. The provincial political élites would obviously play a major role in any union of this kind. Understanding the legal mechanics, how unification might develop in constitutional terms,[50] is less germane to our immediate concerns. We want instead to assess the present sociocultural and political potential for regional union.

Analysts as diverse as civil servants and geographers commonly divide Canada into five 'regions'.[51] Three of the usual five regions, Ontario, Quebec, and British Columbia, coincide with already existing provinces. The other two the Atlantic provinces and the Prairies, do not. 'Regional integration' is usually taken to mean a union among two or more of the provinces in this latter category. (At an earlier time in Canadian history, some considered uniting Upper and Lower Canada. No one seriously proposes it today.)

By contrast, 'The Idea of Maritime Union' was the theme of an important conference held at Mount Allison University as late as 1965. 'One Prairie Province?' was the question discussed at an even larger conference held at the University of Lethbridge in 1970. A few weeks after the Maritime Union Conference, the governments of Nova Scotia and New Brunswick established a commission to look into 'the advantages and disadvantages of a union'. In 1968, after the characteristic lapse of three years, Prince Edward Island gave its support to this project. What are the chances for provincial union in these two regions?

Obstacles to unifying the Western provinces are as numerous as they are hard to deny. In a thorough analysis, Norman Ward[52] buried the idea of one Prairie province under a wheat field of objections. How would provinces resolve the differences among their existing civil and property laws, and health, welfare, and labour legislation? What would happen to the already forgotten minorities in the North amidst the chaos following amalgamation? How would provincial governments divide up the responsibility for vastly uneven amounts of public debt? What would be done to reduce or eliminate the inequalities in social services that each province provides? Would Albertans cheerfully agree to pay higher taxes in order to equalize living conditions among the three provinces? Would people in Manitoba and Saskatchewan, on the other hand, accept domination by Calgary or Edmonton any better than they accept the control of Toronto and Ottawa at present? Of the three political parties then in power in the region, which one would triumph in a region-wide election? The distribution of political strength among parties at the time Ward was writing suggested nothing but a series of minority governments in the event of union.

Ward continued, 'Why even attempt formal amalgamation?' In Western Canada no single major ethnic cleavage stands in the way. But this aside, bringing about regional union would probably prove more difficult than Confederation itself. He argued that almost all of the benefits of union can be gained by co-operating on one issue at a time. In spite of popular beliefs to the contrary, Ward judged that an amalgamated government would enjoy no 'economies of scale'. The new regional government would probably add one more layer to an already expensive system of administration, and would require costly additional communication amongst all the component agencies.

Ward's essay leaves the reader doubting that regional integration has any hope of success, let alone an informed group to champion its cause. But the Royal Commission headed by John J. Deutsch to examine the practicality of a Maritime union concluded that the possible benefits of union in that region far outweighed the expected costs. Their *Report*, finally completed in 1970, strongly recommended following a suggested timetable to union within five to ten years.

Several factors may explain why Deutsch's group reached more optimistic conclusions than Ward did. In the first place, the idea of union arose a century earlier in the Maritimes than in the Prairies, going back at least to 1808.[53] The Maritimes take in a smaller area than the Prairies, less than one-third their size. These provinces are also much poorer; the data in Tables 5.1 and 5.2 indicate as much. Perhaps these factors alone are enough to account for the greater degree of co-operation already found among the Maritime provinces. A 1970 inventory found 181 regional organizations operating there—about four times the number in the Prairies at that time. Their activities ranged all the way from academic to agricultural pursuits. Many of these interprovincial organizations have been helped or even created by the federal government. Much of the co-operative regionalism found here and elsewhere is stimulated by a daily search for ways to solve region-wide economic problems.

Undoubtedly, the scope of the economic and social problems that the Maritime provinces suffer in common influenced the Deutsch Commission's recommendations more than anything else. According to the *Report*: 'The economies of the Maritime Provinces are individually too small and too inter-dependent for the effective planning and execution of development programmes in the face of present-day social and technological trends.'[54] Reviewing the alternative courses of action, the Commission found that some of the necessary changes might be achieved through 'informal co-operation'. A great deal might even be accomplished by setting up *ad hoc* agencies to put specific programs into effect. Yet these new agencies would incur additional administrative and overhead costs, while lacking the authority needed to carry out the desired policies. The only way around these obstacles, they concluded, was through a full political union rather than a lower-level administrative or economic union.

In an opinion survey conducted in connection with the *Report*, the commissioners found that a majority of people supported these recommendations. Sixty-four per cent of those responding indicated that they would vote in favour of 'complete union into a single province'. Significantly, opinion varied in similar ways in all three provinces; this had not been true in the Prairies. Almost all of the respondents felt that Maritime union would bring more industry to the region, provide more jobs, help to develop natural resources, and even make the government more efficient. Whether or not these expectations were justified, they were widespread. That is an important political fact in itself. So persuasive were the Commission's findings that the three Maritime provincial premiers moved quickly to follow the timetable that had been set out for them.

By the fall of 1971, the Maritime premiers were already one year ahead of the suggested schedule in a number of important areas. They had, for example, established a Council of Maritime Premiers. By 1977, however, Nova Scotia's Premier Gerald Regan pronounced Maritime Union 'dead as a door nail'. What had happened is not clear. Perhaps the failure to achieve union validates George Rawlyk's judgement that '[Maritimers] seem content to have their disenchantment expressed in words rather than in effective action. Is there any other choice for a dependent, "colonial" society?'[55]

Federal politics put a heavy price on regional union: this fact alone may go far in explaining why the Maritime provinces failed to unite. Party discipline all but prevents American-style regional 'bloc-voting' in Canada's lower House.[56] In the weak Canadian Senate, representation by region will make no difference to these provinces. If anything, they might lose seats. Current arrangements give the Maritimes nearly one quarter of the Senate seats despite their having less than 10% of Canada's population, Furthermore, under present electoral rules, if either the Maritimes or the West were to unify politically, they would lose some seats in Parliament![57] Amalgamation might strengthen the Maritimes or western voice in some Ottawa circles. But it would certainly reduce the region's representation at crucial gatherings such as federal-provincial conferences, which are ordinarily attended by only one official representative from each province (however large or small it may be).

Another obvious point, too often ignored, is that political unification works against the interests of the provincial politicians and civil servants. Integrating would eliminate positions or reduce career opportunities for the very political élite that is taking the decision to unite. In fact, not only does unification eliminate many positions on the lower levels of government (e.g., MPP or MLA); it also reduces the number of high-level posts (such as premier, cabinet minister, and deputy minister) by about two-thirds. Professional politicians or bureaucrats are as unlikely as anyone else to consciously limit their career or to make it more hazardous. So, in their own interest, they will not support regional integration, no matter how strong the pull to social and cultural co-operation. It is not surprising, therefore, that a recent review of the operations of the Council of Maritime Premiers concluded bluntly that 'Maritime Union is not a viable option for the region'.[58]

Conclusion

Two trends, running in opposite directions, will shape the future of Canadian regionalism. One trend is extending the locus of problem-solving beyond the present provincial boundaries. This can already be seen in decisions about economic development and the protection of the environment. Political leaders are finding out that in many policy areas they must co-operate with 'outsiders' if they are to solve their own problems. The other, opposing, trend is toward increased provincial autonomy and opposition to a sprawling, faceless central bureaucracy that often seems insensitive to local concerns.

These contradictory trends are both powerful and compelling: they make predicting the future of regionalism difficult, if not impossible. The first trend—extended to its logical conclusion—would lead smaller political units to combine into larger ones. In Canada this would mean reducing the number of provinces from ten to five and perhaps even fewer. Projecting the second trend, however, leads one to expect central control to decline and subnational units to isolate themselves more than ever. Confederation might break up into ten or more independent nations.

If the trends balance each other, something in between these two projections will result. *Ad hoc* interprovincial agencies will continue to grow more numerous, responding to specific problems that are regional in nature.[59] When provincial governments are unable to agree on ways of dealing with these issues, the federal government may step in to encourage—even compel—them to co-operate. At the same time, however, many obstacles will block the road to regional amalgamation. Despite the impending achievement of European unification, the present prospects for either Maritime union or a single unified Prairie province are almost nil.

The trend toward greater provincial autonomy seems more menacing. The obvious first question is whether Quebec will remain a part of Canada. At the same time, treating the Quebec case as though unique deflects attention from the fact that friction between the regions of Canada (or in any other federally governed country) is a general problem. Our analysis indicates that the conflict arising from regionalism is not limited to Quebec. Although the manifestation of conflict in Quebec is particularly acute, this problem is truly national in scope and has to be solved in the arena of national politics. The Department of Regional Economic Expansion (DREE) and all of its successor ministries and agencies have not given Canada new policy outcomes in this area. Unlike Australia, which has progressively reduced the economic gap between the wealthiest and poorest states, Canada has merely prevented the gap between have and have-not provinces from widening.[60] Ministerial reorganization has merely brought together under one failing administration policies which previously failed under separate administrations.

But the public policy failure is simply the tip of the iceberg; the underlying problem goes much deeper. For Canada's development, particularly in the twentieth century, can be best characterized as 'region building', not 'nation building'.[61] As Pierre Trudeau recognized, 'The advantage as well as the peril of federalism is that it permits the development of a regional consensus based on regional values; so federalism is ultimately bound to fail if the nationalism it cultivates is unable to generate a national image which has immensely more appeal than the regional ones.'[62]

Even today, the Canadian national identity remains confused and uncertain. Contributing to this are the French-English conflict; the fact that one-quarter of Canada's population belongs to ethnic groups other than the 'charter' British and French majority; and the retrogressive legacy of the Loyalist tradition in Canada. Furthermore, the bonds connecting Canadian regions with the United States are at least as strong as the bonds connecting Canadian regions to one another. These factors all stand in the way of 'the transfer of loyalty from the region to the nation'.[63] They are underscored by real and perceived regional injustices, injustices that are not only economic but political as well.

Hence regional discontent results not from policy failure alone, but from structural inadequacies in the federal system. Any attempt at reform must take account of the problem's full magnitude. Until recently, however, Canadians behaved like the Americans de Tocqueville described a century ago, 'infinitely varying the consequences of known principles and . . . seeking for new consequences rather than . . . seeking for new principles'.

Some attempts to reform our political system held out great promise. In June 1978, the federal government released over the prime minister's signature a document outlining proposed changes in Canada's constitution. Entitled *A Time for Action*, the document proposed a timetable with two phases. In Phase I, to be completed by July 1979, the federal government would make the changes it believes it has the power to introduce unilaterally, without the approval of the provinces. Phase II, to be completed by 1 July 1981, would have made more comprehensive reforms with full provincial participation and agreement. Shortly after circulating *A Time for Action*, the federal government introduced into Parliament Bill C-60, and the process of legislating a new constitution began in earnest.

Both the process of this reform and its timing excited controversy. After failing for a half-century to reform and patriate the BNA Act, why try to rush through the first phase in less than a year? critics asked. And why did the federal government presume to act on its own in a matter so vital to other levels of government? These were but two of the criticisms the proposals evoked. After meeting in Saskatoon, the provincial premiers officially objected to unilateral federal legislation in a letter to Prime Minister Trudeau. The prime minister's response again stressed the urgency of the problem, already hinted at in the draft document's title. In his letter to the premiers, dated 13 September 1978, Prime Minister Trudeau declared that the Quebec situation made speed essential. The federal government must act, he said, 'before the electors of Quebec are called upon by their provincial government to choose between political independence . . . and . . . the status quo which the federal and provincial governments have proved incapable of changing despite 51 years of effort'.[64]

If Quebec regionalism dictated the timing of reform, other regional considerations influenced the substance of changes proposed as part of Phase I. After diagnosing the inadequacies of the BNA Act as a constitution for Canada, *A Time for Action* went on to prescribe the following reforms:

(a) a *'Statement of Aims* which would reflect the understanding of what Canada means to all of us';

(b) a *'Charter of Rights and Freedoms'* designed not only to consolidate existing legal guarantees but also to 'establish new rights for Canadian citizens to live and work wherever they wish in Canada, and . . . provide new protection for minority language rights';

(c) a *'House of the Federation'* to replace the existing Senate. Members of this house would be appointed by both the federal government and by individual provinces in order to represent political parties in relation to the percentage of the popular vote each received in the last election;

(d) changing the size and method of appointment to the *Supreme Court of Canada* to give all of the regions more representation and influence;

(e) (in Phase II) changing the *division of powers* between federal and provincial governments to provide more 'effectiveness of government activity' and greater 'harmony in federal-provincial relations';

(f) clarifying the *role of the monarchy* in Canada, by placing slightly greater emphasis on the governor-general's role as head of state rather than as the mere representative of the monarch;

(g) an *amending procedure* that would allow the constitution to be patriated.[65]

What happened to these proposals is of course well known now. Several provinces successfully challenged in the courts the federal government's threats to resort to unilateral action. The Supreme Court indicated that the BNA Act could not be substantially altered without the consent of a significant number (though not necessarily all) of the provinces. In the end, every provincial premier except Quebec's René Lévesque agreed to a formula to patriate the constitution complete with a Charter. The idea of Senate Reform, changes to the monarchy, and reforms in the process of Supreme Court appointments fell by the wayside. The new Constitution even lacked a Statement of Aims. However incomplete, the patriation of the Constitution in 1982 broke the log jam that had prevented major constitutional change for more than a century.

The attempt five years later to tackle further unfinished constitutional reforms through the Meech Lake Accord also seemed very promising. Unanimously endorsed by all provincial premiers on 3 June 1987, the Accord was designed to 'bring about the full and active participation of Quebec in Canada's constitutional evolution'. In response to a series of 'proposals' (actually demands) put forward by Quebec's Premier Bourassa, the Accord contained provisions affecting the method of selecting Senators and Supreme Court justices, clarified important aspects of the division of powers, and tightened the amending formula by requiring unanimous consent in several areas. The Accord also included a phrase that recognized Quebec as a 'distinct society'. The language of the Accord reveals something very significant about the development of regionalism in Canada. Although it arose in response to demands from Quebec, all of the new powers Quebec demanded were extended to each province, except for the role given exclusively to the Quebec government 'to preserve and promote the distinct identity of Quebec'. To critics who favoured a stronger central government, most notably former Prime Minister Pierre Trudeau, these provisions would 'render the Canadian state totally impotent'. But apart from a promise to convene regular federal-provincial conferences, and include on the agenda the topic of Senate Reform, the Accord did little to transform Canadian federalism by strengthening the representation of the regions in the central government. These structural flaws have yet to be remedied.[66]

Notes

[1] By 1991, while still shut out in New Brunswick and Nova Scotia, the NDP had managed to elect one MP in a by-election in Quebec, one in Newfoundland (1979) and one in P.E.I. in 1974 and 1979.

[2] See H.A. Innis, *Essays in the Economic History of Canada, The Fur Trade in Canada*, and other works cited in Chapter 4. See also Janine Brodie, 'The Political Economy of Regionalism,' in Wallace Clement and Glen Williams (eds), *The New Canadian Political Economy* (Kingston, Montreal, London: McGill-Queen's University Press, 1989); Janine Brodie, *The Political Economy of Canadian Regionalism* (Toronto: Harcourt Brace Jovanovitch, 1990); and Robert Brym (ed.) *Regionalism in Canada* (Toronto: Irwin, 1966).

[3] Donald Smiley, *Canada in Question*: 71. For example, one equalization program, begun in 1967, aims to redistribute wealth 'so that all provinces are able to provide to their citizens a reasonably comparable level of basic services, without resorting to unduly burdensome levels of taxation' (Douglas H. Clark quoting Mitchell Sharp, then federal minister of finance, in 'Note on Equalization and Resource Rent', in Anthony Scott, ed., *Natural Resource Revenues: A Test of Federalism* [Vancouver: University of British Columbia Press, 1975]: 108). Because of the mechanics of the equalization formula, the dramatic financial gains made by oil-producing provinces during the 1970s failed to be included properly in calculating their share of the burden of payment to less fortunate provinces. Consequently Ontario was forced to pay disproportionately. See Thomas J. Courchene, 'Equalization Payments and Energy Royalties', in *ibid.*

[4] Donald V. Smiley (ed), *The Rowell-Sirois Report* (Toronto: McClelland & Stewart, 1963). Other commissions that identified regionalism as a key problem for Canada include the Task Force on Canadian Unity (Pepin-Robarts), and the Macdonald Commission, which assessed the three types of approaches Canadians have taken to reducing regional disparities: market adjustments, compensatory policies, and development policies. See the excerpts from Volume II of the Commission *Report* reprinted in Paul Fox and Graham White (eds), *Politics Canada*, 7th ed. (Toronto: McGraw-Hill Ryerson, 1991): 166 ff.

The Report of the Citizens' Forum on Canada's Future (Spicer Commission) found on the other hand that although the 'forces of regionalism have often been portrayed as stronger than, and detrimental to, the forces of unity . . . this . . . is not the case in 1991 for the vast majority of [their] participants—outside Quebec' (p. 46).

[5] Jean Marchand, 'Regional and National Co-operation', in David K. Elton (ed), *One Prairie Province? Conference Proceedings and Selected Papers* (Lethbridge: The University of Lethbridge and the Lethbridge Herald, 1970). For a balanced view of the origins and accomplishments of DREE, see Anthony Careless, *Initiative and Response* (Montreal: McGill-Queen's University Press, 1977), chs. 10 and 11.

[6] See Roger Gibbins, *Conflict and Unity* (Toronto: Methuen, 1990); and 'From DREE to DRIE', Kenneth Kernaghan, 'Representative and Responsive Bureaucracy: Implications for Canadian Regionalism', in Peter Aucoin, *Regional Responsiveness and the National Administrative State* (Toronto: University of Toronto Press, 1985).

[7] Herschel Hardin, *A Nation Unaware* (Vancouver: J.J. Douglas, 1974): 315, 317.

[8] Mildred Schwartz, *Politics and Territory* (Montreal: McGill-Queen's University Press, 1974): 5.

[9] As quoted in Gibbins, *Conflict and Unity*: 101.

[10] Ralph Matthews, *The Creation of Regional Dependency* (Toronto: University of Toronto Press, 1983): 18.

[11] See Schwartz *op.cit.*: 20. Excellent discussions of the different paradigms of analysis that have attempted to account for regional differences appear in Robert Brym's 'introduction' to his edited book *Regionalism in Canada* (Toronto: Irwin, 1987). and Janine Brodie's 'The Concept of the Region in Canadian Politics' in Shugarman and Whitaker, *op. cit.*

[12] Charles McMillan, *Standing Up to the Future: The Maritimes in the 1990's* (Report of the Task Force on Council of Maritime Provinces, n.p., 1989): 30.

[13] See *Social Trends* (Autumn, 1987): 24.

[14] Alan Cairns, 'The Government and Societies of Canadian Federalism', *Canadian Journal of Political Science* 10 (1977): 696.

[15] See Douglas V. Verney, *Three Civilizations, Two Cultures, One State: Canada's Political Traditions* (Durham: Duke University Press, 1986) especially Ch. 4 and 5.

[16] Cited in R. Cook, *Provincial Autonomy, Minority Rights, and the Compact Theory 1867-1921*: 7.

[17] *Ibid.*: 8. The decline of federal power and rise of provincial autonomy closely resembled the changes that were occurring in the relationship between Britain and Canada, as the following passage clearly indicates: 'the office of Governor-General was gradually transformed from that of an imperial official to a symbolic head of state; the power of the British Parliament to disallow Canadian legislation fell into disuse.' Carl Berger, *The Writing of Canadian History* (Toronto: Oxford University Press, 1976): 33.

[18] Peter B. Waite, *The Life and Times of Confederation* (Toronto: University of Toronto Press, 1962): 325.

[19] *Ibid.*: 5, 323. P.E.I. joined Confederation in 1873, but Newfoundland waited for more than three quarters of a century before joining in 1949. Newfoundland voters approved Confederation by a margin of 52% to 48% in a run-off referendum in the summer of 1948. The Confederation option had been actively debated for several years. Of the 48% who voted *against* Confederation in the two referenda, a substantial group helped to apply for union with the United States after first regaining responsible government, which had been removed by Britain in 1933, when the Newfoundland economy collapsed. See David V.J. Bell, 'The Prenegotiation to Confederation in Newfoundland', paper presented to the Canadian Political Science Association Annual Meeting, Victoria, May, 1990.

[20] Cited in Cook: 8.

[21] 'These powers were used 149 times during the first 40 years after 1867, and only 32 times since.' *A Time for Action: Toward the Renewal of the Canadian Federation* (Ottawa: Queen's Printer, 1978): 13. See also Alan Cairns, 'The Judicial Committee and its Critics', *Canadian Journal of Political Science*

4,3 (September 1971).

[22] Cook: 10, 11. Note as well Smiley, *Rowell-Sirois Report*: 71.

[23] E.R. Black and A.C. Cairns, 'A Different Perspective on Canadian Federalism', *Canadian Public Administration* 9,1 (1966): 27-44.

[24] D. Smiley, *Canada in Question*, ch. 3. Note also that no meeting of federal and provincial first ministers took place until 1906, but in the decade from 1968 to 1978, twenty such meetings were held. This pattern continued throughout the 1980s. Taking into account meetings at other levels (ministerial and senior official), approximately 500 meetings occur each year. See *A Time for Action*: 14.

[25] Richard Simeon, *Federal-Provincial Diplomacy* (Toronto: University of Toronto Press, 1974).

[26] These tendencies are encouraged by 'party asymmetry', i.e., when the provincial party in power is different from the federal. But even when both parties are the same, federal-provincial rivalries often transcend party solidarity, which is weakened by the fact that Canadian parties are themselves federal in nature (i.e., the national party organization often depends on semi-autonomous provincial organizations). For a fuller discussion see Smiley, *Canada in Quebec*: 101 ff.

[27] For a discussion of trends toward increasing provincialism see Donald V. Smiley, 'Territorialism and Canadian Political Institutions', in *Canadian Public Policy* 3,4 (Autumn, 1977): 449-57. Competition between provinces for industrial investment is colourfully illustrated by Hardin.

[28] A study of regional variations in children's political attitudes found interesting differences in level of partisan identification and in children's ability to name various political leaders. Identification with the region itself was not reported. See Alan Gregg and Michael Whittington, 'Regional Variation in Children's Political Attitudes' in David J. Bellamy, Jon H. Pammett, and Donald C. Rowat (eds), *The Provincial Political System* (Toronto: Methuen, 1976). Some data indicate that strong regional identities are nevertheless compatible with loyalty to the nation as a whole.

[29] The argument that regionalism inhibits the development of politics polarized around such horizontal cleavages as social class will be further assessed in Chapter 6.

[30] S.J.R. Noel, 'Consociational Democracy and Canadian Federalism', *Canadian Journal of Political Science* 4,1 (March, 1971): 16, 18.

[31] Douglas Rae and Michael Taylor, *The Analysis of Political Cleavages* (New Haven: Yale University Press, 1970): 22, 13.

[32] Ronald Watts cites reinforced or overlapping cleavages as the first 'critical condition' leading to the 'process of disintegration' in federations. See his article 'Survival or Disintegration' in R. Simeon, ed., *Must Canada Fail?*: 53. One could, however, argue that the most explosive situation occurs where territorial cleavage does not occur but where class, race, and religion all reinforce one another. Arendt Lijphart suggests, for example, that 'because good social fences may make good political neighbours, a kind of voluntary *apartheid* policy may be the most appropriate solution for a divided society'. Arendt Lijphart, 'Cultural Diversity and Theories of Political Integration', in *Canadian Journal of Political Science* 4,1 (March, 1971): 11.

[33] See Roger Gibbins, *Conflict and Unity*: 102.

[34] A.R.M. Lower, 'Canadian Unity and Its Conditions' in Violet Anderson (ed.), *Problems in Canadian Unity* (Toronto: Thomas Nelson, 1938): 11-12.

[35] K.D. McRae, *Consociational Democracy*, p. 241. No more precise measures of the degree to which cleavages reinforce one another in Canadian society have ever been developed. Rae and Taylor (ch. 3) have refined a technique for measuring what they call 'the intensity of fragmentation' in a society. But it is doubtful that applying even these measures would help us much to understand the subjective aspects of negative regionalism. So we must proceed with a somewhat intuitive idea of this important influence.

[36] See Jon H. Pammett, 'Public Orientation to Regions and Provinces', in Bellamy (ed.); and Harold Clarke *et al.*, *Political Choice in Canada* (Toronto: McGraw-Hill Ryerson, 1979), chs. 2 and 3.

[37] Clarke *et al.*, *op. cit.*

[38] Dale C. Thomson, 'The Prairie Provinces and the Canadian Federation', in David K. Elton (ed.), *One Prairie Province? Conference Proceedings and Selected Papers* (University of Lethbridge and the *Lethbridge Herald*, 1970): 45. The North still is a colony of Ottawa. Only recently was the seat of government for the Northwest Territories transferred from Ottawa to Yellowknife, where the new elected Assembly sits.

[39] Smiley, *Canada in Question*: 193. See also his 'The Political Context of Resource Development in Canada', in A. Scott: 65-6.

[40] The Alberta results are probably unique. In the 1974 election survey Saskatchewan and Manitoba respondents display much lower levels of perceived regional injustice than those in Alberta. (See Bell and Pammett, in progress.) A classic focus of western discontent has been freight rates, viewed as symbols of eastern domination because they allegedly discriminate against western entrepreneurs and consumers. See David V.J. Bell, 'Freight Rates and Transportation Policy', University of Toronto/York University Joint Program in Transportation *Research Report* No. 45, March 1978.

[41] Data reported in Gibbins, *Conflict and Unity*: 128, Figure 4.5.

[42] Of course Douglas Harkness from Calgary held two moderately important cabinet posts under Prime Minister John Diefenbaker, himself from Saskatchewan. See Smiley, *Canada in Question*: 195; and M. Schwartz's discussion of regional 'power' in *Politics and Territory*. More significant of course is the election of the Conservatives in May 1979 with Albertan Joe Clark as prime minister.

[43] Bell, 'Freight Rates': 43 ff. Speaking before a Parliamentary Committee, Stanley Roberts, President of the Canada West Foundation, put the point quite bluntly: 'the four Western Provinces . . . do not have in the Government of Canada, in the Parliament of Canada, the kind of political muscle that they must have [; . . . they] have not been recognized in the governing system of this country.' *Minutes of the Proceedings and Evidence of the Special Joint Committee of the Senate and of the House of Commons on the Constitution of Canada.* Thursday, 14 Sept. 1978: 15-16.

[44] See Gibbins, *Conflict and Unity*: 127-30.

[45] George Rawlyk, 'The Maritimes and the Canadian Community', in Mason Wade (ed.), *Regionalism and the Canadian Community, 1867-1967* (Toronto: University of Toronto Press, 1969): 101.

[46] See *The Report on Maritime Union* (Fredericton: Maritime Union Study, 1970), Tables 41, 42, 43.

[47] Gibbins, *Conflict and Unity*: 116, Table 4.1.

[48] Reg Whitaker in David Smith *et al.* (eds), *After Meech Lake*: 112. For a thorough discussion of public opinion survey measuring regional discontent, see Gibbins, *op. cit.*

[49] Philip E. Jacob and James V. Toscano, *The Integration of Political Communities* (New York: Lippincott, 1964): 210.

[50] For a thorough review of the constitutional implications of provincial union in Canada see William F. Ryan, 'Atlantic Union: Some Constitutional Considerations', in *The Idea of Maritime Union*, report on a conference held at Mount Allison University, 5-7 February 1965; Barry L. Strayer, 'The Constitutional Processes for Prairie Union: Some Considerations and Questions', in David K. Elton (ed.), *One Prairie Province?*; W.R. Lederman, 'Memorandum on Constitutional Amendment to Consolidate Two or More Provinces of Canada into a Single Province', Appendix C of *The Report on Maritime Union* (Fredericton: Maritime Union Study, 1970).

[51] Evidently critical of this practice, David Cameron ('Regional Integration in the Maritime Provinces', in *Canadian Journal of Political Science* 4 [1 March 1971]: 25), comments 'However convenient this categorization of provinces may be, and it certainly renders the statistician's task easier by providing only four or five rows of columns per table, it does an injustice to reality by failing to ask whether such "regions" have any meaning. In fact, it simply perpetuates an annoying tendency of Canadians west of New Brunswick to assume the existence of an integrated Atlantic region. As early as 1911 the inappropriateness of this tendency was recognized by a correspondent for the Toronto *Globe* who wrote: "the familiar entity, the Maritime Provinces, is entirely a western creation and has no

existence down by the sea".' Objectively, the Maritimes form a recognizable region. Yet in terms of the perceptions of Maritime residents, Cameron may be correct. According to the 1974 election survey, only about one-quarter of New Brunswickers felt they lived in a Maritime region; the same proportion identified themselves as residents of an Eastern region.

Often omitted from these classification schemes is the neglected region: the North. Increasingly important to Canada's economic future and national sovereignty, the North is going through major internal political change. Native peoples, now linked together by new communication patterns, are striving for political power and autonomy. Many of them resent the colonial-style government to which they are subjected, and the insensitivity of distant federal officials who make policy without consulting them.

[52] Norman Ward, 'One Prairie Province: Historical and Political Perspectives', in Elton (ed.).

[53] J. Murray Beck, *The History of Maritime Union: A Study in Frustration* (Fredericton: Maritime Union Study, 1969).

[54] *The Report*: 30-1.

[55] George Rawlyk, 'Nova Scotia Regional Protest', *Queen's Quarterly* 75,1 (Spring, 1968): 105-23.

[56] For a more thorough comparison of Canada and the United States see Smiley, *Canada in Question*: 211, and his 'Territorialism' article: 451-4.

[57] Ward: 191 f.

[58] McMillan, *op. cit.*: 3.

[59] For an analysis of historical instances of 'interprovincial collaboration in public policy' between Ontario and Quebec, see Kenneth McRoberts, 'An Overview of Ontario-Quebec Interprovincial Relations' published in *Quebec-Ontario Economic Relations*, Report of a Conference held in Toronto, 12-13 January 1978. McRoberts recommends more extensive policy collaboration, and improvement in communications to the 'public at large' in both provinces.

[60] Watts: 46. See also Anthony Careless, ch. 11 and 12.

[61] J.M.S. Careless, 'Limited Identities in Canada', *Canadian Historical Review* 50,1 (March 1969): 9.

[62] Trudeau, *Federalism and the French Canadians*: 193.

[63] Gordon Merrill, 'Regionalism and Nationalism', in John Warkentin (ed.) *Canada: A Geographical Interpretation* (Toronto: Methuen, 1968): 566.

[64] Quoted in the Toronto *Globe and Mail*, 19 September 1978. Very similar opinions were expressed by Marc Lalonde, minister of state for federal-provincial relations, in a speech 18 September to Montreal businessmen: 'If Canadian unity is to be consolidated', he said, 'Quebeckers must have concrete and irrefutable proof that our constitution really can be renewed, that its renewal has already begun and that the constitution can subsequently be amended at any time in response to the aspirations of all Canadians' (*ibid.*). Some Westerners, however, resent this 'over-attention' to Quebec. Stanley Roberts told the Joint Committee on the Constitution that 'It is unfortunate if you have the impression that the Canada West Foundation believes a constitutional reform is something that has been brought about or is necessary because of a "Quebec situation"' (p. 15).

[65] *A Time for Action*: 22-3 et passim.

[66] In the late summer of 1991, the federal government unveiled a new set of proposals for constitutional reform that (unlike the Meech Lake Accord) were put forward for discussion and public comment. They established public hearings and even set up a telephone 'hot-line' to facilitate discussion and feedback. Significant structural innovations proposed to address some of the concerns discussed above included:

• an elected Senate, with increased powers and 'more equitable' representation.
• agreement to 'explore ways and means to strengthen the representation and legislative capacities of individual MPs'.
• a role for the provinces and territories in Supreme Court appointments.
• the addition of a 'Canada Clause' to 'affirm the identity and aspirations of Canadians'.

- devolution to the provinces of some authority 'for non-national matters not specifically assigned to the federal government'.

By the winter of that year, public interest in constitutional reform was overtaken by concern over the economy. Newly elected NDP premier of Saskatchewan Roy Romanow found much support in the suggestion that constitutional matters be put 'on hold' in order to focus governments' attention on economic recovery.

6 | The State, Ideology, and Class Voting

Conceptions of authority and the state are important elements of political culture, and they can vary widely.[1] Should government take an active role in the economy, or should it keep out of the way? Are the needs of the state or individual rights to be the starting point in government decisions? What ideals should inform state policy: a commitment to equality and democracy, or the protection of a privileged minority—an aristocracy—deemed to include the most valuable members of society? Should national authority be concentrated in a single institution or spread among several that check and balance one another? Should government be centralized in a unitary fashion or decentralized according to some notion of federalism? What procedures should guide legislation? Should a written constitution limit the exercise of authority and the right to take part in making decisions?

Discussed in every political system at one time or another, such questions become critical when a constitution is being created or changed. For a written constitution, by its very definition, embodies one particular conception of authority and national purpose. Whether or not the citizens approve, a constitution sets many of the formal rules within which political institutions operate. Constitutions can be changed, of course, but not without a great deal of effort. Because constitutions are so important we must understand how they come into being. This enterprise takes us back into a historical analysis of Confederation as one of Canada's most significant 'formative events'.

John Conway points out that the British North America Act, Canada's 'constitution',[2] was written to unite a disparate assortment of weak dependencies. The colonial leaders took their colonial status so much for granted that throughout the debates preceding adoption of the BNA Act, many of them repeatedly referred to England as 'home'. That the document assumes continued colonial dependency is clear from a number of its provisions. For example, Britain kept control over Canada's foreign policy, at least formally, until the British Parliament passed the Statute of Westminster of 1931. The (British) Judicial Committee of the Privy Council was to serve as the final court of appeal in matters of law, an arrangement that continued until 1949. The Canadian Parliament was given no means for changing the terms of the Act. The British Parliament was to hold this power. (This arrangement obtained until 1982, when Prime Minister Trudeau managed to 'patriate' the Constitution with the support of nine provinces but against the objection of the Quebec government.) In Conway's words, 'the concepts embodied in the British North America Act were perhaps suited to a dependency afraid of being annexed to the United States, but [one that] found emotional security in identifying with Great Britain and the Empire because of the absence of other sources of reassurance, and that had little thirst for a cultural life of its own.'[3]

English-speaking Canadians depended unduly on the mother country for cultural and political enlightenment. And, as we saw in Chapter 4, French-speaking Canadians suffered until recently from a different strain of the same disease. In their eyes, French Canada was an outpost of Catholic fidelity in the sacrilegious New World. Catholicism taught them that only God could authorize rule. Liberalism violated God's will by committing 'the fundamental error of seeking to build a society on other than religious principles.'[4] Theirs was a divine mission: to preserve and where possible spread the Catholic creed in an unfriendly, liberal environment.

Two results of the British North America Act, both errors of omission, remain important today. In the first place, the Act itself and the debate that accompanied its passage failed to address the deeper issues of political philosophy.[5] The Act takes no position on such matters as human nature and the social contract. Even narrower questions related to the bilingual character of Canada went largely undiscussed. Secondly, the document failed to stir the hearts and minds of the new country. Its colonial tone and use of British symbols lacked appeal and failed to distinguish Canadian from British politics and society. In Conway's words, 'For the great majority of English Canadians, unable or unwilling to respond to the symbols of a borrowed British culture, there remains only a view of life refracted through the alien symbols of American culture. This process of refraction has become increasingly negative and distorting as Canadians have grown more critical of American society and its aspirations.'[6]

These weaknesses of the BNA Act betray the true origins of Confederation. Only secondarily the founding of a new nation, Confederation was mainly meant to relieve British North America's political deadlock, economic insolvency, and external threat. Historians disagree about the relative weight of these three factors, but together they account for the lion's share of support given to Confederation by contemporary political and economic élites.[7] One student speaks of the Confederation as, at best, an 'incomplete founding':

> [T]he fathers of Confederation had no intention of founding an 'independent political community'. What they were in fact doing was uniting the four colonies into a larger colonial arrangement. That is why the new constitution had to be an Act of the Imperial Parliament and that is why their new constitution did not incorporate an amendment formula; any amendments would be made at Westminster.[8]

For all its weaknesses, did the BNA Act express a particular ideological viewpoint? Probably not. According to one scholar, 'our political thought is implicit, not explicit. It must be inferred from what we do in and through government, rather than expounded from the text of founding manifestos . . .'.[9] From the policies adopted later by the architects of Confederation, we can infer their ideological preferences.

They seem to have hoped the state would play a major role in developing the new country, and particularly in opening up the West. Because railroads were needed to facilitate commerce and trade, and to serve as the backbone of defence, they were built quickly, assisted financially and politically by the state. Indeed the promise of new railway construction is explicitly set forth in the BNA Act. This set the pattern of strong federal intervention in the nation's economy. In the 1870s, the Conservatives introduced a policy of high tariffs, with the intention of fostering and protecting indigenous industry. The National Policy fomented regional discontent by raising the price of manufactured goods. Worse, it encouraged a great many American industries to set up branch plants in Canada in order to avoid paying these tariffs and to enjoy the preferences trade agreements with Britain gave to Canadian exports. But it did establish the state as a central figure in the economy.

In short, the architects of Confederation saw the state as an instrument of capital accumulation and economic development. Under their direction the state came to embody what Herschel Hardin has called the 'public enterprise culture', but a more cynical observer has termed 'private profit at public expense'.[10]

Conservatism, Liberalism, and Socialism[11]

Yet nineteenth-century politicians were not all agreed on the basic ideological questions. One leading scholar traces Canadian ideological diversity back to the beginning of the anglophone 'fragment'. In an article entitled 'Conservatism, Liberalism and Socialism in Canada',[12] Gad Horowitz has altered the Hartzian approach to take account of what he regards as special features of the Canadian experience. Not only is Canada a 'dual fragment', as Kenneth McRae has argued; the anglophone fragment contains an important ideological impurity, according to Horowitz. This impurity keeps Canada from developing a single uniform ideology of the kind found in societies like the United States or Australia, which emerged from comparatively 'pure' fragments. Thus Horowitz rejects McRae's contention that the Loyalist anglophone fragment is largely a variant of American bourgeois culture. Quoting Hartz, Horowitz points out that the Loyalist fragment was 'tinged with toryism'.

Unlike McRae and even Hartz, Horowitz refuses 'to boil the tory touch away to nothing'. Indeed his interpretation of Canadian political culture stresses its importance. From the presence of Toryism, Horowitz deduces the possibility of many ideologies co-existing in Canada. That is why, in the twentieth century, no single ideology has been transmuted into the 'Canadian way of life'. Rather, competing ideologies—representing almost the entire spectrum from socialism to conservatism—play their parts in Canadian politics:

The most important un-American characteristics of English Canada, all related to the presence of toryism, are: (a) the presence of tory ideology in the founding of English Canada by the Loyalists, and its continuing influence on English-Canadian political culture; (b) the persistent power of whiggery or right-wing liberalism in Canada (the family compacts) as contrasted with the rapid and easy victory of liberal democracy (Jefferson, Jackson) in the United States; (c) the ambivalent centrist character of left-wing liberalism in Canada as contrasted with the unambiguously leftist position of left-wing liberalism in the United States; (d) the presence of an influential and legitimate socialist movement in English Canada as contrasted with the illegitimacy and early death of American socialism; (e) the failure of English-Canadian liberalism to develop into the one true myth, the nationalist cult, and the parallel failure to exclude toryism and socialism as 'un-Canadian'; in other words the legitimacy of ideological diversity in English Canada.[13]

Both conservatism and socialism contribute significantly to the Canadian identity and its distinctiveness. Conservatism, Horowitz contends, provides an important point of contrast between Canada and the United States. American 'conservatives' are simply old-fashioned liberals in disguise, nineteenth-century free-enterprisers. Although this right-wing liberalism also found its way into Canadian conservatism, two other, non-liberal ideological systems—orthodox Toryism and Tory radicalism—have influenced the character of conservatism in Canada.

Canadian conservatives (historically) claimed to value loyalty, tradition, and élitism. Preferring Britain to America, they strongly supported the symbols and practices originating in the British connection—the monarchy, the Empire or Commonwealth, the Union Jack, God Save the Queen, and so on. Conservatives believed that leaders should be given loyalty, deference, and support by the people, and should be permitted to govern as they think best, even at the risk of making mistakes or losing popularity. To the conservative, parliamentary democracy does not mean government by the people but rather 'government by ministers of the crown for the people'. Accordingly conservatives held that 'people should not presume to instruct their governors but [instead] *trust* them to govern well'.[14]

Underlying this élitist view of rule is an organic image of society. Conservative historian W.L. Morton describes it in the following way:

[M]an and his society are organic formations which have birth, growth and decay, and will give way to new individual and social formations, born of the old, but continuing the old in new manifestations and mutations . . . . [Hence] the conservative distrusts not change by growth, or by training the new out of the old, but reform, deliberate change based on the rejection of the old as old and the installation of the novel as new.

Society is hierarchic as well as organic, according to this conception. Social classes, like different parts of the human body, contribute in different ways to the good of the whole. Some parts are more important than others and are meant to govern, as the brain must govern the hand. Nevertheless, the parts need one another. Indeed, 'the good of the individual is not conceivable apart from the good of the whole, determined by a "natural" élite consulting a sacred tradition.'[15]

For this reason, conservatism rejects the liberal's rugged individualism and *laissez faire*; these doctrines ignore the duty of the natural élite to safeguard the whole body politic. In the words of former Conservative Party leader Robert Stanfield, the 'Conservative tradition recognized the role of government as the regulator of individual conduct in the interests of society . . . . Conservative principles of order and stability [can provide] a framework in which enterprise can flourish . . . '.[16] Thus the Canadian conservatives until recently accepted, as necessary for the good of all, welfare state measures that the 'conservative' American Republican would reject.

In liberal thinking, society is composed of free, autonomous people competing, each against all, for economic success and happiness, according to laws and rules set down by the government. What is good for all is simply what is good for each individual, from this point of view. The role of the state must be minimized, limited to keeping the rules that ensure fair play. In its earliest (European) formulations, liberalism was not linked to democracy or any other notions of equal political participation. In the twentieth century, liberals came to conceive of equality as equal opportunity, not equality of condition. Yet so little equality as this has demanded that the state become more than the 'night watchman' early liberal theorists had in mind. Hence the growth of the 'positive state'. Still, the basic 'possessive individualism'[17] of liberal philosophy remains intact.

The liberal's commitment to free enterprise is clearly voiced in statements by members of the 'Canadian Establishment', especially the business élite. Alf Powis, president of Noranda Mines, opined that 'Ideally the government should set the rules under which business operates in a reasonably stable way, rules that aren't subject to violent, year-to-year change.' David Collier, President of General Motors of Canada, warned, 'What the people of North America need to realize is that with the loss of a free-choice, competitive market, it is only a step away from the loss of a free-political choice society.' Hammering this home, Roy Thomson, press lord, bluntly asserted that 'The welfare state robs people of incentive.'

Politicians in the Liberal Party (and increasingly in the Conservative Party as well) have echoed these sentiments. Liberal Prime Minister Louis St Laurent assured the House of Commons on 14 May 1953, that 'I think all of us recognize that there are some things which it is more appropriate to have done by public authorities than by free enterprise. But I think we are all most happy when free enterprise does what is required to be done and public authorities do not have to intervene.'[18]

Despite such insistence that Canada is and must remain a free-enterprise society, the tradition of government intervention is long-standing. Besides providing for public welfare in various ways—old age pensions, medical insurance, unemployment insurance, among others—Canada's economy has a highly developed public sector, especially in transportation and communications. Whatever their misgivings, few liberals would dare to suggest revoking welfare legislation or disbanding the CBC, or Canadian National. Paradoxically, such 'neo-liberal' views have found a welcome home in the Conservative Party under Brian Mulroney. Yet Canadian conservatism once was otherwise. Or was it?[19]

Drawing on some of George Grant's less mournful reflections, Gad Horowitz observes that Canadian conservatism 'uses "public power to achieve national purposes. The Conservative Party . . . after all, created Ontario Hydro, the CNR, the Bank of Canada, and the CBC." ' Yet historian Terry Cook finds problems even in what appears to be a statement of fact, arguing that people have given the Conservatives more credit than they deserved. True, Arthur Meighen (Conservative prime minister) 'did the lion's share of work in creating the CNR, but [his Liberal successor Mackenzie] King was not opposed to the principle of nationalization, and when in power, passed the necessary legislation to complete the system.'[20] Although Conservative Prime Minister R.B. Bennett is credited with creating the Bank of Canada in 1934, the Liberal caucus had suggested it a year earlier. Indeed it was ultimately King, again, who changed the ownership and control of the Bank from private to public.

Likewise, the idea behind the CBC arose in the first instance from the report of the Aird Commission, which King had set up in 1928. Originally called by Bennett the Canadian Radio Broadcasting Commission, the organization had little clout until reorganized in 1936 as a crown corporation (The Canadian Broadcasting Corporation) and given added support by King.

However interpreted, these facts suggest that the two major parties differ little in the ways they view the role of the state. Both parties have often intervened in the economy even if, as Cook hints, they have done so for different reasons. 'Conservatives have tended to devise policies that were meant to allow Canada to function as an organic unit . . . . The Liberal's . . . use of state intervention has often been motivated by regional or individual considerations.'[21] Yet the result is the same as if they did not differ ideologically at all.

Contrasts between the two major parties were historically somewhat more pronounced in respect to Canadian foreign policy. Unlike the Conservatives prior to the advent of Brian Mulroney, the Liberals typically preferred the United States to Britain. 'Sir Wilfrid Laurier's Reciprocity campaign in 1911, Mackenzie King's lifelong suspicion of the British, and Laurier's campaign for a Canadian fleet independent of the Royal Navy demonstrated the Liberal's traditional view of Britain,' Peter Newman remarked of the differences between Canadian Liberals and Conservatives.[22] Even this statement exaggerates Liberal-Conservative differences, however. As a description of tendencies and sentiments, it has some basis in fact. But these preferences have not consistently been translated into policy and action. For example, when Britain entered the First World War,

Laurier himself declared that Canada should be 'ready, aye, ready' to assist in any way that was needed.[23]

Expressions of nationalism by the two major parties reflect how differently they regard foreign policy. Conservative nationalism at one time meant loving England and hating America. Liberal nationalism[24] has meant the opposite, sentimentalizing our many banal links with the United States, and talking dreamily about the 'partnership' with 'our great neighbours'. Following World War Two, Liberal nationalism was epitomized in the policies of C.D. Howe, which openly encouraged American investors to take over Canadian manufacturing. (Nationalism as fire sale!) Liberal nationalism also led Canada to support NATO. Conservative nationalism, by contrast, was signified by Diefenbaker's refusal to arm the Bomarc missiles. Yet even in foreign policy the parties' positions have sometimes been reversed. In 1957, Diefenbaker (a Conservative) signed the NORAD agreement committing Canada to a North American joint defence system controlled by the United States. And in the early seventies Trudeau (a Liberal) began to explore 'third options' in order to wean Canada away from the traditional ties to both the United States and Britain. In fact during Trudeau's last term in office, Canada's relations with the U.S. reached a startling nadir.[25] Under Mulroney, they became almost embarrassingly cosy, not only in economic matters through the Free Trade Agreement, but even to the point of Canadian involvement as an ally of the U.S. in the Gulf War. But these were deviations from the rule. Leaving such exceptions aside, for much of Canadian history, choosing between Conservative and Liberal versions of nationalism has meant choosing between British and American domination. What could better demonstrate the colonial thinking of both major parties?

Yet historical change has influenced both parties' views of Canadian nationalism. Whatever their party, most members of the Canadian élite opposed nationalism-as-independence in the 1950s. Conservatives, Liberals, and even many CCFers felt Canada had to tie its future to the United States in military and economic matters. Co-operation was largely voluntary, not done with teeth clenched and eyes scanning the ceiling. The Liberal Party stated that it aimed to welcome foreign investment warmly. The interdependence of Canadian and American economies was taken for granted, despite the bargaining imbalance that favoured the latter. Most of the political élite assumed a continuing partnership was in force. (This recalls the cartoon depicting Uncle Sam, fatherly and confiding in an innocent Canada, 'I propose a continental energy policy: you provide the energy and I'll provide the continent.') They simply wanted Canada and the United States to get along with as little friction as possible. To this end the Canadian-American Committee was formed in 1957, backed financially by the American Carnegie Foundation. The keynote was flexibility and an absence of ideology.

The 1960s saw several important changes. Universities and state bureaucracies expanded, creating a 'new petty bourgeoisie'. The interests of this class lay in strengthening the Canadian state and reducing American influence. Tough new economic measures adopted in the United States denied Canadian investments a special status and the Vietnam War provided emotional issues around which anti-American nationalists could rally. Élite opinion, once indifferent, had grown concerned about the increasing American domination of Canada's economy and cultural life. This newly awakened Canadian nationalism expressed itself most significantly in Liberal government policies to regulate foreign investment through the Foreign Investment Review Agency (FIRA); maintain a made-in-Canada energy price system through the National Energy Program (NEP); and generally protect aspects of Canadian culture and communication from American domination.

Under Mulroney the Conservatives abandoned any plausible conception of Canadian nationalism and took up instead what at times seemed like American hero worship. Privatization and deregulation became the favourite buzz words. Mulroney disclosed that Canada was 'open for business' and scrapped FIRA, replacing it with Investment Canada. The NEP was dismantled with the solemn assurance that no Conservative government would ever introduce so heinous a policy.

On matters of nationalism and continentalization, the Liberals and Conservatives have changed positions so completely that no coherent ideological outlook can be identified for either party. Both are clearly pragmatic parties that treat ideology as a means to electoral success rather than as an end in itself. But there are other parties that claim they have a different character and ideological persuasion than the two old main line parties.

Socialism came to Canada by way of the United States and Britain.[26] Its earliest exponents were labour activists who held to orthodox Marxism and predicted the coming of a class war. Yet partly because Marxist socialism lacked the support of Canadian intellectuals, it remained electorally marginal, particularly after the unsuccessful Winnipeg General Strike, when government suppressed the radical unions involved. Marxist socialism did, however, influence the 'democratic socialists' who modelled themselves after the British Fabians and the example of the Labour Party.

Democratic, not revolutionary, socialism shaped the Co-operative Commonwealth Federation, Canada's socialist party. Founded in Calgary in 1932, the CCF became a viable political force almost at once. According to Horowitz, CCF socialism 'stresses the good of the community as against possessive individualism; equality of condition as against mere equality of opportunity; the co-operative commonwealth as against the acquisitive society'.[27] Canadian socialism therefore combines the conservative's organic view of society with a desire for equality inspired by reform liberalism, but expressed in more radical terms.

The Regina Manifesto, which set forth the ideology of the new CCF Party, grew out of at least four distinct strains of leftist thought: Marxism, rural revolt, the policies of the British Labour Party, and Christian ethics. Revolutionary notions found no haven in CCF ideology. Instead of historical materialism and class struggle, the Manifesto spoke of peaceful change and human compassion. The triumph of the moderates, led by J.S. Woodsworth, testifies to the strength of bourgeois ideology in Canada and the fidelity to British rather than German or Russian socialist models (another legacy of Loyalism). In addressing the delegates, Woodsworth acknowledged the party's heritage of notions of 'individualism common to all who live in North America', and also the heritage of British institutions and Christian ethics. The new party spoke out in favour of parliamentary democracy. Socialism would come about through the ballot box, not through armed struggle.

While attempting to maintain consensus among the members, party leaders felt they had to work to attract voters as well. This required modifications that moved the party further in toward the ideological centre. In 1944, the party adopted a resolution endorsing private enterprise as a legitimate part of social democracy. Further changes of this kind found their way into the Winnipeg Declaration of 1956; in 1961 the founding convention of the New Democratic Party reaffirmed them.

Yet, during its first three decades in existence, the CCF/NDP could not respond effectively to Canada's two most serious problems: French-English conflict and foreign domination. The failure stemmed, according to David Lewis,[28] from two rigidities in party ideology: the first, a doctrinaire rejection of nationalism, the second, an insistence that one capitalist is just like another.

Growing out of the first belief was an insensitivity to the national consciousness maturing in Quebec. A few francophone activists joined the party but they neither forced the issue of French nationalism onto the party agenda, nor redirected the party to appeal for francophone support. As a result the party was overwhelmingly Anglo in its membership and its point of view. Its Regina Manifesto only indirectly referred to francophones in an obscure clause promising to respect ethnic rights. The ideological revisions of 1944 and 1956 did no better. Throughout this period the CCF won little of the popular vote in Quebec; it got its few votes mainly in urban anglophone areas. Not until the NDP was founded in 1961 did the French fact receive serious debate, just as the Quiet Revolution was beginning.

Aware of the natural affinity between conservatism and socialism, NDP supporters hoped that an ideological awakening in Quebec would help the party's fortunes. Gad Horowitz reported that in the 'Quebec of the quiet revolution' a 'change of political culture, from old style to new style collectivism is proceeding at a breath-taking speed'. Unlike English Canada, where 'American ways of thinking about politics [i.e., liberalism] . . . have prevented socialism from becoming a major power . . . Quebec's collectivist background leads far more certainly to the growth of a socialist party'.[29]

But to succeed at the polls, socialism in Quebec would have to speak *en français* exclusively. When Pierre Bourgault, the founder of the socialist predecessor to the Parti Québécois, the Rassemblement pour l'Independance Nationale (RIN), was addressing a group of Toronto socialists, one of his audience invited him to make common cause by joining the NDP; Bourgault demurred. 'I am a nationalist first and a socialist second,' he answered. In this way he expressed the feelings of most of his compatriots. Partly because it failed to win significant support in Quebec, the CCF/NDP has remained a third party nationally, never gaining more than 20% of the vote in a federal election.

Cataclysmic political change in the 1980s—including economic boom and bust, deindustrialization, constitutional upheaval, regional, linguistic and ethnic conflict, the rise of the women's movement, rapid changes in international geopolitics, clashes over aboriginal rights, land claims and the quest for native self government—have quite understandably shaken the Canadian political firmament to its core. The electorate has become more volatile than ever before. Loyalty to and identification with the major parties broke down as the party system experienced 'dealignment'. These conditions provided a rich culture for the growth of alternative political parties. In rapid succession the Christian Heritage Party, the Confederation of Regions Party, the Reform Party, and the Bloc Québécois appeared on the scene. Of these, the latter two seem to have the greatest likelihood of winning federal seats in the short run. The B.Q. was formed in March 1990 when the senior Quebec cabinet minister in the Mulroney cabinet, Lucien Bouchard, defected from the Conservative Party in anticipation of the defeat of the Meech Lake Accord. A small number of Quebec MPs joined him. Despite the total absence of a political organization or a platform (beyond the separation of Quebec from Canada), the party rose almost instantly to first place in the polls in Quebec.

The Reform Party's rise is more complex.[30] It was originally formed in Winnipeg in 1987 out of a sense of frustration with the Tories, who had been given strong electoral support in the West in the expectation that their policies would be much more palatable than those of the hated Trudeau Liberals. Preston Manning, son of a former Social Credit Alberta premier, easily won the leadership. The party drew on U.S. populist democratic ideas of referendum and recall to highlight its commitment to represent the voters' wishes more faithfully than the old-line parties. The substance of its appeal include opposition to big government and heavy spending (with its seemingly inevitable deficit implications), opposition to multiculturalism policies, a hard line vis-à-vis Quebec, and Senate reform. The party attracted a number of extremists, particularly in response to its position on Quebec and multiculturalism. (Preston Manning attempted to minimize this aspect of the Party's development by pointing out that 'A bright light always attracts moths'.) The spring 1991 decision by the membership to expand into Central Canada resulted in predictable attempts to modify some of the party's rhetoric and distance itself from extremists. Its grass roots membership and support in the polls rose accordingly, and by summer 1991 it had surpassed the Conservatives in the polls (despite its lack of support in Quebec) and was challenging the faltering NDP.

Parties, Ideologies, and Voting

It should be evident by now that with respect to the major parties, a party's name does not reliably identify its ideology. In fact, the Conservative Party has changed its name five times since Confederation, using among others the name Liberal-Conservative and the current Progressive Conservative. ('Progressive' is meant to offset the right-wing implication of 'conservative'.)

A leading political commentator, Peter C. Newman, complained that Canadian voters get little clear choice in elections, on account of 'The Lack of Conservative-Liberal Differences in Canadian Politics'.[31] Recent research into the ways Canadians view political parties revealed a near inability to distinguish, on ideological grounds, between the Progressive Conservatives and Liberals. In some regions the Conservatives are even thought to stand slightly to the left of the Liberals.[32]

This is not to deny that a few 'small-c' conservatives still exist, still holding on to the principles of organicism and privilege. Such people may not, however, dominate or even necessarily belong to the Conservative *Party*. The most articulate of these philosophical conservatives, Professor George Grant admitted his ideological loneliness when he lamented 'the all-pervading liberalism' of North America.[33] What better proof that true conservatism is a minority viewpoint, perhaps an endangered species in Canada?

In truth we simply do not know the number of philosophical conservatives. One disgruntled critic has even called the red Tory a 'myth'.[34] The difficulty is twofold. First, major political parties consciously try to minimize ideological issues to avoid alienating voters, so as to draw from the largest possible pool of potential supporters. This strategy is apparently quite successful. When asked detailed questions about how they view federal political parties, Canadians have typically placed ideological concerns at the bottom of their list. In both the 1984 and 1974 national election studies, fewer voters mentioned ideology as the dominant aspect of federal party images than mentioned policy/issues, style/performance, leader/leadership, or other vague categories including general characteristics of parties or something to do with area or group.[35] Ideological differences may even be greater among members of the same party than between different parties. For example, many Western conservatives fervently support free enterprise and oppose Eastern 'red Tory' notions of government intervention. The regional political cultures discussed in the last chapter show up even *within* the major parties, though they have on occasion given rise to small regional parties.

Though voting behaviour is a weak indication of ideology, available data suggest that *strong* party identifiers do differ ideologically, one set from another. A recent article concludes that 'Canadians, in spite of their greater volatility of party identification, see the parties more distinctly than do the Americans and are more likely to use party as an ideological organizing device than are Americans'.[36] Does this mean that Canadians are more likely than Americans to vote according to their social class? Americans aside, to what extent do Canadians vote by class?

Class Conflict and Voting

It stands to reason that people who make their livings differently will have specific interests to protect. Different interests will lead people to different ideologies and, in turn, to supporting different parties. Capitalists will want to guard their investments against the demands of labour, against civil strife and competition from abroad, and will look to the state for help in these regards. They have often gotten it: the Canadian state has played an historic role in suppressing strikes and harassing protestors.[37] It has also provided industry with tax incentives and protective tariffs (the 'public enterprise culture' discussed above).

On the other hand, labour will try to get the state to safeguard it against employers by permitting union activity and strikes, by enforcing fair labour practices, protecting pension funds and the like. Labour must unify itself in order to gain the best deal possible from government and from employers of labour. Conversely employers will prefer to see labour disunited, unaware of its shared interests, and lacking leaders.

Out of the clash between labour and capital comes either revolution or, as in Canada, the political culture of the welfare state. The selection of William Lyon Mackenzie King as leader of the Liberal Party gave a clear sign of the latter. The leadership convention of 1919 took place shortly after the Winnipeg General Strike, which had focused attention on the new militancy of labour and had aroused fears of a socialist revolution. Most delegates felt the relationship between labour and capital needed to be examined anew; and it called for a creative political response. Mackenzie King had been both deputy minister and minister of labour; he was a labour expert and the author of a revolutionary if impenetrable book titled *Industry and Humanity*. King emerged as the new leader, and was to hold this post for nearly thirty years.

Opinion remains divided about the link between King's authorship of the book and his victory in 1919. King felt that the book had helped him win the support of 'labour men' at the convention, and he used it later in appealing for middle-class support. But in his introduction to a reissued edition, historian David Jay Bercuson speculates that 'it is doubtful that more than a tiny minority of the voting public ever read it'. Whatever the impact of *Industry and Humanity*, King's reputation as a labour expert no doubt influenced party delegates in this troubled period. In many respects King's major achievement as prime minister was to reform industrial relations. Again in Bercuson's words: 'Canada began the King era in 1921 convinced that *laissez faire*, piecemeal approaches to the problems of modern industrialized society were sufficient and ended in 1948 as a welfare state with a powerful trade union movement and a collective bargaining process guaranteed and protected by law.'[38]

New policies and legislation brought in by the King ministry included old age pensions, Family Allowance benefits, the Wartime Labour Relations Order of 1943, and veterans' benefits. Liberals adopted many of these policies in order to win the support of left-wing voters and cut into the electoral strength of the CCF. But whatever their origin, these policies became part of the political culture of contemporary Canada. If only symbolically, King's choice as party leader dramatized the shift toward social welfare measures in the Liberal Party and in the country as a whole.

By adopting such measures, non-socialist parties hope to produce consensus by appearing to be impartial mediators between society's competing groups. By contrast, the socialists argue that such practices of compromise and 'splitting the difference' invariably favour the establishment and work against the interests of the disadvantaged majority. But even while articulating this critique of consensus politics, the noted socialist intellectual Charles Taylor admitted, with exasperation, that 'consensus has stolen the day' in Canadian politics.[39] The evidence backs him up. Instead of voting to intensify the 'politics of polarization', most Canadians apparently disregard their class interests when voting.

One of the earliest analyses of this tendency was Robert Alford's comparative study of voting in Canada, Australia, the United Kingdom, and the United States. Of all of the voters he studied, Canadians were the least likely to vote along class lines. Those who voted Liberal did not appear to differ by class from those who voted Conservative. The NDP tended to draw a largely working-class vote, but workers were far from voting for the NDP *en masse*. Alford concluded that in Canadian federal elections voters did not support their 'own' parties very consistently.[40]

This finding seems to fit in well with some popular notions about Canadian society. Canadian voters are not guided by class interests, the argument goes, because the society is so divided along regional and ethnic lines. If Canadians are not 'class-conscious', we should not be surprised to find them voting for interests unrelated to class. Yet we cannot be completely certain that the failure to vote along class lines indicates a lack of class-consciousness or an acceptance of the politics of consensus. Other factors may be involved, such as lack of choice.

Obviously voters can only choose among the parties and policies that are offered to them at election time. Imagine, for example, that the Liberals and Conservatives line up on opposite sides of the Quebec question but present similar policies on employment, social services, taxes, and so on. This keeps the electorate from voting on issues about which the social classes would certainly differ in their thinking. In this case, we could not tell from voting statistics whether people were conscious of their class interests, or eager to serve them.

Alternatively, people may not vote by class because they feel that their votes will make little difference, or they believe that the party they prefer cannot be elected, or they doubt that politicians, whatever the party, will pay them any attention once elected. People may fail, it is true, to vote in their own class interests through what Marxists would call 'false consciousness'.[41] They may not be aware of their best interests, or of the political choices that would serve them best. Yet, for the reasons outlined above, we must not conclude too hastily that a failure to vote by class proves a lack of class awareness in Canada. Before speculating any further on the explanations for Canadian voting patterns, we ought to get our facts straight.

Do Canadians Vote by Class?

The first task in assessing class voting is deciding how to distinguish the political parties by the class interests they serve. Alford was convinced that the Progressive Conservatives and the Social Credit stood in the right wing of Canadian politics. After all, the Progressive Conservatives acknowledged by their name that they were 'Conservatives'. Like the Social Credit Party, they received a lot of their support from rural Protestants. Similarly Alford supposed the Liberal Party was as 'liberal' as its name, which in the United States translates as 'left'. Of course, the NDP had stated its intention to further workers' interests. Therefore Alford took the Liberal Party and NDP as together making up the Canadian 'left wing'. Workers ought to vote for either of these in their own interest.

Alford more or less correctly identified the NDP as a workers' party.[42] But did he label the other parties correctly? The two largest parties seem to differ less in their policies than in the regional, ethnic, and religious basis of their constituencies. (For example, the Liberals have customarily gotten their greatest support from urban areas, Quebec, francophones, and Catholics.) Indeed both the Liberals and the Conservatives had helped the underdog at some times and big business at other times. Once in power, they have behaved pragmatically, incorporating into their own platforms the more appealing ideas of the opposition parties.

Some students have even argued that in the period of interest to Alford, roughly 1955-65, the Conservative Party moved to the left of the Liberals. Led by John Diefenbaker, the party changed its program to appeal more than in the past to people who conventionally supported third parties. The appeals worked: in 1957, the Conservatives came into federal power after twenty-two years as the official opposition.[43]

So Alford's analysis classified Canadian parties in a highly questionable fashion. In reality, Liberals and Conservatives had almost exactly the same class appeal in this period; in some respects, the Conservatives held out more promise of reform, more concern for the disadvantaged than the Liberals. The misclassification resulted, in part, from failing to ask voters what *they* thought they were voting for. The same might be said of Alford's confusion over Social Credit, a populist party that has great appeal to farmers and small businessmen as well as some workers. The meaning of a vote for Social Credit is rarely self-evident. Like support for the Parti Québécois in 1976, it may just as well be a vote *against* something as *for* something. For example, it could be a vote against political corruption or against rule by Toronto and Montreal bankers, with which even 'leftist' NDP voters could sympathize. So party positions and voter intentions are not easily reconciled, whatever Alford might believe.

Rick Ogmundson has used different measures of party position than Alford's to analyze voting patterns. When parties are arrayed along a left-right continuum defined by the voters themselves, the result reveals more class-interested voting.[44] Moreover, the degree of association between class and vote seems to vary from one province to another. If, as Alford argued, Canadians failed to vote by class because of a traditional 'national character' or even cross-cutting loyalties, then Canadians in different parts of the country would be about equally likely to vote on class grounds. Yet, this is not what seems to happen. A majority of 1965 voters for the NDP identified with the working class west of the Ottawa River, but not east of it, for example.[45]

Other doubt is raised by the many observations that Canadians in different classes respond differently to given political issues. The appropriate question to ask is not 'Why do Canadians lack a class-consciousness?' but rather 'Why don't Canadians translate their class-consciousness into class voting more consistently?'

Ogmundson answers that the Liberal and Conservative parties, like the Democratic and Republican parties in the United States, have not wanted to offer themselves up to this kind of battle. Each wants to stake out the safe middle ground. Each oscillates slightly to the right and left around a centrist position. By the same token, of course, many voters in this situation will not support third parties simply because they doubt these parties can win. The sense of inevitable failure may also explain why workers participate in politics—and even vote— less often than middle-class people. As surveys by Meisel and others have shown, how much individuals involve themselves in politics depends a lot on how much effect they think they will have. And the sense of being effective, or having 'political efficacy', increases with each step up the social hierarchy.[46]

In short, people of different classes may hold attitudes and values that differ but do not always get translated into different styles of voting. Still, even this conclusion is not completely secure. Perhaps a particular kind of data lead to this conclusion, and other data would lead to another one. When we turn our gaze from aggregated national statistics to local ones, whether they concern a federal or other election, another conclusion is suggested: more people do appear to vote along class lines.[47]

People of different classes vote differently from one place to another. Class-based political activity by workers demands a strong local party organization, a strong sense of worker solidarity, opportunities to discuss politics and plan strategies, and so on. Rex Lucas has shown that workers in company towns, where typically political institutions are underdeveloped, tend to be politically inactive.[48] Some observers have said this inertia proves a lack of interest or education, or a lack of commitment to the town. Yet the inertia is far more easily explained once we consider the way power is distributed. In a company town the workers are vulnerable in every sense and they depend for their survival upon the good will of a single employer. Also, they are largely isolated from class-based institutions that might otherwise help them overcome their dependency and feeling of inefficacy.

This observation can be generalized as follows: workers are most likely to vote in their own interests when they take part in organized working-class institutions. Raymond Breton has coined the term 'institutional completeness' to explain why immigrants retain their native culture.[49] Without such institutional completeness, an individual—whether as an immigrant or as a working-class person—is assimilated into someone else's institutions and culture. To observe that people vote against their class interests is without meaning until we know what else they might have chosen. In a company town, for example, where even unionization is controlled by the company, a worker may only be able to choose either assimilation to the town (company) culture or isolation. Voting for the 'wrong' party may have a similar explanation, but often we cannot tell from the data that are available.

Developing institutions based on class depends on many factors. Some of these are outside the control of individuals, at least in the short run. The development of institutions requires a certain density of similar people with easy access to one another. It may require money; it certainly requires leadership, and it may demand that workers have some time and energy left after work to spend on political activity. But much personal sacrifice is needed. So it would be unfair to accuse workers who have failed to develop working-class institutions of having no class-consciousness.

Regional variations in political behaviour are due not only to institutional differences, but to broader cultural difference as well. The previous chapter discussed various claims that political cultures have developed to different stages across Canada. This difference in political development is demonstrated by greater class voting in some regions than in others. By and large, in provinces with the highest level of 'political development', one finds the most complete set of workers' institutions. Surely this is no mere coincidence. Workers' institutions foster a political culture of class-consciousness and a politics of polarization in Taylor's sense. In fact, neither class-culture nor institutionalization can survive without the other.

Dominant Ideologies and Counter-Ideologies

At many points this book has emphasized that Canada has many political sub-cultures. The political culture of anglophones outside Quebec is quite distinct from that of Quebec francophones. Closer examination reveals many political cultures, differences among Canada's many socially and economically defined 'regions': Newfoundland, the Maritimes, and the West most prominent among them. In each case, cultural differentiation has its historic roots in founding fragments and formative events, but also in relationships of dominance and subordination that may have persisted from the very beginning.

The English-French cultural difference is not merely an artifact of differences in world view arising at the time of first settlement and perpetuated through linguistic barriers, religious distrust, and/or differences of temperament—the tight-lipped English versus the flamboyant French and so on. This cultural difference reflects English-Canadian superiority in all important areas of Canada's existence: superior numbers, greater assimilation into the American world empire and its associated liberal culture, and most of all, economic control. English Canadians have, since the very beginnings of the Canadian state, controlled the major sectors of the Canadian economy, especially the banks and other money-lending institutions. French Canadians have until recently had to adapt their needs and wishes to that fact of life.

The regional differentiation of world views—the regional cultures discussed in the last two chapters—likewise reflect inequalities, particularly the metropolis-hinterland relationship of Ontario to the rest of Canada. Until recently southern Ontario and the area around Montreal have dominated Canada's social, cultural, and economic life; they have done so ever since Confederation. This small region has determined the course of development in all the rest of the country, except when unmediated influence has been exercised by outside powers, primarily by American investors.

Because this cultural differentiation results from differences in power, the growth and persistence of alternate political cultures, for example, in Quebec, in the West, and in the Maritimes, can also be understood, perhaps most profitably, as the growth of counter-cultures. Such cultures not only organize and give meaning to the daily lives of people living in what are dominated areas: they also 'make sense' of the condition of subordination or domination per se. Thus English-Canadian and French-Canadian cultures are not equals, co-celebrants of Canadian nationhood: rather they are opposed to each other, mirror images in some respects, devoted antagonists so long as their economic relationship is asymmetrical. Unequal power must lead to opposed, as well as different, cultures.

Likewise, Western Canadian culture and Maritime culture do not simply differ from Ontario culture. True, different patterns of settlement, different climates, staple industries, and relations to the United States make for interesting, even amusing contrasts between regions. But the conflicts that occur at federal-provincial conferences are more than colourful and amusing, because they result from serious matters like regional inequality, especially the subordination of the West and the Maritimes to the central region of Canada, whose interests are represented best by the federal government. The pious hope that multiculturalism—state-supported tolerance and appreciation for ethnic, religious, racial, and regional variations—will somehow bring Canadians together fails to address this central issue: namely, different cultural groups have a different amount of say in the way the country runs. The subordinate groups want more say, not merely more tolerance of their folkways. The often militant declaration of their cultural distinctness is no plea for tolerance: it is a demand for equality. The militance of a group's counter-culture is directly proportional to the subordination that group has suffered at the hands of the central Canadian establishment.

Nowhere, perhaps, is this more readily understood than in relation to social classes. An entire literature about dominant ideologies and counter-ideologies in respect to class conflict has grown out of the work of Marx and Mannheim (see Marchak's *Ideological Perspectives on Canada*[50] for a fuller statement of this theme). In writings by the 'political economy school' this notion of the dialectical relationship between dominant and counter-ideology has been applied, in discussions of monopoly capital, imperialism, and underdevelopment, to studying oppressed regions and oppressed nations. Every struggle for power, even an 'un-ideological' struggle for control of the economy, gets played out simultaneously on the cultural-ideological, as well as on the material, levels. The more powerful or dominant contenders eventually seek to impose their point of view on those they would subordinate. Those who resist must, if their resistance is to succeed, develop their own ideology or culture to counter, to unmask, to neutralize the dominant ideology. Otherwise they fall prey to what Marx called 'false consciousness', a point of view that serves the interests of the ruling class. Conformity to the prevailing order is far more commonly secured by such 'false consciousness' than by threats or physical force.[51]

As noted throughout this book, unlike the American political culture, the Canadian political culture was able to make room for conservative and socialist, as well as liberal, perspectives. Yet, one cannot deny that the liberal perspective dominates Canadian society, just as it dominates American society. It dominates, first, in the sense that most citizens endorse the liberal point of view, as evidenced by the voting patterns just examined. But liberalism is not only numerically dominant. It dominates because it is the ideology of the dominant class: it has the full force of the state, church, media, and educational system behind it: it has been trained into all of us.

We should have no difficulty understanding why the dominant ideology is liberal. After all ours is, like the Americans', a capitalist society founded on private property and a belief in the right of individuals to choose how to dispose of their property. What C.B. Macpherson called 'possessive individualism' is the quintessence of liberal philosophy, and it is also the ideological legitimation of capitalist accumulation. That is to say, there is an 'elective affinity' between liberalism and capitalism: they seek each other out. Any ideology defending private property will most benefit those who control the most property. That is why the economic élite, with the most property at stake, is the most committed to liberal capitalism.

Why the Canadian mass culture is so dominated by liberalism is harder to say. Of course, voting statistics alone do not demonstrate this dominance adequately, for people's choices are limited by the available candidates. However, a great many workers—white-collar office workers as well as blue-collar factory workers—who might be expected to vote socialist in their own interest, choose not to because they seem to have accepted the liberal point of view, the dominant ideology.

In part this is because they have not been convinced of the merits of the socialist position. Liberalism is better at 'accounting for' certain portions of their daily reality than socialism. 'Marx predicted the steady impoverishment of the working class and the loss of skill differentiation amongst its members. What has occurred, instead, is an increase in the numbers of workers who are steadily employed, and who are employed in white-collar and lower managerial positions.'[52]

If socialist doctrine seems inappropriate in explaining daily life to blue-collar workers, it seems even less relevant to white-collar workers. As Marchak observes:

> The working middle class is mobile. Its upper regions are becoming affluent, and their affluence is being used to purchase a never-ending array of consumer goods and services. They have not needed to invest, to scrimp, to build an empire in order to live well. Why indeed should they concern themselves with the long-term defects of monopoly capitalism? That is simply not a real-life experience for them, and their ignorance is compounded by a studied absence of information on the economic structure in their schools.[53]

The demise of authoritarian regimes in Eastern and Central Europe, and the dissatisfaction with the 'command economies' throughout the so-called 'socialist' world, has further discredited socialism and given a boost to the capitalist 'market economy' everywhere.

Marchak notes the growth in popularity of a 'do your own thing' ethic, combined with a search for 'roots' and religion, for meaning through superstition. Rootlessness is the down-side of possessive individualism: it results from a war of each against all, in a society constantly transforming itself to increase material wealth. But it also seems to accord with people's experience of life in large organizations: in schools, in bureaucracies, in careers. There people find 'universalism', justice of a kind (if not mercy), and a contest that legitimizes the outcomes that are already programmed into our social fabric: 'Individualism as a creed provides an explanation for differences in wealth and status: we make it on our own, and deserve what we get . . . . Do these people see their situation in class terms? It seems most unlikely that they do, or even that they see themselves as having anything in common. The young still expect to get ahead if they can just get into the mainstream.'[54]

Marchak has argued, in effect, that the dominant ideology dominates because it accords with people's daily experience. But it does so because it has programmed people to see certain things and not others; and to want certain things, not others. Bernd Baldus puts this position even more forcefully in his discussion of 'complementary periphery' behaviour.[55] The time has passed, he contends, when dominant groups need to train the masses to believe in the same things they believe in; all that is needed is the illusion of choice. The masses need to feel free to choose, but they need to be led to choose among alternatives which do not affect the distribution of power. In that sense, behaviour by the masses, at the 'periphery' of society's power structure, is 'complementary' to élite behaviour: it is not identical, but it reinforces élite initiatives and never threatens them.

Consider consumerism and the common practice of buying on credit. North American people undoubtedly consume more luxuries than any people who ever lived: gadgets for the home, clothes, cars, vacations, houses, boats, and so on. Easy credit has put these luxuries into almost everyone's reach; accordingly, indebtedness has risen progressively to higher and higher levels. Credit buying is a good example of 'complementary periphery' behaviour. While giving consumers the illusion of significant choice, it puts them in debt to the country's lending institutions and, indirectly, to the economic élite. This indebtedness significantly reduces their potential for radical behaviour: people with debts tend to become cautious. They don't want to risk their jobs, their homes, their standard of living by non-conformity, let alone by social protest or revolution. The monthly payments to VISA, to the mortgage company, the credit union, and assorted other creditors no doubt exercise greater social control over Canadians than all the police, judges, and clergy put together.

How did we come to that pass? The mass media and advertising agencies contribute by turning wants into needs, getting people to want luxuries, making luxuries seem indispensable instruments of happiness and fulfilment.[56] The schools help out by teaching us that 'progress' is the growth of material technology and that a high 'standard of living' means luxury consumption. Underlying such 'complementary periphery' behaviour there is, as Baldus tells us, a broader though less obvious socialization that makes us value free choice, respect private property, and show obedience to authority. Given these three general orientations and a mass media that keep us envious and insecure, we are led to embrace a life of materialism, opportunism, and conformism.

Why does the dominant ideology, liberalism, dominate? Because it does indeed make sense of many facts of our daily life, whatever our social class. Where we have difficulty 'making sense' on our own, the schools, mass media, even government will step in to 'clarify' our thinking in liberal terms. The socialist, alternative explanation is almost never heard, certainly never with the same force and authority. But also, the myth of free choice, which is the root of liberalism, is the hook inside the worm: once swallowed, it only allows us a range of behaviour that conforms to, and never challenges, the existing order.

As Baldus has shown by his research based on interviews with Toronto school children[57] by the time we are teenagers we have already learned that rich people—people with white-collar jobs, who drive nice cars and live in big houses—are more upstanding, more honest, more likable than poor people. This belief will make us honour and obey the rich, make us strive to be rich and despise the poor, and hold the poor responsible for their own failure. Perhaps this helps to explain why even working people frequently vote for the liberal, and not for the socialist, political candidates, and why the materialism so prominent in our culture has captured the majority of our citizens, creating in them what Herbert Marcuse calls 'commodity fetishism'.

Conclusion

In the 1970s, advanced industrial societies everywhere experienced new tensions between labour and management with every new challenge to continued economic growth. Canada was no exception. The Keynesian economics that promised to reduce the fluctuations between boom and bust no longer seemed to work by the mid-1970s. Governmental measures intended to regulate the trade-offs between unemployment and inflation failed disastrously. Not even wage and price controls, introduced in 1975, could put a stop to this painful combination of high inflation and high unemployment. Workers complained, justifiably, that while wages were being suppressed profits were allowed to soar. All the while the economy limped ahead, growing hardly at all.

After the 1976 PQ victory, a lack of confidence in Canada's political stability combined with poor export performance (particularly in manufactured goods) to weaken the Canadian dollar's value abroad. By late 1978, the dollar had slid to its lowest value since the Depression, even when measured against the declining American dollar. Canada's prodigal past had taken a toll. Like all dependent economies (someone once described the country as a 'banana republic without the bananas'), Canada was paying for the failure to balance, and control, its own economy.

Economic difficulties translate into political problems in a number of ways. The most visible manifestation in Canada was increased labour unrest. From 1960 to 1975, the number of strikes and lockouts in Canada grew fourfold; the number of workers involved, tenfold. Person-days lost rose from 738,700 to nearly eleven million![58] Even if little of this militance was reflected in voting patterns, confrontation was the order of the day. The state's role in regulating class relations has become increasingly central to the society's well-being. As the largest single employer in the country, the federal government is involved directly as well as indirectly in labour-management disputes. Since collective bargaining was introduced into the public sector, government employees of all kinds—nurses and meteorologists, air traffic controllers and postal workers— have gone out on strike. Inept at handling disputes in the public sector, the government not surprisingly failed to provide leadership or guidance in the private sector as well.

The state in Canada and elsewhere was experiencing what James O'Connor called severe 'fiscal crisis'. A shift in thinking regarding the role of the state, a transformation of the nature of political discourse seemed inevitable. At first it appeared the left would benefit from this instability but in fact the opposite occurred. In both Britain and the United States, right wing policies of tax cutting for the rich, privatization and deregulation were introduced under the leadership of Margaret Thatcher and Ronald Reagan. Called neoconservatism, but more accurately labelled neoliberalism, since it involved a harkening back to nineteenth-century classic liberal notions of *laisser faire*, this outlook took hold in the Canadian conservative party and helped Brian Mulroney unseat Joe Clark as party leader in 1983. The following year Mulroney triumphed over the faltering Liberals, now led by John Turner. The political discourse of the welfare state gave way to a new anti-statist pro-free-enterprise language, whose most enthusiastic champions were the new breed of young, upwardly mobile professionals—the Yuppies.

Meanwhile, the disintegration of communist regimes in Eastern and Central Europe, and upheaval in the Soviet Union as its leaders attempted to achieve restructuring and renewal (*perestroika* and *glasnost*) spelled the end for socialism and marked the beginning of a new triumphant epoch of capitalist democracy, or so it seemed.

The actual situation was much more complex. Neoliberalism was not an unmitigated blessing. The promise that tax cuts for the wealthy would ultimately produce financial benefits that would 'trickle down' to the poor went unfulfilled. Despite promises to cut spending, deficits soared. Deregulated industries became unstable to the point of chaos. Free Trade led to deindustrialization, particularly in Southern Ontario. Mulroney's campaign slogan of 'jobs jobs jobs' applied more accurately to their disappearance than their creation. After several years of impressive growth, the economy sank into a slump nearly as painful as the depression-like conditions at the beginning of the 1980s.

But Canada also faced other problems at least as severe as these economic difficulties. The long suppressed claims of native peoples erupted in confrontation and violence. Ethnic and racial tensions flared up. Violence against women, bloodily epitomized in Marc Lepine's massacre of 14 women at the Ecole Polytechnique in Montreal, continued unabated. With the failure of the Meech Lake Accord and the surge of support for independence in Quebec, Canada appeared to be facing disintegration and chaos.

Alternative ideologies provide different 'pictures' of the problems facing a society. Each picture is necessarily selective: it characterizes some problems as crucial, others as less important, and still others as non-existent. An ideology also links problems to strategies of change. Liberalism, especially in its early formulations, imagined that private property, the market economy, and the destruction of feudal institutions would save society. Soon, however, liberalism's heroes became socialism's villains. Socialism redefined entrepreneurs as parasites preying on the surplus value of labourers, whom socialism idealized as the salt of the earth. Only public ownership of the means of production could overcome the ills engendered by a liberal society. That people with competing ideologies could portray the same societies so differently illustrates the extent to which an ideology makes up an entire *weltanschauung* or world view.

Despite the variety of ideological traditions in Canada's political culture, no existing ideology appears able to solve our present problems. Some sort of cultural mutation is needed if we are to regain economic prosperity and develop more harmonious class relations. The alternative to this—increasingly virulent conflict—is at least as probable and as threatening today as when Mackenzie King laid the framework for the social welfare state nearly half a century ago.

No one can tell whether the future's new ideology will grow out of an existing ideology, as social welfareism emerged from liberalism; or will synthesize from elements scarcely noticed today. We are forced to agree with Marchak's observation that many current patterns of thought and action 'do not fit' either of the main two, liberal and socialist, ideologies.

> There are statements that question the virtues of equality—which both liberals and Marxists accept. There are statements that express contempt for the democratic framework, not, as in Marxist literature, because it fails to express the will of the people, but because it fails to represent efficiently the interests of the ruling class. There are statements that question the usefulness of nation states and their governments and call on corporations and other governments to impose their will on recalcitrant populations. There are statements that say, in effect, cultural genocide is all right if it is undertaken in the interests of greater efficiency and profits . . . . They are the ideological statements of a society that is past and ritually buried, yet they refer to a society that may succeed the liberal democracy. In both, there is a ruling class which does not pretend to be something else.[59]

Not only in Canada, but throughout North America, something reactionary, in all the various meanings of that word, took shape in the 1980s. We saw a growth in racism, a resurgence of ethnic and religious solidarity, a quest for family 'roots', and at the same time, a new selfishness or 'narcissism' as Christopher Lasch called it: all of these in reaction to the threat to personal integrity that economic difficulty and rapid social change pose. People retreated from the 'mass society', whose promises of opportunity and well-being were broken and, in any event, bought at the price of personal happiness. People were ripe for a new ideology, yearning for belief. Some reverted to religious fundamentalism. Others turned to various 'new age' beliefs. By the 1990s, the culture of greed and conspicuous consumption was giving way to a new value system.[60]

This chapter began with a discussion of the critical importance of constitutions to the establishment of conceptions of authority and national purpose. Constitutions have another equally important function in relation to political culture. The constitution becomes a crucial touchstone of political discourse. The language embodied in the constitution provides the key terms and definitions for political discussion, debate, and conflict. Since all legislation derives its authority from, and must be compatible with, the constitution, both proponents and opponents of legislation will turn to the constitution as a kind of sovereign dictionary. Moreover, disputes over meaning and constitutionality will be resolved by the Supreme Court, which is given the opportunity and the responsibility to make authoritative judgments to resolve such disputes.

Prior to the adoption of the Charter in 1982, the constitution (i.e., the BNA Act) defined in great detail areas of jurisdiction for the federal and provincial governments, and enshrined a very few other key policy areas such as transportation (the railroad), language rights, and jurisdiction concerning aboriginal peoples. In view of the preponderance of attention in the BNA Act to the federal division of powers, it is not surprising that the major focus of political discourse in Canada centred precisely on this topic. The classic Canadian political joke highlighted this obsession: 'The Elephant—is it a matter of federal or provincial jurisdiction?'

The Charter has transformed Canadian political discourse by extending almost infinitely the range of political concerns that can be related directly to the constitution. Federalist discourse—which still retains importance, and is still invoked in particular by governments in their jurisdictional struggle with each other—is being eclipsed by a discourse about rights that has taken off from the various pronouncements in the Charter. Now virtually any aspect of public policy might conceivably lead to a 'Charter challenge.' Governments and agencies devoted millions of person-hours to a review of all areas of their activity to attempt to anticipate any possible Charter violations in the few years following its adoption. The Charter has become enormously popular among the general public in most parts of the country. To some extent this has helped nationalize political discourse, and provide a common national focus to political debate. Instead of focusing on intergovernmental relations this rights based discourse concerns the relations between citizens and the state, and with each other. Some groups have been accorded special status by virtue of their being specifically mentioned in the Charter. Thus as Alan Cairns points out,

> The written constitution has become a symbolic document of great importance. It hands out differential status to Canadians in terms of sex, ethnicity, language, indigenous status, and other social categories singled out for explicit constitutional attention.[61]

Notes

[1] See Samuel Beer's discussion of 'conceptions of authority and purpose' in Samuel Beer and Adam Ulan (eds), *Patterns of Government* (New York: Random House, 1958).

[2] The BNA Act embodied only a portion of what would properly be described as Canada's constitution. Many basic features were omitted entirely or referred to only in passing. The Act states that Canada shall have 'a constitution similar in principle to that of the United Kingdom', thereby importing a complex set of practices and arrangements related to the parliamentary system. See Kenneth McNaught, 'History and the Perception of Politics', in John H. Redekop (ed.), *Approaches to Canadian Politics* (Scarborough: Prentice-Hall, 1978): 106. Some but by no means all of these unwritten provisions were further codified in the Constitution Act of 1982.

[3] John Conway, 'Politics, Culture, and the Writing of Constitutions', in Harvey L. Dyck and H. Peter Krosby (eds), *Empire and Nations* (Toronto: University of Toronto Press, 1969): 4. In Conway's view many of the limitations of the BNA Act stemmed from the lack of refinement and education of the founding fathers who drafted it. He points out that 'of the thirty-seven Fathers of Confederation only four had a college education and of these only one—Charles Tupper—had a university education in the sense in which we would use the term today' (p. 5).

[4] Louis-François Laflèche writing in 1868, as quoted in *ibid.*: 6.

[5] Cf. Edwin Black, *Divided Loyalties*: 5.

[6] Conway: 17.

[7] Reg Whitaker, 'Images of the State in Canada', in Leo Panitch (ed.), *The Canadian State: Political Economy and Political Power* (Toronto: University of Toronto Press, 1977): 44-6; Donald V. Smiley (ed.), *The Rowell-Sirois Report* (Toronto: McClelland & Stewart, 1963): 29-33.

[8] Vaughan, 'The Political Philosophy of the Canadian Founding': 24. To some these features of the BNA Act are precisely its strengths and advantages. See, for example, McNaught.

[9] Black: 3.

[10] See Herschel Hardin, *A Nation Unaware*; Whitaker: 65.

[11] These analytical categories are drawn primarily from the experience of institutional and ideological development in Europe. Consequently, they apply less than perfectly to North America, where important mutations have occurred. In using them, we must be aware of what Sheldon Wolin calls 'the fetish of ideological interpretation which compels us to look at past theories through constrictive peepholes' (*Politics and Vision* [Boston: Little, Brown, 1960]: 358). Wolin has forcefully opposed the reduction of political theories to the status of ideological symbols. Thus he would argue that Marx's work cannot be reduced to Marxism; indeed Marx himself denied that he was a Marxist in any narrow sense. However inadequate for classifying complex, esoteric theories, the categories are helpful in discussing the simpler, exoteric ideas found in the political culture. Despite the theoretical potential for almost unlimited permutations and combinations, in practice political values, beliefs, and assumptions tend to cluster or cohere into relatively few combinations. Three such clusters are the ideologies we call conservatism, liberalism, and socialism.

In the Canadian setting, relatively unique variations have appeared in the doctrines of Social Credit, progressivism, etc. Space limitations preclude our analysing these ideological variants. Although they have had a very minor impact on federal politics, their importance at the provincial level has been much greater.

[12] Gad Horowitz, 'Conservatism, Liberalism and Socialism in Canada: An Interpretation', *Canadian Journal of Economics and Political Science* 32,2 (May 1966). Later revised and published as chapter 1 of Gad Horowitz, *Canadian Labour in Politics* (Toronto: University of Toronto Press, 1968). Note that we are here picking up some issues left unresolved in Chapter 2.

[13] *Ibid.*: 9. Horowitz's description of the un-American features of English-Canadian political culture is substantially correct, but his explanation of these features places too much emphasis on the Tory streak. Our interpretation stresses instead the importance of the continuation of the colonial tie, the

subsequent importation of socialism from Britain, and the confused identity resulting from Loyalism's attachment to British symbols.

[14] *Ibid.*: 21.

[15] W.L. Morton, 'The Possibility of a Philosophy of Conservatism', in *Journal of Canadian Studies* 5,1 (February 1970): 8. See also Carl Berger, *The Writing of Canadian History* (Toronto: Oxford University Press, 1976): 252 ff.

[16] Quoted in William Christian, 'Ideology and Politics', in John H. Redekop (ed.), p. 129. In the 1980s, however, American-style 'neo-conservatism' has made considerable inroads in Canada, particularly among members of the Progressive Conservative Party.

[17] C.B. Macpherson, *The Political Theory of Possessive Individualism* (Clarendon: Oxford University Press, 1958). By the term Macpherson refers to the impetus in liberal theory toward accumulation as a measure of virtue.

[18] Peter C. Newman, *The Canadian Establishment* (Toronto: McClelland & Stewart, 1975): 157 ff.

[19] Very few systematic data are available on attitudes to social welfare measures among the political élite. Two studies, however, deserve mention. Allan Kornberg surveyed about two-thirds of the MPs elected to the twenty-fifth Parliament of Canada. Among his survey items were three questions from which he constructed a 'Welfare-State Index', measuring support for federal government activity in public works, unemployment, and medical insurance. He then reported his findings by party affiliation, combining Liberal and New Democrat responses into 'Left-Wing Parties' and Conservative and Social Credit responses into 'Right-Wing Parties'.

He found that clearly 'left-wing' MPs show much stronger support for welfare-state measures than 'right-wing' members. Two difficulties complicate this observation, however. First, the contrasts between Liberals and Conservatives are probably exaggerated by the inclusion of responses of New Democrat and Social Credit members respectively. Second, the wording of the questions emphasized federal as opposed to provincial government activity, and may have tapped into an anti-centralist bias among some MPs, thereby misrepresenting their views as anti-welfare state when they instead merely opposed the federal government's activity in these issues.

Robert Presthus also conducted a survey of the political élite in Canada (and the United States) in which an index of 'economic liberalism' was included to measure general support for big government, and particular attitudes toward government measures providing 'economic security', federal aid to education, to 'national medicare plan', and lower rates to unemployment. Again these items can ruffle the feathers of strict constitutionalists in Canada (where for example education is a provincial responsibility) and thus the responses must be interpreted with caution. Furthermore, Presthus treats politicians (whom he calls 'legislators') as a single group, and does not break down their responses by party affiliation. His data do provide interesting insights into contrasts between the two countries, among certain regions within each country, and among bureaucrats, politicians, and directors of interest groups. See Robert Presthus, *Elites in the Policy Process* (London: Cambridge University Press, 1974): 371.

For an assessment of the fate of public ownership in the new economic era see Jeanne Kirk Laux, 'Shaping or Serving Markets? Public Ownership After Privatization', in D. Drache and M. Gertler (eds), *The New Era of Global Competition: State Policy and Market Power* (Montreal and Kingston: McGill-Queen's University Press, 1991).

[20] Horowitz quoting Grant, *Canadian Labour*: 10. Terry Cook, 'The Canadian Conservative Tradition', in *Journal of Canadian Studies* (November 1973): 33. Note as well Christian and Campbell's discussion of the 'conservative streak' in *Canadian Liberalism*: 37. In another writing, William Christian suggests that a 'new toryism' began to emerge under Robert Stanfield, who was at least aware of the need for synthesis of the 'welter of contradictions found in the Party during Diefenbaker's tenure'. William Christian, 'Ideology and Politics': 128-9.

[21] Cook: 37.

[22] Peter C. Newman, 'The Lack of Conservative-Liberal Differences in Canadian Politics', in Gordon

Hawkins (ed.), *Order and Good Government* (Toronto: University of Toronto Press, 1965): 97. Cf. William Christian and Colin Campbell, *Political Parties and Ideologies in Canada* (Toronto: McGraw-Hill Ryerson, 1975): 170-1. For a more recent and better documented assessment see Richard Nadeau and André Blais, 'Do Canadians Distinguish Between Parties? Perceptions of Party Competence', *Canadian Journal of Political Science* 23, 2 (June 1990)

[23] Garth Stevenson, 'Foreign Policy', in Winn and McNemeny: 254.

[24] For some Liberals, nationalism is in principle unacceptable because it rests on 'emotionalism'. That directly contradicts the liberal commitment to 'cold, unemotional rationality' that alone can serve as the basis for governmental authority in modern society. Thus according to P.E. Trudeau (*Federalism and the French-Canadians*: 202): 'Nationalism will have to be discarded as a rustic and clumsy tool.' But liberal anti-nationalism has in effect led to the growth of continentalism and continued absorption of Canada by the United States, according to conservative George Grant: 'the capitalist politics of cybernetics which [Trudeau] so admires must inevitably work against national identity' (Foreword to Laxer and Laxer: 11). See also Christian and Campbell: 179, 187.

[25] See Charles Doran, *Forgotten Partnership*; and Stephen Clarkson, *Canada and the Reagan Challenge* (Ottawa: Canadian Institute for Economic Policy, 1982); and Lawrence Le Duc and J. Alex Murray, 'A Resurgence Of Canadian Nationalism: Attitudes and Policies in the 1980s' in Allan Kornberg and Harold Clarke (eds), *Political Support in Canada: The Crisis Years* (Durham: Duke University Press, 1983).

[26] Norman Penner, *The Canadian Left* (Scarborough: Prentice Hall, 1977).

[27] Gad Horowitz, 'Tories, Socialists and the Demise of Canada', in *Canadian Dimension* 2,4 (May-June 1965): 12.

[28] David Lewis' speech at York University, Fall 1977.

[29] Gad Horowitz, 'Tories, Socialists and the Demise of Canada': 16. Note also Christian and Campbell. 31: 'Quebec's collectivist past provided receptive and fruitful soil for socialist ideas once the invasion of liberal capitalism had broken the monopoly of the old conservative ideology.'

[30] See Christopher Adams, 'The COR and Reform Parties: Locations of Canadian Protest Party Support.' Presented to the CPSA Conference, Kingston, Ontario, June 1991.

[31] Newman, *The Canadian Establishment*.

[32] David J. Elkins, 'The Perceived Structure of the Canadian Party Systems', *Canadian Journal of Political Science* 8,3 (1974).

[33] George Grant, *Technology and Empire* (Toronto: Anansi, 1968): 43.

[34] Rod Preece, 'The Myth of the Red Tory', *Canadian Journal of Political and Social Theory* 1,2 (Spring-Summer 1977): 3-28.

[35] See Harold Clarke *et al.*, *Absent Mandate*. (Toronto: Gage, 1991): 51 ff.

[36] Beck and Pierce: 40.

[37] See, *inter alia*, Stuart Jamieson, *Times of Trouble: Industrial Relations in Canada* (Toronto: Macmillan of Canada, 1973). Canada's record of working days lost due to strikes and lock-outs is among the worst of advanced industrial societies. This fact indicates a high level of class conflict notwithstanding peculiarities of voting behaviour discussed below. One observer even attributes the high rate of strikes, walkouts, and absenteeism to the political emasculation of Canadian worker institutions and the 'business unionism' of large American-based unions. The predictable result of this orientation is that 'the more militant sections of the working class have been forced to find other outlets for their political energies'. Daniel Drache, 'The Enigma of Canadian Nationalism', *Australia and New Zealand Journal of Sociology* 14,3 (Part Two, October 1978): 319.

[38] David Jay Bercuson, 'Introduction' to W.L. Mackenzie King, *Industry and Humanity* (Toronto: University of Toronto Press, 1973): xx, xxi.

[39] Charles Taylor, *The Pattern of Politics* (Toronto: McClelland & Stewart, 1970): 1.

[40] Robert Alford, *Party and Society* (Chicago: Rand McNally, 1963).

[41] See the discussion of this issue in N.H. Chi, 'Class Cleavage', in Winn and McNemeny: 103-6.

[42] The NDP was formed in 1961 out of the CCF Party and with the formal support of most of the Canadian labour movement. Trade union workers provide nearly 50% of the votes obtained by the NDP, but a majority of trade union votes go to the major parties. (Even the Social Credit, despite its right-wing enterprise ideology, draws a substantial working class vote.) Furthermore, nearly half of the NDP electoral support comes from non-working-class voters. The closer the party gets to winning political power, the more it attempts to moderate its ideology toward the comfortable centre. See Chi and Drache.

[43] Jane Jenson, 'Party Strategy and Party Identification: Some Patterns of Partisan Allegiance', in *Canadian Journal of Political Science* 9,1 (March 1976). The Conservative Party gradually modified its platform to include more social welfare issues from 1919 to 1948. The 'Bennett New Deal' was largely modelled after the policies adopted by President Franklin Roosevelt in the United States. For a thorough study see Larry Glassford, 'The Conservative Party and Policy Change' (unpublished seminar paper, York University, 1978).

[44] Rick Ogmundson, 'Mass-Elite Linkages and Class Issues in Canada', in *Canadian Review of Sociology and Anthropology* 13 (February 1976): 1-12; 'On the Measurement of Party Class Positions: The Case of Canadian Political Parties at the Federal Level', in *Canadian Review of Sociology and Anthropology* 12 (November 1975): 565-76; 'Party Class Images and the Class Vote in Canada', in *American Sociological Review* 40 (August 1975): 506-12; 'On the Use of Party Image Variables to Measure the Political Distinctiveness of a Class Vote: The Canadian Case', in *Canadian Journal of Sociology* 1 (Summer 1975): 169-77. Note, however, that in a re-analysis of these and subsequent (1968) comparable data, Lambert and Hunter conclude that Ogmundson may have exaggerated the importance Canadian voters attach to class in labelling political parties, or in voting. See Ronald D. Lambert and Alfred A. Hunter, 'Social Stratification, Voting Behaviour and the Images of Canadian Federal Political Parties', *Canadian Review of Sociology and Anthropology* 16 (1979). Note as well that a careful examination of the 1965, 1968, and 1974 survey data led a group of researchers to conclude that 'several measures of social class were but weakly related to voting behaviour, and no clear trend towards an increase in class voting could be detected' (Harold Clarke *et al.*, *Political Choice in Canada*: 127).

[45] See Chi. In *Crisis, Challenge and Change: Party and Class in Canada Revisited* (Toronto: McGraw-Hill Ryerson, 1985) Janine Brodie and Jane Jenson develop the hypothesis that the pattern of class voting reflects the historical period during which the working class was mobilized into politics. Note as well the data from the 1965 survey discussed in Mildred Schwartz, *Politics and Territory*, p. 135.

[46] See Rick Van Loon, 'Political Participation in Canada: The 1965 Election', in *Canadian Journal of Political Science* 3,3 (September 1970): 376-99.

[47] Nelson Wiseman and K.W. Taylor, 'Ethnic vs. class voting: the Case of Winnipeg, 1945', in *Canadian Journal of Political Science* 7 (June 1974): 314-28.

[48] Rex A. Lucas, *Minetown, Milltown, Railtown: Life in Canadian Communities of Single Industry* (Toronto: University of Toronto Press, 1971). See also Janine Brodie and Jane Jenson, 'Piercing the Smokescreen: Class and Brokerage Politics in Canada' in A. Gagnon and A.B. Tanguay (eds), *Canadian Parties in Transition: Discourse, Organization and Representation* (Toronto: Nelson, 1988). An excellent analysis of the lack of class voting in Canada appears in Jon Pammett, 'Class Voting and Class Consciousness in Canada', *Canadian Review of Sociology and Anthropology* 24 (1987).

[49] Raymond Breton, 'Institutional Completeness of Ethnic Communities and the Personal Relations of Immigrants', in *American Journal of Sociology* 70 (May 1964): 193-205.

[50] M. Patricia Marchak, *Ideological Perspectives on Canada* (Toronto: McGraw-Hill Ryerson, 1975).

[51] This point is developed by the Italian Marxist Antonio Gramsci into a theory of ideological 'hegemony'. For an excellent overview of Marxist approaches see Jorge Lorrain, *Marxism and Ideology* (London: Macmillan, 1983).

[52] Marchak: 98.

[53] *Ibid.*

[54] Marchak: 99.

[55] Bernd Baldus, 'Social Control in Capitalist Societies: an Examination of the Problem of Order in Liberal Democracies', *Canadian Journal of Sociology* 2,3 (Summer 1977): 247-62.

[56] See Stephen Kline and William Leiss, 'Advertising, Needs and "Commodity Fetishism"', *Canadian Journal of Political and Social Theory* 2,1 (Winter 1978): 5-30.

[57] Bernd Baldus and Verna Tribe, 'The Development of Perceptions and Evaluations of Social Inequality among Public School Children', *Canadian Review of Sociology and Anthropology* 15,1 (February 1978): 50-60.

[58] David Wolfe, 'The State and Economic Policy in Canada, 1968-1975', in Panitch.

[59] Marchak: 116-17.

[60] Canada is not alone in this experience. As Inglehart argues, 'During the past few decades, economic, technological, and sociopolitical changes have been transforming the cultures of advanced industrial societies [including Canada] in profoundly important ways. The incentives that motivate people to work, the issues that give rise to political conflict, people's religious beliefs, their attitudes concerning divorce, abortion, and homosexuality, the importance they attach to having children and raising families—all these have been changing. One could go as far as to say that throughout advanced industrial society, what people want out of life is changing.' Ronald Inglehart, *Culture Shift in Advanced Industrial Society* (Princeton: Princeton University Press, 1991).

[61] Alan C. Cairns, 'The Charter, Interest Groups, Executive Federalism, and Constitutional Reform' in David E. Smith *et al.* (eds), *After Meech Lake: Lessons for the Future* (Saskatoon: Fifth House, 1991): 14-15.

Conclusion: Problems and Prospects

Political culture consists of the ideas, assumptions, values, and beliefs that condition political action. It affects the ways we use politics: the kinds of social problems we address and the solutions we attempt. For political culture serves as a filter or lens through which political actors view the world; it influences what they perceive as social problems and how they react to them. Political perception and political action are mediated through language and speech. Political culture is the language of political discourse, the vocabulary and grammar of political controversy and understanding.

This book has applied the political culture approach to some of Canada's most pressing problems: Quebec's drive toward independence; the disenchantment of Canada's regions with Confederation; conflicts involving class, gender, ethnicity and aboriginal rights. Each of these problems—duality, regionalism, and the politics of identity and status—has transformed the fragment cultures that founded Canada. A chain of formative events has brought about mutations in these cultures, redirecting them toward new concerns, values, and beliefs.

To some extent class conflict in Canada has recreated in miniature the ideologies and conflict found in Europe. A few Canadians embraced European-style conservatism, and found in monarchy and the Empire usable symbols of a hierarchically ordered society. Others took up socialist doctrine and with it attacked privilege and inequality, using the powerful rhetoric of class warfare. But all Canadian parties have been centrist, heavily influenced by small-l liberalism and, especially in recent years, by American-style neo-liberalism. In electoral politics, ethnic, religious, and regional solidarities have persisted, blocking the development of nation-wide class solidarity. Not only do Canada's social classes avoid warring, they scarcely vote differently.

For this and other reasons, conservatism, liberalism, and socialism are simply inadequate to conceptualize the cultural substance of Canadian politics. Nothing consistently connects these three ideologies with views on Anglo-French relations, regionalism, or identity. Nor do Canadians agree about the way to approach these issues. Instead the political culture comprises contradictory values, which can be grouped into broad categories of co-operation and conflict. The co-operative formula for Anglo-French relations has combined accommodation, compromise, partnership and friendship. The determined quest for mutual compromise and understanding was epitomized by the truck driver from Ontario who invested thousands of dollars of his personal funds to put up billboards stating 'Mon Canada Comprends Québec/My Canada Includes Quebec.'

(The French word *comprends* has a double entendre: it means both include *and* 'understand'.) By contrast assimilationism (or its flip side, separatism), rigidity, hatred, and hostility have provided a recipe for conflict symbolized by the trampling of the Quebec flag in small town Ontario, or the burning of the Canadian flag in Quebec. Regionalism has likewise raised contradictory tensions between centralization and greater regional autonomy, between justice-as-re-distribution and bald selfishness, between a harmonious vision of Canada as a 'community of communities' joined together in national reconciliation, and a picture of squabbling political leaders engaged in 'province bashing' or 'ganging up on Ottawa'.

Canada's regions have developed differently, transformed by foreign invest-ment that was never effectively co-ordinated under a national policy of eco-nomic development. Today, as always, gross regional inequality remains despite countless policies aimed at equalization. Moreover, Canada is dominated by outsiders, as it was in earlier days by the French and British empires. So suc-cessfully have American influences penetrated English Canada, both economi-cally and culturally, that the American way of life is widely and strongly preferred in this country. American 'mass culture'—food, books, clothes, and television programs—is prevalent enough to erode and homogenize even the rich regional diversity of Canada.

Canada's relationship with the United States has been ambivalent from the outset: a mixture of admiration and disdain, co-operation and conflict, flattering imitation and self-righteous distinctiveness. In the 1950s, the political culture of Canadian-American relations settled on partnership-as-dependency; we wel-comed American popular culture and unlimited direct investment. Although the pendulum began to swing the other way in the next decade, the new Canadian nationalism born in the turmoil of the 1960s soon lost much of its energy. Instead, initiative shifted to the provincial level, where strong governments began to intervene in the economy as instruments of new regional bourgeoisies often competing for American investment. The Free Trade Agreement cemented con-tinental economic ties between Canada and the US.[1] When followed by the GST, it helped create a new type of ambivalent Canadian: the cross-border shopper.

Victimized by a sense of cultural inferiority, Canadians failed until recently to encourage or even acknowledge Canadian art, letters, and other forms of 'higher culture'. Efforts to overcome the legacy of indifference have had little success. Concern over these matters dates back at least as far as the Massey Commission and the establishment of the Canada Council in the early 1950s. Despite a host of policies, agencies, and inquiries intended to stimulate and nurture Canadian arts and letters, a recent study of the 'Canadian cultural marketplace' concluded that '[l]ess than thirty per cent of books and magazines sold are Canadian, less than three per cent of film screen time is filled with Canadian films, less then ten per cent of sound recordings, less than thirty per cent of all programming in the English language available on television screens'.[2] Many Canadians still

regard Canadian music or writing or drama as automatically inferior and unde-
sirable. In this respect we continue to display a colonial mentality.

Similar problems have complicated efforts to strengthen national feeling. A
full century after Confederation, Canadians were just starting to change the most
basic symbols of national self-image—flag, anthem, constitution—in hopes of
strengthening solidarity. Such halting steps, a little too late, a little too small,
were reflected in how most Canadians identify themselves with the federal state.
When asked in 1974 to which level of government they felt closest, most Canadians replied 'the province'; only in Ontario did a majority report feeling
closer to the federal government.[3] Strong regional or provincial loyalties have
tended to supplant national loyalties, keeping truly national institutions and
alliances from coming to fruition.

Canada's political institutions have not dealt effectively with these problems.
In adapting the British parliamentary form of government to a federal state, the
founders of Confederation underestimated the strength and persistence of regionalism. Moreover, judicial interpretations of the BNA Act gave the provincial
governments much more autonomy than drafters of the Act had intended.[4]
Restricted as they are by party discipline, Canadian federal politicians have
proved incapable of resolving regional conflicts through mutual compromise at
the federal level. Instead, these conflicts are fought out between federal and
provincial leaders, who increasingly think of each other as antagonists rather
than compatriots.

The resulting harm is both obvious and profound. Partly in response, an entire
layer of intermediate political institutions grew up, like a scar tissue on a wound.
By smoothing relations between governments, these new institutions of 'executive federalism' gained considerable power in their own right; but they function
very much as a closed society. Only a tiny fraction of what transpires at their
meetings is subject to any form of scrutiny or review, and the public knows little
about them. These new institutions have done little to heal the severed ligaments
of national good-will, or inspire a sense of national purpose and commitment.

After Quebec elected (in 1976) a provincial government committed to gaining
sovereignty-association, federal-provincial conflict sped to a crisis. The Canadian federation threatened to dissolve before our eyes. Consequently, politicians
turned their attention to changing the Canadian federation in ways that appeal
to Quebec, while at the same time soothing discontent in other regions.

For all their importance, federalism and constitutional reform were not the only
problems facing Canada. Such concerns tended to preoccupy our political thinking, crowding out reflection on other important issues. The Canadian political
culture, already rich in concepts and insights into the workings of federalism,
had little to tell us about class conflict or about humanitarian and civil libertarian
issues. The poor, the old, the jobless, aboriginals, women, ethnic minorities,
disabled people, stood or sat at the back of Canada's bus, second-class citizens.

In the 1960s and 1970s, most Canadians knew little about these issues, and indeed seemed to suffer from a kind of cultural blindness or insensitivity to them. But change came rapidly, especially in Quebec. The 'ice' that Siegfried said encased Francophones' political culture, melted quickly in the heat of social change. Many new ideas surfaced. Two formative events in Quebec—the 1960 election that ushered in the Quiet Revolution, and the 1976 victory of the Péquistes—transformed the political culture. The people of Quebec sensed the exhilaration, or the profound disappointment, that major political change brings with it.

The defeat of the Quebec referendum in 1981, and the subsequent unravelling of the Parti Québécois a few years later—coupled with the return to power of Liberals under Robert Bourassa—lulled many Canadians into a false sense that Quebec nationalism was dead forever. Then followed the Meech Lake Agreement and the re-election of the federal Conservatives in 1988. But Meech died, the PQ survived, and Bourassa shifted rapidly away from a pro-federalist stance, egged on by articulate nationalists in his own party, and pushed further by the recommendations of the Belanger-Campeau Commission his own government had established. By 1991, Canada faced its most profound constitutional crisis ever.

But the painful dilemmas of constitutional reform now extended far beyond the Quebec issue, or the division of powers between the federal government and the provinces. English Canadians had been politically awakened to the realization that the Constitution is not simply a matter of underlying governmental structures: 'the plumbing,' as Keith Spicer called it. The Constitution embodies the key symbols of political identity. Its language enshrines a particular understanding of Canada: it privileges a definition of the country, its people, the fundamental political issues, and the political processes by which they may be resolved. It legitimizes a particular type of discourse about Canadian politics. What the Constitution fails to include is thereby implicitly excluded from this privileged status. Hence the attempt to remake the Constitution has generated new stakeholders profoundly concerned that their issues be addressed. Groups that fail to win recognition in the Constitution thereby lose to those that do. The stakes are higher and much more extensive than ever before. Hence the bitter contests over the substance of constitutional reform, and also the process by which it is carried out.

All of this is taking place against a backdrop of cultural change and symbolic transformation, permeated by a deep anger toward and distrust of our political leaders and even our political institutions.[5] However rapid the changes that occurred during the Meech Lake period and its aftermath, they seemed modest and restrained in comparison to the cataclysms that swept through the Soviet Union and eastern Europe in the same period. Canada is redefining itself both structurally and culturally. The politics of identity has forced itself into the national agenda, and has changed the political culture throughout the country. Many forces are responsible, not least of which is the transforming impact of the

Charter, and the appearance of what Alan Cairns has called 'Charter Minorities'. Canada is changing. Gone forever is 'British North America' and the myth of two founding peoples. What will emerge is far from clear. Anger and frustration are poor foundations on which to construct a new political edifice. Many have lamented the absence of strong national feeling, of shared values and abiding commitment. But few have attempted to correct the underlying structural and institutional failures that account for the situation.[6] The educational system virtually ignores 'political education', the cultural system eschews national commitment that would entail further governmental 'interference'. We face the future uncertain of our past and with a fragmented national consciousness. This is a crisis in which the dangers are numerous and extensive, the opportunities few and limited.

Notes

[1] For an excellent analysis of the impact on Canada of continentalization and global economic force see *The New Era of Global Competition: State Policy and Market Power*, edited by Daniel Drache and Meric S. Gertler (Montreal and Kingston: McGill-Queen's University Press, 1991) especially chs. 1 and 5.

[2] John Hutcheson, 'The Context of Cultural Policy: English Speaking Canada' *London Journal of Canadian Studies* 7 (1990): 5. See also Richard M. Merelman, *Partial Visions: Culture and Politics in Britain, Canada, and the United States* (Madison: University of Wisconsin Press, 1991).

[3] Data drawn from the 1974 federal election survey as reported in H. Clarke *et al.*, *Political Choice in Canada*: 72.

[4] This point is set in a fascinating comparative context by Ron Watts:

The contrast in the cumulative result of the historical trends in Canada and the United States is clearly illustrated by the proportion of total revenues and public expenditures attributable to the national, as opposed to the state or provincial, governments in the two federations. While federal revenues and expenditures prior to intergovernmental transfers have in the United States in recent decades represented between 65 and 70 per cent of the total, in Canada from 1955 to 1979 they declined from 74.3 per cent to 45.9 per cent. When the federal share of total government expenditure is adjusted to account for transfers, the net federal share in the United States is 56 per cent, whereas in Canada it is less than 34 per cent. Furthermore, the portion of federal transfers to states that is unconditional or only semiconditional is very much higher in Canada, representing 73 per cent of all transfers as compared with less than 20 per cent of all transfers in the United States. Canadian provinces are not only responsible for a higher proportion of revenues and expenditures, but in the transfers they receive from the federal government their relationship is also a much less dependent one. ('The American Constitution in Comparative Perspective: A Comparison of Federalism in the United States and Canada', *The Journal of American History* 74,3 [Dec. 1987]: 777.)

[5] For a comparative analysis of this phenomenon in more than two dozen countries including Canada see Ronald Inglehart, *Culture Shift in Advanced Industrial Society* (Princeton: Princeton University Press, 1990).

[6] Organizations that have been active in trying to promote Canadian nationalism include the Pro-Canada Network and Council of Canadians. Perhaps the most articulate and energetic leader of this movement is Maude Barlow. See her book (with Bruce Campbell) *Take Back the Nation*.

See also Sylvia Bashevkin, *True Patriot Love: The Politics of Canadian Nationalism* (Toronto: Oxford University Press, 1991).

Index

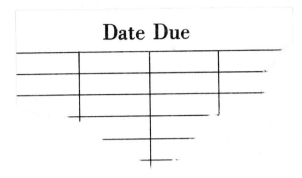

Date Due